PRAISE FOR CONSCIOUS NATURE

Early Reviews

"**Josh Lane has set the new gold standard for the how and why of mindfulness. This book will help you achieve balance using simple techniques that are easily integrated into your every day life.** Josh offers tangible takeaways for personal nature connection, helping relieve stress and increase health. Backed by science and story, Josh's writings are an easy, informative and fun read. This book is the perfect place to start your journey to true connection and happiness."
— Nicole Apelian, Ph.D.

"**At last! A revolutionary book that ties together the healing power of nature connection with mindfulness, at the cutting edge of neuroscience.** Josh has dedicated his life to practicing and teaching these skills. Adding to his clear explanations and the magic of his storytelling, there are tried and true exercises, audio meditations, and online tools that take us to a deeper level, one of action and experience, where the reader can live into the practices leading to nourishing changes in the brain, emotions and senses. *Conscious Nature* is a book that is more than a book, because it takes you on a journey of a lifetime and shows you how Nature is healing and transforming your brain along the way."
— Ruth Cory, Naturopath & Counselor

"*Conscious Nature* **by Josh Lane is a real gift to humanity in a time when a book like this is so critically needed.** Josh draws from a life dedicated to tracking and deep nature awareness. He reveals the secret doorways to entering wild places and knowing them intimately. He reminds us of who we are as a species and how we are adapted to move and think in the wilderness. This book, if studied well, has the capacity to transform lives, and connect people back to the state of mind that kept us joyful for thousands of generations."

— Craig Foster, author of *Sea Change: Primal Joy and the Art of Underwater Tracking*

"The journey to regular nature connection is empowered in some surprising ways through Josh's book, which powerfully motivates each of us through the contexts of science and story-telling. Josh is a genial guide and companion whom it's easy to trust to achieve what he calls the 'pure awareness that is our core.' Both veteran and novice outdoors-people will find intriguing and valuable ideas and methods."

— Jim Lowery, author of *Walk With the Animal* and *The Tracker's Field Guide*

"For those seeking practical ways to increase their connection to the natural world, look no further than *Conscious Nature*. With easy-to-follow exercises to get yourself out of the house and into the woods, this book will help you to strengthen your relationship with the outdoors. It will also help you understand the science behind nature's impact on the brain. A much needed antidote to our screen- and phone-filled world... Josh's stories inspired me to get outside right away!"

— Ben Weiss, LICSW

"*Conscious Nature* takes us on an amazing journey of connection... Josh's experience as a deep nature connection mentor and thoroughly skilled practitioner of tracking really shines through the words of this book. With attention to detail, Josh has assembled a wonderful collection of research, exercises, and techniques... a bundle proven to get results. Thank you Josh for laying a practical pathway and a very useful bridge to connecting with ourselves and the power of meditation in nature. This book will be an indispensable tool for the nature connection movement."

— Jon Young, author of *Coyote's Guide to Connecting with Nature* and *What the Robin Knows*

CONSCIOUS NATURE

THE ART AND NEUROSCIENCE OF MEDITATING IN NATURE

JOSH LANE

CONSCIOUS
NATURE
LLC

Publisher's Cataloging-in-Publication Data

Names: Lane, Joshua M., author.
Title: Conscious nature : the art and neuroscience of meditating in nature / Josh Lane.
Description: Includes bibliographical references. | Stone Ridge, NY : Conscious Nature LLC, 2019.
Identifiers: LCCN 2019903116 | ISBN 978-1-7337971-0-8 (pbk.) | 978-1-7337971-1-5 (ebook)
Subjects: LCSH Meditation. | Meditations. | Nature. | Mind and body. | Spirituality. | Consciousness. | Self-consciousness (Awareness) | Awareness. | Perception. | Experience. | Philosophy of nature. | Nature observation. | Well-being. | Conduct of life. | Mind and body therapies. | Mental healing. | Self-help techniques. | BISAC BODY, MIND & SPIRIT / Mindfulness & Meditation | SELF-HELP / Meditations
Classification: LCC BL65.N35 .L36 2019 | DDC 202/.12--dc23

ISBN-13: 978-1-7337971-0-8 (Paperback Edition)
ISBN-13: 978-1-7337971-1-5 (E-book Edition)

Cover design: Rebecca LeGates | *Cover photo:* Melissa Glorieux
(TheRitualMandala@Instagram)
Content editing: Melissa Kirk

Printed and bound in the United States of America
First Printing 2019

Published by Conscious Nature LLC
P.O. Box 82, Stone Ridge, NY 12484

READER'S EXTRAS: YOUR FREE
MEDITATION COURSE

.

Get FREE access to Conscious Nature guided meditations and awareness practices:

https://www.consciousnature.net/readers-extras

CONTENTS

INTRODUCTION

> The Force is an energy field created by all living things. It surrounds us and penetrates us; it binds the galaxy together."
> — Obi Wan Kenobi, Jedi Master

Yup, we're going full nerd here. Just wanted to get that clear from the start. You know, set the tone and all.

The fact is, as we connect with Nature, we are immersing in a sea of energy. The meditations I share in this book are designed to help you connect with this energy. Through them, you can grow a deeper awareness of the currents of life moving within and around you.

With this awareness, you can access greater peace and harmony, and more effectively harness the power of intention to support your life. Nature has lessons to offer that will help you to do this, and the practices shared here will help you learn from this most amazing teacher.

Meditating in Nature directly connects you with the vibrant life force that literally gives you each breath you take, and the very body you experience it with. By meditating outdoors regularly in a favorite spot, you'll become attuned to the natural rhythms and cycles of your place in the world, no matter whether you're in a city park, a backyard garden, or in the deepest wilderness.

The energy of Nature flows through all environments, available and awaiting your participatory attention. The calls of the birds and animals, the murmur of the wind in the trees, the trickle of quiet brooks and the roaring of mountain streams are all powerful living mantras that transform your awareness, when you mindfully attune to them.

Some of the awareness practices contained in this book have been passed down from long ago, used by people who literally depended on them for survival. Most were known by all of our ancestors at one time or another, though largely forgotten today. Certain of these skills and concepts have even been declared illegal at different places and times around the world for various reasons, often due to religious censure or political schemes.

Yet, these practices of awareness have helped us to become what we are, though in our Digital Era it's easy to forget our connection to the wellspring of Nature.

It's time now to remember these perceptual gifts, and consciously reawaken to our primal connection with the power of Nature. This infusion of ancient wisdom will give us the grounded foundation we need to move forward in balance with the cycles of life on this planet.

The Goal & Dedication of This Book

By attuning to the essence of Nature that is our foundation, we can enhance our lives in many ways.

In the pages of this book, I weave together ancient wisdom and modern research to show you exactly how the practices of Nature

Awareness and Meditation work synergistically to heal us and help us be our best.

This book is dedicated to those adventurers who seek to remember and awaken their own vital connection with the Nature within and around us all.

This is the journey of *Conscious Nature* — to make what was once unknown, known; to open an understanding of that which was once hidden or overlooked. As the old Taoist saying goes, "Through practice, that which is hidden becomes subtle. Then, that which is subtle becomes obvious."

In these pages, you will find stories and practices that guide you step-by-step into a deeper awareness through meditating in Nature.

You'll learn effective tools to release the stresses of modern life, tend your Being, and learn to read and participate in the language of Nature in a way you may have always longed for but not known how to achieve.

This longing comes from the ancient genetic inheritance of earth connection that fills your very bones; may the cup of Nature fill your thirst.

What Does it Mean to "Meditate in Nature"?

As we'll explore in the chapters ahead, meditation brings us a variety of benefits, ranging from stress reduction all the way through beneficial immune response and actual healing changes on the epigenetic level. At the most basic layer, meditation is like a handy reset button that wipes away stress and gets us out of our usual thoughts and attitudes.

Meditation can also be grander in purpose; Mystery Schools from around the world have long used meditation as a route towards unification with the timeless and eternal. In fact, the word *yoga* means "union," and its goal is the realization of the Self

Within with the Grand Self that moves through all Being and beyond all form. If one takes the view that all of life is Sacred and connected to the Great Mystery, then all of Nature becomes a doorway to the Infinite.

Whether you are simply looking to reduce stress and support your well-being, or you're seeking a sense of deeper meaning and a feeling of connection with all of Life, meditating in Nature can help you.

The Power of Concentration...

> " *Focus, Daniel San!"*
> — *Mr. Miyagi, in the film, The Karate Kid*

Mr. Miyagi said it best. The most basic element of meditation is *concentration*, focusing the mind on a quality or subject of attention for a period of time. This relaxed focus changes the pattern of electricity moving through your brain, synchronizing large neural regions and allowing the overtaxed mind to quickly restore its functions.

The relaxed brain more easily attunes to subtle signals from its environment, opening to the creative inspirations that bubble forth from the unconscious mind and instincts. Meditation tunes you into the language of the Nature around you, and propels your dive into the landscapes of the Nature within.

The Practices - A Quick Overview...

Many people think of meditation as sitting on a cushion and counting breaths, which certainly is a common focusing technique. However, you can enjoy meditation outdoors, too, in a variety of ways that enliven your senses and inspire your day.

On our journey into *Conscious Nature* we will explore many focal points for concentration, from the breath and heartbeat moving within you to the songs and calls of the birds vibrating around you. You'll gain tools that help you deepen your awareness of your own *Being*, on every level. You'll also learn how Nature provides instant feedback about your inner state, and discover that you are indeed constantly participating in the larger story unfolding on the land around you, whether you know it or not.

You'll also learn how to choose a Meditation Spot, a special place in Nature where you can use the practices in this book; think of it as your own outdoor meditation studio. These practices can be used in a backyard, local park, or favorite wilderness area. In fact, many of the techniques can be adapted and utilized just about anywhere you go; some of my favorite Nature experiences have been in the city.

The practices we will cover include both sitting meditations and dynamic moving meditations. Nature's outer appearance is ever shifting and transforming, yet the sages say that within our Core Nature is a place of stillness and repose. Thus, we learn by mimicking Nature in all its stages and transformations, finding out how these qualities of action and stillness move within ourselves, too.

A Path of Discovery...

In these pages, I share stories from my own journey into Nature's mysteries, gathered from over two decades of adventures and intensive explorations on the inner and outer landscapes.

Since the age of sixteen, my path has led me to various mentors and Wisdom Keepers, including a ten-year-plus apprenticeship in the ancient arts of wildlife tracking and deciphering Nature's language, in a lineage of trackers that reaches far back into the shifting sands of time.

Some things can only be learned experientially; fueled with the questions of my mentors, my best guide was the Nature surrounding my Meditation Spot, located under a red maple tree at the edge of a Western Massachusetts farm field that I visited and sat beneath every day for many years. Many of the stories in this book come from the 800-acre patchwork of forest and fields surrounding that tree. The stories from that place serve to illustrate a bundle of transformative principles and techniques that will help you as you set out on your own journey into the mysteries of Nature.

There at my Meditation Spot, I learned to still myself and blend into the flow of the woods, while at the same time expanding my senses to the natural patterns around me. I learned to decode the calls of the birds to deduce the location of hidden animals and distant people, and discovered how to avoid triggering the forest alarm system myself, so that I could observe animals in their natural state.

As I explored each day on my wanders to and from this spot, my ever-growing curiosity empowered my senses and enlivened my *sense of place*; over time, I came to know each forest patch and rivulet, to the point where I could find my way on the darkest night. I also learned to bring the deep level of mindfulness that I was cultivating at my Meditation Spot with me as I moved through the forest. This dynamic meditation allowed me greater access to my capacities of intuition and instinct, leading to many memorable and mysterious encounters with animals and other aspects of Nature.

Ultimately, I discovered that these experiences in Nature transferred powerfully into my everyday modern life, offering me a deep sense of creative engagement with my work and the capacity to examine situations from many perspectives, infusing me with a sense of full aliveness brought about by my passion and curiosity.

Most importantly, I've found that meditating in Nature helps me feel connected to the flow of Life and to my highest creativity wherever I happen to be; when I feel connected this way, I know that I can better help those around me to enjoy a deep, conscious level of this connection, too.

A Transformative Journey

Mentoring and coaching others in this journey of awareness is one of my greatest joys and fascinations. Over the years, I've had the opportunity to share the art of mindfully connecting with Nature with clients from around the world, ranging from executives, busy professionals and parents, to real honest-to-goodness 16th-level ninjas. I've seen how the journey into Nature transforms each person in unique — but often predictable — ways.

Sensory connections engage and expand. Familiarity with the local patterns of Nature develops, as the senses take in the sinuous shapes of oak leaves here, and the raspy call of a jay there. Comfort in the outdoors and all its varied conditions gradually develops, along with an affinity and empathic connection with the land.

At the same time, an inner journey ensues as Nature's stillness offers a reprieve from the busyness of the daily grind. Stress begins to shed and a greater feeling of relaxation and poise comes to life. Simply put, a person sitting quietly under a tree suddenly has time to face his- or her-self, and to attune to the deeper longings and callings of the soul.

This is why the journey into Nature is transformative — as we connect with the Nature around us, we can't help but connect more fully to the Nature moving within us.

In this book, you'll learn proven techniques for supporting a positive engagement in Nature, and for tending the inner transformation that comes along with it.

These are tools I use with my one-on-one coaching clients. I've included them here because they are invaluable for helping you forward when you bump up against your own walls and inertia.

You'll find techniques for honing your motivation, awakening an unbridled curiosity, developing a keen sense of place in the outdoors, and even for releasing old programs of thinking that no longer serve you because you've grown past them on your journey.

The Neuroscience of Meditating in Nature

Over the years of mentoring others through these transformations, I became curious as to what was happening in the brain while these changes occurred. *What kind of neural circuitry gets engaged as we connect with Nature? What internal mechanisms are at play as we experience the various stages of meditation and awareness? How could such knowledge help us on our journeys in Nature?* Fascinated by these questions, I spent several years surveying a variety of neuroscience-related research journals for clues and answers.

Interestingly, I found that many of the age-old mentoring strategies I had been steeped in match up perfectly with the latest cutting-edge findings in brain-based education and current understandings of how the brain works.

Pursuing this research, I also noted the great number of cognitive and health-related benefits that have been recorded in relation both to meditation and time spent in Nature; the intentional fusion of these two helpful sources of well-being yields results in personal transformation that are truly extraordinary.

So, along with discovering a variety of techniques and practices that are designed to lead you into your own deep engagement with Nature, you'll also find insights peppered throughout this book about what's happening "under the hood" in your brain each step of the way.

You'll get a glimpse at the amazing ways your brain constantly maps and makes sense of the world of Nature. You'll learn how you literally carry your sense of place with you in your neural web, and why the mentoring tools shared in this book are so essential in helping the strands of this web to reach out and make meaningful, conscious connections with the Nature within and around you.

My hope is that this information will encourage your practice as you see the many benefits of developing your own routines of meditating in Nature.

How to Use This Book

I recommend reading the entire book through and trying out the techniques as they are shared, one chapter at a time.

Many of the practices are built sequentially, depending upon the understandings and techniques shared earlier in the text. This structure builds your skills of awareness a bit further each step of the way, just as a mentor would help you to do in a one-on-one setting.

Read, dabble, and have fun. Most importantly, put these skills to use. Adapt the practices so that Nature can nourish your life in the way that works for you. Reach beyond the concepts to taste the Reality. "He who tastes, knows."

In Section One, Chapters 1-10 provide you with inspiring foundational techniques for meditating in Nature that you can get started with right away, including a review of the health benefits and brain functions related to meditation and time in the outdoors.

You'll learn how by going into Nature with intention and mindful awareness, you can invite the power of the archetypal Hero's Journey into your life to bring positive transformation and new heights of discovery.

You'll also learn about the *five key brain states* that we use in everyday life, and how to balance them by using the practices in your growing meditation toolkit. The *arts of journaling and questioning* will be explored as a method to track and support your new awareness skills.

Importantly, we will cover the various *fears, doubts, and misconceptions* that are common to this transformational journey of awareness, and how to put them in perspective and keep your practice on track.

In Section Two, through Chapters 11-15, you'll learn how to bring together the foundational skills you've been practicing into a complete four-part awareness cycle that you can use at your Meditation Spot.

With continued practice, you can learn to access these meditative states whenever you need them. Then, you can shift your mindstate as desired to help you accomplish your goals with a foundation of peace and the power of Nature-inspired creativity.

Finally, in Part Three, Chapter 16, you'll learn an advanced technique called *Being Nature* that draws upon all of your Conscious Nature experiences for cultivating creative inspiration and insight at those times when you need it the most.

Through all of this, you'll be learning to attune to the flow and patterns of Nature's primal energy.

Get ready, young *padawan* — it's time to learn the ways of the Force and become a *Nature Jedi*. It's what you were born to do. Our journey begins as we step out the door... and face the Wall of Green.

SECTION I

FOUNDATIONS

In this first section, learn and practice essential skills for creating a nourishing meditation practice in Nature:

- **Explore a toolkit of enlivening sensory meditations** that help you tune into Nature's dynamic patterns within and around you

- **Discover the many benefits of meditating in Nature that support well-being,** and the 5 key brain states you can harness to optimize your mindset

- **Learn fun, engaging mindful awareness techniques** for both seated and moving outdoor meditations

Let's get started! Here we go, out the door and into the Wall of Green...

1

WE ARE NATURE

"The Wall of Green" is the term my friend and longtime nature mentor Jon Young uses to describe not knowing the plants growing on your lawn.

As a kid growing up in the suburbs, I often encountered this wall, though I didn't have a name for it at the time. You see, when I explored my local outdoor areas, I looked at the plants and trees in the yard and forest and wondered longingly what they were.

I liked climbing trees and collecting rocks, and playing hide and seek and ninja games with my friends in our little patch of woods at the edges of the town park. Yet, that was as far as I knew how to go in my experience of the outdoors. But I wanted more.

Nature was calling to me, but where I grew up it was hard to find anyone that knew about the woods.

Just about the only trees that stood out to me were the camouflage-like bark of the sycamores, which I knew because my grandparents had one in their backyard. However, there weren't many of these majestic trees in our local woods.

When I looked at the forest, I didn't know what I was looking

at. Everything was a blur... I couldn't tell an oak from a beech tree
— all I saw was a big Wall of Green.

The "Wall of Green" phenomenon isn't just green, though.
This lack of awareness rippled out to all the other aspects of
Nature around me.

Although I was surrounded by the calls of the birds, the tracks
of the animals, and the life force of countless other beings, their
presence appeared more as a blank spot in my map of the world.

I just didn't know how to make a meaningful connection to the
life around me, so I couldn't perceive it. Like Luke Skywalker
during his youthful days in *Star Wars*, I was surrounded by the
wonders of the Force, but I didn't even know it.

The Wall of Green is a Modern Invention

Looking back, I realize that people learn to pay attention to what
which is important to them. The local culture reinforces this.

What was important to us kids at the time? Left to our own
devices, for an eight-year-old boy in my suburban peer group it
was all about baseball, video games, BMX bikes, and comic books.
That was our world.

Meanwhile, for an eight-year-old growing up in a hunter-gatherer culture, the focus is very different.

When I visited with a San community in the Kalahari Desert
who still maintain many of their ancient traditions, I saw how
deeply attuned the youth are to the language of Nature.

Because these kids live in an environment filled with lions,
leopards, and other aspects of Nature that demand respect, their
senses are extremely connected to each nuance of the landscape.

If a small songbird alarms a hundred yard away, each child
instantly stops what they are doing and listens to assess any
danger. To find food in the desert requires that they know how to
identify every leaf and twig. A single shriveled leaf of a certain

plant can indicate the presence of a huge taproot filled with life-giving water, which means survival in the dry season.

There is no Wall of Green for these kids, because the culture they grow up in is filled with rich connections to the earth. Their elders tell stories every day of the tracks they've followed, and the hunters mimic the antics of the animals around the fire.

From a young age, these children learn the nuances of each animal's behavior through dances and songs, and they learn about the edible (or dangerous) plants and trees by helping to gather alongside expert eyes.

When they get older, these kids won't need to go to a yoga class to learn mindfulness or reduce stress — they are living in their fully embodied awareness every second, and their ancient cultural dances and healing ceremonies help them make sense of the world and release any regular trauma that comes up in daily living.

For most of humanity's long history (300,000 + years), this is how we all lived.

Only recently have large portions of the world's population turned to a more sedentary agricultural lifestyle (circa 10,000 years), and later to industry (200 years), increasing urbanization, and now, the digital lifestyle (20 years).

It's easy in many places today to forget just how intimately connected with Nature we really are, being surrounded by concrete and wi-fi and the myriad gadgets of modern life.

Yet, as today's Paleo Diet proponents like to say, *we are still hunter-gatherers in body and mind.*

The sensory acuity we enjoy, the mental pliancy and emotional resilience we harness to thrive, and the creative visionary gifts we shape our lives with all come from the adaptive hunter-gatherer experience that honed our species over a vast period of time.

We can't simply step away from the diverse, complex interactions with Nature that have breathed life into our species and expect to do well for very long. We need Nature in our lives, because we <u>are</u> Nature.

―――――――

Towards a Natural Ecology of the Imagination

66 *Nature holds the key to our aesthetic, intellectual, cognitive, and even spiritual satisfaction."*
— *E.O. Wilson*

AS WE EXPLORE THE NOTION THAT WE <u>ARE</u> NATURE, LET'S CONSIDER a helpful teaching from the Tzutujil Mayan community of Guatemala, recounted by the shaman and seed-tender of the indigenous soul, Martín Prechtel.[1] The teaching begins by saying that *we live within the dreams of the Ancestors.*

This is a way of observing that the state of humankind in the present emerges from the quality of the lives and imaginations of the Ancestors that came before us. We build our ideals and dreams for the future upon the foundations of thought and connection that we are steeped in, bestowed upon us from those who have come before.

Reaching back further, it's said that *the Ancestors emerge from the great Dreaming of Nature.* The present emerges from the past, which arises from the primal wellspring of Nature, the ultimate source of the inspiration and energy that moves through humanity.

Relationships Require Tending...

This relationship with Nature is one that needs tending and awareness to remain in balance.

For a long time, the human Dream was in harmony with the essence of Nature. People lived close to the land and because of this, their cultures reflected Nature's patterns. The dances, songs, tools, and even the qualities of the languages themselves all provided linkages to each group's local ecology, providing an intimate sense of place within the natural world.

However, some of the Ancestors surrounded themselves with enough of their own inventions and ideas that they began to lose touch with the spirit of the land and the other beings in Nature; like a bubble whose inside is no longer permeable to the outside air, they insulated themselves within the ever-tighter confines of their own human Dreaming, cutting themselves off from the full nourishment of Nature that is their source and birthright.

The air inside the bubble has grown stale. These self-limiting ties have been dreamed forward to the present, where we find ourselves facing the many potent challenges unique to the modern experience: increasing rates of depression, anxiety, information overload, a lack of meaning and purpose, and many other signs of imbalance.

At the same time, the larger realm of Nature calls us to pay attention to our relationship, which has become heavily one-sided. Resource extraction, widespread pollution, massive biodiversity loss, and all the other inimical side-effects of modern Culture are begging for attention. We need to re-orient ourselves to where we are and what is truly important, so that we can healthfully navigate forward.

Dreaming Forward...

Alan Watts put it well: "You didn't come *into* this world. You came *out* of it, like a wave from the ocean. You are not a stranger here." It is time to expand our vision once more to encompass the healing and nourishing Dream of Nature, and to echo this restored ideal forward into the future. For, we who are here now will become the Ancestors of tomorrow.

What are we collectively dreaming forward as a gift to those yet to come? What does it mean to be conscious of this Dreaming? How are we bringing the gifts and teachings of Nature forward in our own creativity?

This book is designed to help you discover fun and meaningful pathways towards a fulfilling, conscious connection with Nature. The practices and stories offer a bridge that introduces the modern mindset to the gifts of the Earth Awareness that our ancestors all knew and enjoyed. Abounding peace, inspiration, and increased wellness are just a few of the gifts that we can discover as we meditate within Nature's dream, if we choose to look.

The Deer Woman, and Making Nature Relevant

When I look back to my childhood experience with the Wall of Green, and then think about the children of the hunter-gatherers that I've met, I realize that this kind of intimate connection with Nature was what my eight-year-old brain was adaptively craving. My culture just wasn't geared to support this biological desire, though.

Fortunately, there was one day when an elder finally appeared that sparked a fire in me, inspiring me on a path that has taken me to where I am today in my life. It was fourth grade, and the public school had some curriculum devoted to learning about the indigenous cultures of our area, along with the earth living skills that all people at one time have depended upon.

A guest teacher came and brought our class outside. She taught us how to make a small stone hatchet with wood and sinew. Also, she showed us how to stalk silently, and we played a game of sneaking up on "deer" (each other) as she played a soft rhythm on a handmade drum.

The morning passed quickly, but I held onto that hatchet for a long time. It was really just a child's toy, barely more than a toothpick with a flake of slate tied on. However, it opened a doorway in my imagination to an ancient world.

I would go searching for other stones that could make good tools, and whittle away with them on sticks to make spears and arrows. The forest took on a new dimension as I imagined life as a hunter-gatherer.

The little hatchet would eventually end up on my shelf and grow dusty for many years, as other interests took over. But the connection with the land that opened from that experience, however small, would stay with me.

With the help of many mentors alongside my own explorations, I eventually learned to see through the illusion of the Wall of Green.

In its place, I found myself surrounded by many friends and worthy companions of the natural world: dandelion, oak, ash, and all the other beings of Nature that were always there waiting for me to discover them.

The Beginning of a Journey...

Little would I know that later on, many years of my life would become devoted to learning the arts of living with the land, tracking, tuning to Nature's language, and sharing these skills with others around the world.

My journey would also take me to seek shamans, martial artists, mystics, and healers of many traditions, as I sought the essence of Nature's creativity moving through its many forms of human expression. Through all of this, my life has been enriched as an infinity of new connections with Nature's Mysteries continues to open out.

Thank you Deer Woman. On that day almost thirty years ago, you opened a moment of relevance that directed my youthful attention to the importance of Nature.

You continue to teach me how impactful a single moment of role modeling can be, and how this simple gift can powerfully support a person's passion and path in life. Thank you.

Thank you to the many mentors of earth connection, vision, and healing that have supported my path.

Thank you to my family for your endless support as I've followed my vision, even when you've wondered what in the world I am doing, or tried to explain it to others.

Thank you also to those who have given me the gift of allowing me to share these skills forward with you, because you have taught me so much in the translation.

Connecting to the Nature Within and Around Us

As a teenager, I discovered a passion for consciousness exploration in the form of *raja yoga*. My practice developed a consistent force, and I was very pleased with the peace and inner resolve that arose through the routine. However, as I turned further to the deeper layers of Nature within, I couldn't help but notice that my connection to the Nature *around* me was not developing at the same rate.

My awareness training seemed lopsided - yoga and mindfulness meditation on its own, and directed inwards, was not an immediate antidote to the Wall of Green. The sensitivity and intu-ition that the practice generates certainly helps (and at advanced levels offers key insights into Nature's patterns), but I found myself searching for an equivalent "outer awareness" practice to supple-ment the internal skills I was learning.

I wanted to feel as intimately connected to the land and animals as I did to the thoughts, emotions, and sensations running through my being. This seemed to me like it should not only be possible to achieve, but should be a basic requirement of living on the Earth! Why didn't anyone know this? To my teenage mind, the modern lack of connection to the landscape felt alien, as if a whole global techno-culture had just suddenly plunked down here from some other planet without regard for the natural cycles and patterns around us.

Discovering Scout Awareness...

When the student is ready, the teacher appears. I came across the books of a wildlife tracker named Tom Brown, Jr., an outdoorsman who was raised in his boyhood by an Apache scout. The scouts were the eyes and ears of the tribe, hidden sentinels who surveyed the mountains and forests for distant danger, highly trained in Nature's language in order to keep their people safe.

For me, Tom's stories highlighted the deep connection with the land, the animals, and the greater ecological web that it is possible to enjoy — and which is, in fact, a level of personal connection with the Earth that all of our ancestors once knew and practiced.

I had finally found a pathway towards outer awareness devel-opment that would complement my inner meditations. This set me on a twenty-year journey that would propel my interests and research through the remainder of high school and into college, then across the country to apprentice for over a decade with

Tom's first protege, the tracker and mentoring specialist, Jon Young.

Along the way I would meet many elders and Wisdom Keepers of different traditions, from shamans of indigenous tribes to meditation masters, Taoist priests, and Qi Gong healers. Combined with persistent inquiry and experimentation, the teachings I encountered would help me find my own place in relationship to the Earth and to the larger realms of Spirit and Awareness that surrounds us.

Throughout my journey, I've sought and learned meditative skills that help us to connect not just with the inner landscapes of the Nature *within* us, but with the language and energy of the Nature *around* us in the land, water, and sky. Every day offers new lessons and discoveries. Ultimately, the inner and outer aspects are different manifestations of the one Primal Nature that encompasses all of life.

Remembering the Dream of Nature

How do we remember our connection with Nature's Dream? We turn to the wild. We seek out those hidden, mysterious and oft-forgotten sanctuaries of the wilderness that offer a contrast to our own overly-patterned modern existence. In these places, Nature's complex, myriad patterns and forces are at play, waiting for us to immerse our senses and come alive.

Some of these pockets of undiscovered wilderness are hidden right under our noses: in backyard hedgerows teeming with bird-song, tucked away on the outskirts of town parks in overlooked brambles and forest patches, and even underfoot in the microscopic jungles of the front lawn.

A Return to the Wild...

The word *wilderness* comes from the Old English for "wild deer," and translates as "a place of the wild animals." The wilderness is beyond human control. It's a place of adventure and mystery, and of vision and healing. The wild places bring us to a sense of humility (related to the word *humus* — literally, "of the earth") as we revel in their vastness, power, and beauty.

Many cultures have come to understand the vitalizing power of the wild. Gary Nabhan, in his thought-provoking book *Cultures of Habitat*, shares how the Piman-speaking peoples of the American Southwest have very similar words for *health* and *wildness*; both terms stem from the root-word *doa*, which means "to be alive" or "to be cured."[2]

As we step into the wilds of Nature, we strip away the dross of daily life and remember the wild places inside ourselves. With this remembrance and unification, we find new sources of energy to heal and empower our lives.

Experiencing the Unity of Life...

Meditating in Nature opens us to experiencing the basic unity of life. When we connect with the primal energy of the elements, breathing in the pure mountain air or immersing in the crisp cool waters of an alpine stream, we realize we are part and parcel of Nature. There is no separation.

The same air that flows across the mountain trees reaches into our lungs to give us life; the same water that cascades down the forest streams feeds into every cell in our body, a body made of the minerals and very stuff of the earth that forms the mountain trails. The warmth of the Sun reaching down from above touches our skin, mingling with the metabolic fire exuded with each step we take.

This understanding is basic, but essential. In this return to our foundations, we find a certain peace that nourishes and inspires our own Inner Nature.

A Hero's Journey

As we heal and nourish ourselves in Nature, we can bring our newfound peace and insight back with us to our daily lives. In this way, the energy and experiences we find in Nature can inform the human Culture that we contribute to.

This kind of quest is the root of the classical Hero's Journey. Such a journey itself is transformative, with key stages that unfold in a predictable pattern. By understanding this cycle, we get insights into some of the things that can happen as we go forth on our own journeys into Nature.

Learning From Old Tales...

Think about the story of Hansel and Gretel. Old myths and fairy-tales like this one send their leading characters out into the unknown, on a Quest that carries them beyond the borders of the home or village. The Questers travel past their known maps of the world and into raw experience, carrying only their need to solve an urgent problem.

In this case, two kids are booted out of their home by their mother and left in the woods, far from home (not the best way to be introduced to the outdoors...). Nature propels the rest of the story, helping the two journeyers to unlock previously unknown gifts and abilities. The messenger of Nature, a mysterious white bird, leads the children to a magical gingerbread house deep in the forest, where they must face an ordeal with a hungry Witch who wants to eat them for dinner.

Faced with this outrageous situation — one like they've never faced before — the kids must rely purely on their wits and quick thinking to succeed. After they catch the Witch in her own trap, the children serendipitously find a stash of jewels and make their way home, led by another emissary from Nature in the form of a white duck. Returning home, they find their mother is gone, and the children happily spend the rest of their days with their father, who had missed them dearly since their disappearance.

We can see in the story how a kind of inner alchemy is set into motion within the anvil of Nature, as the elemental forces distill and purify the characters of the heroes-to-be. The protagonists are led step-by-step into a situation that will change them forever. Nature is all about transformation, and Going into Nature is a potent way to invoke these primal forces of change.

Hansel and Gretel appear at first to be in a desperate situation, left all alone in the unknown woods. Yet, the white bird appears and guides them, visiting in the guise of two distinct forms at two key points in the story; once, to lead them forward to their moment of challenge with the Witch, and again, to triumphantly lead them home.

The appearance of the bird shows how Nature provides boons along the way to help with a Quester's awakening. Supportive guides and innovative solutions appear at just the right moment, propelling the journey along. The heroes discover something essential about their own values and capabilities as they face Reality.

At some point on any Hero's Journey, the protagonists have to release their old notions of egoic control and simply surrender to the flow of life. What worked in their lives before at home doesn't work here in the Wild, and so they must expand their notions to embrace the new opportunities before them. Hansel and Gretel have to go with the flow, trust their instincts, and keep alert for messages and opportunities from the world around them. This is the crux of the transformation process: the Questers become present to the numinous power of moment. They begin consciously co-creating their pathway in unison with the dynamic flow of Nature.

Through this expansion of perception, the newly actualized Journeyers tap into their previously unknown inner resources, realizing the gifts they have to offer the world. In this case, Hansel and Gretel must overcome the Witch, a character of adversity who forces them to turn within and find their inner strengths and determination. Then, they return home with these gifts (symbolized by the jewels), transforming their daily experience with a new threshold of meaning and understanding. Such Journeyers are bringing the Dreaming of Nature's raw experience back with them to infuse their culture with something vital.

Nature Helps Us Face (and Free) Ourselves...

We all have our own version of the Witch that needs to be understood and integrated into our experience. For some, it might be the voice of a fierce inner critic that dampens their creativity; for others, it could be a fear or worry, or limiting belief. Nature can help us transform these qualities to find the gifts hidden within.

Nature provides a place to simply go and *be*, to get out of our usual ruts and comfort zones. When we slow down from the fast pace of daily life, immersing in the peace and quiet of Nature, we become still enough for these old inner voices to surface and be resolved. Instead of carrying these burdens with us everywhere we go, we can finally release them and achieve a new understanding of ourselves and where we are headed.

We All Need a Journey Into Nature...

Every generation needs this Journey anew. The old Wisdom Traditions have understood that Culture has a tendency to get wrapped up in itself, amazed at its own inventions and ways, often to the detriment of the land and ecosystems the culture itself depends on for sustenance.

Ancient rites of passage emerged to help remove this veil and face a culture's emerging adults with the basic understanding that the well-being of the land is our well-being, too. Through a potent encounter with the wild, individuals populated the ecology of their imaginations with the textures and voices of the natural world. This understanding informed citizens' choices and actions. Now, it's time for a large-scale remembrance of our interdependence with the rest of Nature.

Starting on the Hero's Journey...

How do we get started? The Hero's Journey into Nature can be initiated in small ways. It begins with the opening of mindfulness and sensing what's happening in the moment, within us and around us. Because of this need for attunement, meditation goes hand-in-hand with this natural awakening.

Meditation relaxes us, providing a needed daily reset to the nervous system that counteracts the stress of modern life. Meditation also teaches us to becomes centered in the moment, and the moment is where Nature's transformative power dwells. If we are caught in thoughts about the future or past, we can easily miss the gifts that are surrounding us *right now*.

By developing some simple practices that get us out into Nature each day, and into the moment, we can open our awareness to the Mysteries that are waiting there to inspire us. We can each step foot on our own Hero's Journey, knowing that Nature is with us every step of the way.

To bring these pieces together, I will end this beginning chapter with a true story from my own journey. This story highlights how Nature becomes our best teacher and guide towards a deeper awareness and connection with the flow of Life. This is what happened at my Meditation Spot, many years ago...

A Mystery On the Wing

Soaking in the golden glow of a crisp mid-autumn sunset, I sat peacefully at treetop level on a small hill, overlooking the valley surrounding my Meditation Spot. The sky was clear and the air became brisk as the day grew to a close. Most of the nearby song-birds had already begun settling down for the approaching evening, leaving the finger-like strips of second- and third-growth forest that bordered the farm fields silent and still.

Having sat with my senses attuned to Nature's sights, sounds, and feelings for the past twenty minutes or so, my body was deeply relaxed; I now felt at one with the slight swaying of the trees that my high perch overlooked. I had never sat here in this exact spot before, my usual Meditation Spot of the last year being just fifty yards away to the north, posted along the narrow rivulet of a creek that trickled through a stand of red maples. But today something particular had drawn me to this spot at this sunset hour, and I was about to find out what it was...

Awakening the Instinct...

Suddenly, instinct drew me from my stillness and into unexpected motion. A wordless sensation of *inner knowing* caused me to peer back over my shoulder; something was coming towards me, fast... There was no sound of anything approaching, only the soft breeze moving across the treetops just beneath me. Yet as my head turned, my eyes made immediate contact with the large form of a great horned owl, flying at eye level right towards me!

The owl was flying parallel to the edge of the meadow at the start of his hunting shift, hoping to snag any hapless rabbits that ventured out too far from the sumac and raspberry shrubs at the forest's edge. Our eyes locked with a spark of mutual recognition, yet he did not change his course, continuing to glide the remaining fifteen feet right towards me. I simply remained as I was, gradually turning my head forward again as my eyes tracked his silent path in the air.

My body filled with energy as the owl swooped and passed by over my right shoulder, the edge of his left wing trailing within inches of my face... and a puff of air from the quiet wingbeats moving across me. The mysterious visitor continued deftly ahead down the valley, swooping into the red maple swamp to the southeast, vanishing amidst a flurry of alarms uttered by complaining blue jays disturbed from their roosts.

A Larger Pattern...

This encounter had been long in the coming — the meeting with the owl was not an isolated event, but rather another node on a much larger trail of a specific mystery. The perfection of the moment felt like a clear gift from Nature, an answer to a long-held question that had been brewing deep within me over a period of several months.

To experience the encounter, and therefore behold the answer to my quest, meant being in the right time at the right place; I recognized that the learnings leading up to this moment had enabled the meeting to take place such as it did. Each step led to another, a progression of unfolding experiences in Nature that were each part of the larger story between myself and the mystery that is the owl. The meeting was the expression of a conscious connection between the worlds of Nature *within* me — the fusion of my awareness, senses, and intuition — with the movement and patterns of the Nature *around* me.

Months before, a friend had shown me a large flight-feather left behind by a great horned owl, and I was instantly fascinated. The top face of the feather was covered in a smooth, fur-like velvet, making a non-reflective surface. Studying the feather more deeply, I saw how the leading edge was faced with tiny baffles that muted the sound of air as it passed over the surface of the airfoil, rendering a silent flight. The architecture of Nature...

As I held the totem in hand, the mystery of the owl moved into my consciousness — *who was this being that had left this feather? What does this owl know, and how does this animal relate to the world? How could I see this owl, and experience a real connection with Owl as an emissary of Nature? How could such a connection help me and help others as I walk my path?*

In time, I would come to appreciate that Owl is a connoisseur of the subtle and transformative, appearing in the dreamy interim between day and night, a shadow at best and generally unseen by most eyes.

By day owls remain hidden, tucked away against the comforting bark of a conifer, blending into the tree as just another part of the forest. When twilight calls, this tufted predator stirs, traversing the edges of the forest and meadow, flying on silent wings. Offering a few sparsely resonant calls to its mate or nearby colleagues, Owl patrols the wilds, silent and aware. This is the Being that would become my teacher for a time.

On the Trail of a Burning Question...

Having just arrived back at college, the autumn season stepped into gear and I found myself immersed in a sea of classes and activities. Yet every day I thought about the owl, and continually felt the mystery pulling me towards it. I knew this was a trail to follow up on, and I made it a point to do so.

I had established a special place to sit and meditate outdoors a couple years before, where I went just about every day to explore the wilds and simply be in Nature. Occasionally I had heard the distant calls of the great horned owls as I sat there, yet had not had any encounter of substance. It wasn't enough to see a far-off owl; I needed to interact with one at close hand, to be in the bird's presence. I began to research the natural history and habits of the owl, learning its yearly cycle and hunting strategies, where it slept and what it ate.

During my regular tracking outings, I kept a map of any owl sightings or sign that I encountered, slowly forming an idea of the places these majestic birds would frequent. Pellets and whitewash became beacons that spoke volumes about the owl's activity. Unlike hawks, which powerfully spray their whitewash of excreted uric acid against a tree trunk like an explosion from their roost, owls drop their whitewash straight down, leaving the forest floor beneath their resting places and hunting perches littered with bright white paint.

Owls eat rodents and other small mammals or birds, and the indigestible bits get spit out in the compressed form of a pellet, many of which can accumulate beneath favorite roosts. Their presence told me not only where I might find a sleeping owl, but also what was being hunted in each season; by finding the food sources, perhaps I could find the owl...

Even as I researched the lives of owls and actively sought their presence on the land, I also began attuning to their unique voices and calls. I learned to differentiate the great horned's deep "who-who-whooo, who-who," calls from the barred owl's eerie "who-cooks-for-you?" refrain.

Smaller owls began to reveal their presence to my ears, too — the neighing whinny of the screech owl, and the "truck backing up" high pulse of the saw-whet owl (a diminutive bird that remains still enough to be picked up by hand, should you encounter one in the daytime).

Soon, I even realized a difference between the hoots of the male and female great-horned owls, as their duets revealed the pairing of higher and lower voices echoing together through the quiet night.

A Mysterious Attunement...

More and more often, I would hear the great horned pair calling, and make my way towards them in hope of a glimpse. Often I would run, quickly covering an eighth or a quarter of a mile in an attempt to reach them before they moved on, slowing down as I approached and slipping quietly towards their perch. Usually they would be gone, and I would listen intently into the distance for jay alarms and other clues of their passage.

Through this routine, my ears became highly attuned to the great horned's unique sound. One night around a loud community campfire, I suddenly had an image in my mind's eye of an owl. Wondering why, I stepped back from the din of the fire circle. After a moment, I felt a subtle pressure moving in my ears, not audible as any recognizable sound, yet meaningful in some way... I listened into the night, and realized the pressure was pulsing in a familiar rhythm...

A friend was curious as to what I was doing, so I invited her to come from the fire and listen into the distance with me. "Do you hear an owl?!" I asked curiously.

"What? No, I don't hear anything."

Intrigued, soon the others stepped forward and started listening with us, too. Alas, no one else heard anything, either. I invited the group to slowly step further forward, listening intently. After we had moved a good 20 yards, the soft pulsing in my ears came to resolution, and I heard the ever-so-faint staccato of the great horned owl's call.

"Listen — I *definitely* hear an owl! Can you hear it?" I asked again.

Now, people were looking at me askance as if I had gone crazy, as no one else heard a single sound. Most of my compatriots finally shook their heads and returned to the fire. Just as I had given up hope that anyone else might hear the owl and verify that I wasn't going crazy, an excited voice called from the darkness ahead — "Hey, there really *is* an owl! I can just hear it! How *the hell* did you know it was there?" My friend was truly mystified.

Soon everyone was back for another listen. The group moved further forward until finally, everyone could hear the distant resonant hooting. My friends were at a loss for words, either amazed or unsure of what had just taken place.

It seemed my acute search for the owls had awakened a deeper sensing faculty, one that linked incoming subtle sensory information with my memory and mind's eye. Some part of my inner consciousness had recognized the owl's presence, activating an image of the owl on my mental screen, even though I couldn't consciously hear the owl around the loud campfire. This would become a handy tool in many other areas of life, an understanding I would carry forward with me beyond this experience, just one of the many gifts of the Owl...

The Owl as the Teacher...

This moment of recognition of the Owl's teaching would lead to other moments of discovery, each layering upon each other in a tapestry of insight as I stepped further into the world of Nature. These and other moments flashed briefly in my mind as I sat now upon the hill at sunset, reveling in the wake of the owl's passage.

The owl had become my teacher, my focus of meditation,

helping me learn about the unity of Nature, teaching me to recognize the subtle stirrings of intuition and the state of mindful presence that reveals its quiet voice. Through the owl, I learned how to be "in the right place at the right time," immersing in the moment and trusting the subtle call of instinct and intuition in a way that forever transformed my understanding of Nature's language.

By meditating in Nature each day, the lessons of the owl had become apparent for me, deepening towards their fruition in that moment atop a small hill as the day transitioned to night, at the time of Mystery when things are not always what they seem, and there is more to be revealed than is first apparent.

The Empowerment...

The foundation that empowered the Quest of the Owl was a passion to know, to connect with, and to touch a greater Mystery. In following this passion, my senses came alive to the stories of the land and of our wild neighbors that dwell alongside us on this Earth.

Such Mysteries are available and waiting for us all, if we will embark upon them... and when we do — when we touch the Mystery — we realize that the Nature within and around us is truly one. We are one with Nature, and the Mystery moves within us beyond and through all time.

Stand at the threshold and listen...what Mystery is calling to you?

Flying Forward...

In this first chapter, we explored our ancient biological legacy of connection with the Dream of Nature, and how our longtime lineage as hunter-gatherers has shaped us to become what we are today as a species. Through this we see that we <u>are</u> Nature, leading us to discern how we actively need Nature's presence in our lives to help us heal, nourish, and grow to our fullest potential.

We also covered a quick overview of the many gifts that meditation in Nature can offer us in the modern experience, ranging from stress reduction to a restored connection with the pure creativity of Nature's Dreaming. Finally, we painted a picture of where we're headed and some of the key topics we'll cover along the way.

Next, it's time to boot up your laces (or just take off your shoes!) and Go Into Nature...

In chapter two, we're going on a field trip. Amongst other things, we'll dispel some urban myths about Nature, visit Yoda's cave for sage advice, and shine light on the internal transformations that go along with a journey into Nature. Get ready, it'll be a party!

2

GOING INTO NATURE

Before we dive into the practices and techniques of meditating in Nature, there's a few basics we need to explore first. I want your meditation practice to prosper for the long haul. Getting a few essentials in place here at the outset will ensure you have a great experience. Then, you'll want to continue your practice far into the future.

In this chapter, I introduce some outdoor basics that every Conscious Nature explorer needs under their belt. We'll also look at the not-so-obvious mental traps that stop many people in their tracks without their even realizing it, and how to avoid these internal pitfalls. Finally, I share some common sense "musts" about meditating in the outdoors that are all too easy to overlook.

Into the Paradox...

One of the strange effects of growing up in the suburbs is adopting the idea of "Going Into Nature." As a suburbanite, when you go for a hike or go camping, you leave your house, and what do you do? You *go into Nature.*

It's as if Nature isn't there already in your neighborhood, but is lurking somewhere "out there," beyond the comfortable confines of paved asphalt and electric streetlights. It's certainly not in your house (remember all the trees that have contributed the floorboards, joists, and frames of your house? No? Not to mention the toilet paper you use every day?).

Nature is certainly not in the flame of the propane stove that warms your eggs for breakfast, or the chlorine-purified water that somehow magically comes out of the kitchen sink. Nature definitely isn't in the electricity pulsing through the copper wires in the walls, or in the rare-earth minerals powering the cell phone you use very day. It's definitely not in the air that fills your lungs with each breath you take.

Or so it seems. Because Nature is "out there," and you are "in here" — in your house, in your car, on the highway, at school, in the shopping mall. How often are you surrounded by four walls, a roof, and a floor? How many times are you bombarded with flashing screens, loud sounds, and the rumble of heavy vehicles roaring past? I suppose it could be easy to forget that all of this manmade hustle and bustle is actually part of Nature. A simple oversight. A matter of semantics, even.

As a matter of fact, you share about 60% of your genome with the broccoli on your dinner plate, and about the same with the tree you relax against in your yard. Compare your genome with that of a chimpanzee, and you're at a 96% match.[1][2] Heck, you even share about 70% of your genome with the marine acorn worm, with whom we all share a humble common ancestor.[3] Simply put, we *are* Nature.

Still, it seems for many that you have to get dressed up to "go into Nature." You have to lace up your hiking boots, fill your water bottle, get on the regular bug spray (plus spray Permethrin on your socks for ticks), then put on the extra-breathable UVA-resistant, nanoparticle shirt (!), and then lather on a final coat of sunscreen. It's like you're going to the moon instead of the trail just down the road. In the suburbs, Going Into Nature is a freakin' *process*.

Then, once you Get Into Nature, there's a whole slew of new challenges to contend with. Is that annoying guy with the off-leash, ridiculously large dog going to be there? Are the ticks out? Is it too hot for the gear you've brought, or too cold? It just rained, and do you really want to get your new shoes muddy on that one section of trail? Or maybe you should rush back because you just remembered you were supposed to meet someone for dinner?

If you even get past these basics and go deeper into the woods, more troubling thoughts emerge. *Hmm, it's awfully quiet in here. Too quiet?* After all, your senses are used to a barrage of flashing lights and sounds. The sudden aloneness and quiet is jarring.

Is it safe to be alone? Are these trees looking oddly at me? What if I get lost? Is that overly-friendly squirrel rabid? Didn't I hear my cousin's neighbor say when I was a kid that some ax murderer lurked around over here?

After all, your TV shows you all kinds of crazy stuff every day from around the world, and it's probably all happening in this patch of woods, too, right?

Now, these are true thoughts and concerns that often come up for people who haven't spent much time outside when they first consider "Going into Nature." Maybe a few of you reading this have even experienced some of these thoughts. These concerns create blockages that can keep us from really enjoying our connection with the outdoors.

In part, we have these thoughts because of our own unfamiliarity with the natural environment, from media-driven perceptions that may be blown out of proportion, or because of the frightening power of the unknown. In contrast, in many traditional nature-based cultures, each generation saw a special opportunity in facing these kinds of fears and instead of avoiding them, used them as a rite of passage.

Truth or Dare on Dagobah: Facing the Unknown

Remember what happened to Luke Skywalker on *Empire Strikes Back*? This is actually quite an instructive tale for suburbanites and city-dwellers who are newly Going Into Nature. There's a scene in the film that shows how this process works, and what it takes to move through these kinds of perceptual barriers and into a thriving sense of connection.

Luke, a Jedi in training, goes searching for Master Yoda to teach him the ways of the Force. Luke ends up on a far-away planet called Dagobah. What he found there was a mud-puddle of mysterious jungle swamp, something Luke had never encountered in the desert world where he grew up.

This place was totally outside Luke's comfort zone. There were spooky sounds everywhere, fog, dark water, and even snakes. He had to camp there because his X-Wing had crashed in the swamp. So Luke's first challenge was to adapt and acclimatize himself to this strange place. Luke simply had to experience the mud, wet, dark, cold, and unknown of the place. It was a total rite of passage.

Fast forward, and now Luke has found his mentor. Yoda is a cantankerous little curmudgeon. The little green guy is working Luke like crazy, making him run every day through the jungle and do handstands while he levitates rocks with his developing Jedi powers.

Clearly, Luke has gotten used to the place by now. He's probably encountered a lot of things during his training (dangers to avoid, places to find food on the land, and many runs-ins with the local flora and fauna), and he's learned how to find his way and blend in. By this point, the young Jedi has learned to stretch his senses in all directions, while becoming present to the moment. Yoda is attuning Luke to the greater Nature around him through the Force; he's learning to trust his intuition and inner resources. All foundational stuff.

What's Yoda to do next? The old master senses it's time to send Luke down into the spooky cave. He knows Luke must now dig deeper into his Inner Nature and shine the light of awareness into this place of hidden emotion and belief, just as he did with the mysteries of the outer landscape. There's nothing like spending time alone in the dark to bring out those inner demons.

So, Yoda shows his young protege the way into the Cave. Just outside, he gives Luke an epic pep talk — "This is a place of great Darkness..." — you know, all that wonderful kind of stuff that you want to hear right before you crawl alone down into a dark, mysterious pit. And by the way, you can't bring your lightsaber. Gotta do this one on your own, buddy.

Luke musters some courage and goes into the Cave. Out of the swirling mists comes his worst fear, which he has to face. In the end, we see his fear is really telling him something about himself that he has to come to terms with (but that journey ends up taking him a whole other movie to actually accomplish, because it's a "trilogy"). Eventually, though, Luke figures out the lesson and steps fully into his own sense of mastery. He's learned to flow with the Force and becomes a true Jedi. Now, he's working in partnership with the balance of Nature. Pretty cool stuff.

So, what can we learn from this story for our own situation? If we start to track fear, one of the things we might notice is that there are two different types.

Understanding the Faces of Fear

One kind of fear is that very visceral sense that actually arises beneath the conscious mind, from the more ancient parts of the brain and body. It's a direct response to a signal in the environment that some part of your sensory system is picking up — even when your conscious mind might not be aware of it.

This visceral signal of fear could manifest in the gut as a really tight sense of warning; or the whole body can activate with tension and intensity. This is actually a very useful survival mechanism to help us become aware of nearby threats, such as the presence of a large animal in the brush. Sometimes the body *knows* when there's a real danger.[4]

The other (and more common) type of fear is projected by the mind. This is to do with the kind of stuff Luke had to face in the Cave.

It's not unusual for fear to come up when we get out of our familiar routine and into a new situation. This is the brain's warning system at work, simply urging you to pay attention in the new place. If you haven't spent a lot of time out of doors, your brain might get into an overactive warning mode so you don't step off an unseen cliff, or impulsively wolf down a brightly colored poison dart frog for a snack during your vacation to the tropics. Because we don't know what to expect in a new place, the brain goes crazy — *What's that? What's that?*

Here's where the projected fear comes into play. The old saying "the greatest fear is fear itself" is right on the money. Because the untrained brain is not calibrated to the new environment, it begins drawing on any spare, two-bit piece of data it can find to match to what's happening.

The rustle of a mouse in the dark becomes the padded steps of a mountain lion you read about in *National Geographic*. The shadow of a gnarly tree becomes a cloaked monster you saw once in a scary movie. The warning mode has a way of hijacking brain function. You need to be able to recognize that your fight-or-flight system has been activated, and if there's no real threat, to tone it down (see the "Presencing With the Complete Breath" exercise in Chapter 11 for a powerful way to restore your inner calm).

Separating Fact from Fiction

So, fears and worries might come up, but how will you manage them? Luke had to work through these fears; in fact he had no choice, since his ship was sunk in the swamp and he was stuck camping. Appreciate the sensation of fear for what it is — a call to be aware. Apply common sense, and use contemplation to assess the truth of your fears so you can face them head on.

Nature Jedi Brain Tip: When you use your prefrontal cortex by rationally examining what's happening, you actually help yourself shift out of the instinctive response state.

Some fears, upon inspection, reveal themselves to be groundless and irrational. *The ax murderer in the woods? The evil clown in the trees that is going to steal your soul?* Let these ones go.

For dealing with real human safety concerns, hike or even meditate outdoors with a friend or two; find a time to get out together regularly each week, and make it a thing. Bring your dog as backup if you need to. Carry pepper spray if it helps get you out there. Tell someone where you're going and when you'll be back.

Of course, pay attention to your surroundings. Are there other people hiking — families, couples? Does it feel good to be there? Does it look like troublemakers loiter there? Do you have phone reception if you needed to call for help? Make choices based on some data and observation rather than letting your life be ruled by blind fear.

Other fears appear from the germs of loose facts, amplified and distorted beyond proportion. *The rabid animal waiting to bite me? Snakes in the trees?* Again, use common sense and avoid anything or anyone that seems to act strangely. If a slobbering raccoon swaggers up to you in the daytime, don't try to pet it. And not many snakes live in the trees, at least in the suburbs. Only black rat snakes climb trees in North America, and they're more interested in rats than they are in you. A big one lived in my friend's kitchen for years.

Shrink these kinds of blown-out fears back to what they really are: half-truths and statistical exceptions. Some fears might have merit, but when appropriate, offer yourself a chance to step up and shine the light of truth on urban myths about the outdoors. The woodsperson learns what it takes to avoid or deal with the real situations that can come up in Nature. This gives you a chance to learn about the nature of your place and how to respect it and flow with it.

We'll be returning to the topic of fear as we explore a set of advanced Nature Jedi tricks for working with the mind in Chapter 9, after you get some field experience in. Now, it's time to focus on some foundational Nature know-how; like Yoda did for Luke, we're going to attune your awareness to some essential basics of your local landscape.

Be Prepared

Don't become a candidate for the Darwin Awards. Do some research. You can bet that Luke had to learn about all the things that could eat him or harm him when he first landed on Dagobah. In North America at least, that list is pretty short. It's more about learning to avoid the things that can *irritate* you, though there are likely a few "must-knows" for actually dangerous hazards in each region. If you live in places that have big cats, hundreds of dangerous spiders, snakes, and other goodies, you have more research to do.

For sure, in suburban North America you'll want to learn about ticks and how to avoid them (the CDC website has great info and can quickly get you up to speed; just search "CDC ticks"). Those little buggers are abundantly common and are vectors for Lyme's Disease and other pathogens. You *need* to learn strategies for tick hygiene, so that you can detect them and keep them off of you. It's pretty simple. As the cover to the *Hitchhiker's Guide to the Galaxy* says, "Don't Panic."

With ticks, it comes down to good routine. Tuck your socks over your pant legs so they can't crawl inside. If you're sitting down to meditate or just relax, put down a groundcloth first to sit on. Check your pant legs periodically, especially if you've gone through tall grass or brush. Ticks can crawl up pretty fast! Throw your clothes in the dryer on high for ten minutes when you get home to kill any hangers-on. Do a full body check, too (especially armpits, groin, behind the ears & around the hairline).

Keep your wits about you, just like Luke learned to do. If there's other obviously hazardous stuff in your area, learn about it. Duh, right? Alligators? There's none where I live, but if you live where they are, you should obviously know how to avoid them. Same goes for anything else that can take a chunk out of you, or that bites, stings, or causes rashes. It's usually a pretty short list to be aware of. If you're going to be spending a lot of time connecting outside, do your due diligence.

In the Northeast, my "biters and stingers to avoid list" mainly includes ticks (several species, but they are all obviously tick-like), yellow jackets (don't step on the ground nests in the summer), and black widow spiders (mostly in untended corners of the attic, etc.). Poisonous reptiles include the copperhead and timber rattlesnakes; none of these snakes are very common around my home, and they tend to be localized where they hang out. Ask around your local hiking club or nature center to find out what to watch out for in your area (pro tip: if a place is called "Rattlesnake Mountain," there might be a reason for it).

My "everyday irritating plants list" includes poison ivy (duh — but good to know both when it has leaves, and even when it doesn't), and stinging nettle. Usually poison ivy is the first thing I get a bead on when I set into a new area. I'd really rather not have to deal with it, and since I like walking at night and at other odd times in the woods when I'd prefer not to discover it by accident after the fact, I tend to memorize where it grows. And I love to eat nettles, but I also watch where they grow so I don't accidentally walk through them with shorts in the summer.

Removing the oil from accidental contact with poison ivy, by the way, can be done with cold water and laundry detergent, and a good amount of pressure with a towel (think of the way you need some pressure to pull grease off your skin). If I'm harvesting wild edibles or medicines, then I'll have to be aware of other poisonous look-alikes, but if I'm just tromping around, those two are the main concerns.

Also, I keep an eye out for other basic stuff like "widowmaker" branches that are dangling and waiting to fall. If I'm off trail and barefoot, I also note old barbed wire fence lines, broken glass, and sharp branches. During lightning storms, I avoid ridge lines and standing under (or being) the tallest object. When it's hot I drink plenty of water, and when it's cold I bundle up. Pretty basic.

For mammals, I avoid getting between mother bears and their cubs, and I don't get too close to male moose in the rut, or near mother moose and their young. I also avoid wearing a porkchop necklace around the dog park. It's really a manageable list, and is mainly to do with common sense.

If you go to a state or Federal park, usually there will be signs up about any hazardous species or local conditions you should know about. Ask a ranger for more information if you're unsure. For your home turf, ask other locals and do some research in field guides and on the Interwebs.

~ Practice: Researching Local Hazards ~

It's time for a scavenger hunt. The mission: gain knowledge of your basic local hazards. This is stuff any little kid in a hunter-gatherer culture would know. Spend a half hour on this, you'll be glad you did. Make Yoda proud.

Get out the field guides or the ol' Google browser and do some research. Check your nature section in your local library for resources. *Peterson's Field Guide to Venomous Animals & Poisonous Plants* is a handy resource for North America. Skim the range maps in that guide to quickly learn what to pay attention to in your area. Take notes and learn about:

1. **Poison ivy (east coast)/poison oak (west coast)**, or other plants that cause irritation.
2. **Ticks.** Which ones are in your area? How can you avoid them? How do you remove them safely? (Again, see the CDC website).
3. **Snakes & other reptiles.** Any venomous/dangerous ones in your area? How do you identify them? Where do they hang out? How common are they?
4. **Spiders.** Know how to identify black widows, the brown recluse, and their webs.
5. **Wasps, Hornets, Bees.** Which ones live nearby? What do their nests look like?
6. **Mammals.** Any ornery ones? What times of year are

they especially aggressive? What times of day? How common are they?

~ Practice: Scanning for Natural Hazards ~

Nature Jedi Skills 101: When you select an outdoor area for your meditations, whether you'll be sitting there or mindfully walking through, observe the place first in good light for any natural hazards to be aware of. Make a mental map of anything you'll need to avoid.

Sweep your eyes up above for hanging tree limbs or branches that could snap in the wind. Examine the ground for uneven terrain, sharp rocks and broken glass, or barbed wire from old fence lines. Learn how to identify poison ivy (east coast) or poison oak (west coast) and make sure it is not growing anywhere you intend to tromp around. It can grow up a tree with its tendrils, so don't lean against any hairy looking vines. At home or at the park office, research any unique local hazards and how to avoid them (flash floods in canyons, Komodo dragons, etc.).

Refresh your mental map with a quick spot check each time you visit the area. With just a little practice, you will learn to rapidly assess any area you move through. Potential dangers need not cause you fear if they are understood and properly respected.

Tuning the Mind to Nature's Channel

The point of all this talk about what's a real danger and what isn't is that *we have to tune the mind*. Half of getting to know the nature of a place is learning *what* to pay attention to and *where* it is;[5] the other half is just showing up and being present. Both sides of the coin require attunement. This zone of attunement (or at-one-ment) is where meditation and the art of awareness come into play.

When you are attuned to your surroundings, and you are equally attuned to your inner state of being, then you can move with more harmony and understanding. As you keep your awareness expanded, you will naturally encounter and learn new things about your environment.

Culture and Attunement With Place...

A culture that is connected to the land helps support this kind of integrated awareness, because the activities and way of life require the people to know their surroundings. This makes the experience of Nature frictionless. Then, your senses attune to Nature every day because your life depends on it — there is no option not to do so.

When a culture *doesn't* support an intimate connection with the land (i.e. most of modern life), then we have to work harder to break through the inertia caused by this social gap. We have to create our own self-motivation and commitment to engage with the practices that will help us realize our personal connection with the natural world. That said, let's unpack what this actually means:

The cultures that have lived close to the cycles of the land for thousands of years have figured out that in order to survive, they need to teach their kids to pay attention to what's around them. Through mentoring and role modeling, kids learned how to gather wild foods, how to hunt, how to build shelter, make herbal medicines, and how to live well with what the land could offer them. Each generation added to this understanding of place.

After a while, the people got to know their place really well. The songs, dances, art, and crafts of the culture all reflected the unique patterns of the place the culture sprang forth from. The culture's *ecological imagination* became finely tuned, inspired by the place. Through the culture, the peoples' minds attuned to the Nature of their place.

This, in fact, is the story of all of our ancestors. For most of the 300,000 plus years that we have been identifiably human, and for the millions of years leading to that moment, we as a species have had our senses tuned to the patterns of Nature's singular channel. Each sensory adaptation, every neural firing pattern, and each metabolic function of the human body has been through Nature's sorting process over this long time span.

Over much of this vast time period, a variety of cultures sprouted up from the land, attuned in various ways to the rhythms of their places. Some persisted, others didn't. All were transformed in one way or another by Nature's changing dynamics.

The Acid Test...

Only recently have humans taken over so much of the planet that we can (seemingly) ignore most of what's happening around us in the natural world. Consider a few questions that would be basic knowledge to a hunter-gatherer, literally "kid's stuff":

What phase is the moon in right now, and where it is in the sky in this moment? What direction is the wind blowing from right now? What is the closest natural drinkable water source, and how much water does it yield each day? Where is the nearest edible or medicinal plant, and how can it help you in this season? What are the birds telling you about the location of large carnivores in the area?

For many of us today, we don't have a direct reason to have such keen relationships with the world of Nature. We can slide by, it seems, without making the primary sensory connections that our ancestors depended on — connections that empower us to be in conscious relationship with the land, that lead us to viscerally understand how to exist in balance with the natural places that support us.

To paraphrase one of my own longtime nature mentors, Jon Young: "Not paying attention is a luxury of modern living." Four walls, a floor, and a roof provide a certain sense of protection and comfort. One can generally get away with playing video games or streaming Netflix without having to listen for the distant bird alarms that signal approaching danger. We can become self-absorbed in our own imaginings and to-do lists, and never even notice the direction of the wind that carries our scent as we walk down the trail, or the cry of the blue jay alerting us to the cat hidden in the thicket.

A Culture of Amnesia...

When enough generations of people in a place manage to go through their entire lives from house to work and back each day without ever having to step foot on the living earth, the Dream of Nature starts to slip away from the Dream of Culture. Then, the culture gets short-sighted, and it begins to do things that aren't sustainable. That's when Nature steps back in with a dose of reality:

Fuel loads from hundred-year "no fire" forestry practices build up to become incendiary blazes; rivers that are dammed and siphoned for agriculture and consumption in arid regions get tapped out as water demand increases; richly biodiverse habitats are displaced in favor of vast mono-crop plantings, which become highly susceptible to disease. These are just a few examples of short-sighted practices that serve immediate needs without enough long-term forethought. When these kinds of temporary strategies fail, Nature tips the scales back towards balance. Such practices come about when a culture imposes its own ideas on Nature, rather than collaborating with Nature's tendencies and principles.

The practices in this book, of course, are intended to help

break that cycle. When we meditate in Nature, then natural cycles become part of our regular world view. With this awareness, we can bring Nature's wisdom back into our community experience through our own creativity and interest. Nature then starts to positively infuse and regenerate the cultures that it supports. This new cycle of earth awareness is supported in a million different small ways, through the stories and inspiration shared by each person who goes on a journey of exploration into Nature's mysteries.

If you're reading this, then you no doubt enjoy Nature already, and may have some active connections of your own with the outdoors. Or, perhaps you want to learn how to get started in this direction. Fortunately, getting started is easy. Why? Because as we've seen, you're already part of Nature. Now, you're simply going to deepen that understanding.

Fortunately, much of this journey can happen at your Meditation Spot, right in your backyard or local park. We'll get into how this all works as we move further in the book. For now, take a moment to consider: *How would it impact your life to feel more consciously connected with Nature?*

Take a walk and ponder this question. Really dig into it.

I'm asking you to do this now because I know that before you undertake a journey, it helps to first understand your true motivations. After all, these inner longings are the source of the emotional power that will fuel your quest over the long haul. When you clearly know what you're after, and why you're going for it, you have a truly valuable Powerbar of motivational energy to help you through those moments when you feel stuck. So, get out into Nature and sit with this question.

Adapted for Mindfulness in Nature

Now that we've established that we (including you) are part of Nature, it's a good time to mention that we're also already setup for achieving a mindful connection with the natural world.

Mindfulness is one of those modern buzzwords that seems to be everywhere today. For some people, the idea of dropping fully into the moment seems arduous, or akin to reaching some impossibly enlightened state. However, this skill stems from our ancient primal inheritance of needing to pay attention in order to survive.

Over those hundreds of thousands of years and beyond, our ancestors had to contend with all kinds of hazards. People learned to use all of their senses to detect danger. They had to be ready to respond at a moment's notice in order to stay safe. Hunter-gatherers have to be mindful and aware, not as a hobby, but as a way of life. We can learn to tune our senses to Nature's channel through mindful awareness, too. We just have to find the right teachers.

A cat is a great awareness teacher. Your cat knows all about mindfulness and when to apply it.

After a good meal, you'll notice your cat lays around, content and purring. Those are moments to enjoy the luxuriousness of comfort and ease. When the night arrives, your cat's instincts kick in. It's time to prowl and hunt. The second the door opens, the cat seems to come alive at a whole new threshold, with the complete array of feline senses penetrating into the night for any glimmer of sound or movement. If you watch a cat at these times, you can see an animal that is fully in the moment. When in doubt, watch the animals. You'll be sure to learn something.

Though the practices that lead us to this state of primal awareness are quite simple, there will be a bit of a journey in bringing this mindful connection "online." The modern mind does have a bit of adapting to do to get back in tune with the rhythms of the land and the animals. As Yoda said, "You must unlearn what you have learned." You'll have to go on your own journey to Dagobah, and eventually, into the Cave...

Up Next...

So far, we've explored how we are adapted to mindfully pay attention to Nature, and that in fact, we as human beings are part of Nature's complex patterns. In the next chapter, we'll discover the many benefits of actively connecting with Nature for our health and well-being, including the restorative effects of meditation and mindfulness training.

3

HOW MEDITATING IN NATURE HELPS US
FEEL & BE OUR BEST

According to a recent report, the most common health concern that's Googled in the United States is *stress*.[1] When you get stressed out, your fight-or-flight system gets activated. This system evolved to help us deal with things like the sudden appearance of saber-toothed tigers or large snakes. When triggered, a cascade of stress hormones float through your bloodstream, preparing your muscles and respiratory system for a life-or-death sprint away from danger.

Now, a tiger is either going to try to eat you or not, but one way or the other, eventually it's going to go away. Most predators succeed with the advantage of surprise, and once that element is gone, it becomes too dangerous to stick around. The human nervous system is adapted to cope with periodic bursts of this kind of stress, but it really needs time to wind down afterwards and reset. The brain needs to recuperate from these adrenaline bursts by relaxing, whether that means going fishing, taking a walk, or just staring up at the clouds.

The problem with the stress of modern life is that it hangs around like an angry rain cloud that doesn't want to stop soaking you. A barrage of to-do lists, appointments, texts, Tweets, IM's, and bills requires your ongoing attention. Each stress moment that is not resolved begins to compound, multiplying into a chronic condition with potentially severe health effects.

Our social media and other tech is built around addictive neurological responses that can add to the stress effect. The pleasure chemical dopamine gets triggered when we receive texts or make a post online. This is the same stuff that gets released in a rat's brain when it beats the maze and gets the cheese. What happens to a rat that learns about the cheese? It gets really good at going through the maze. What happens when the rat doesn't get to go through the maze and get the cheese anymore? Withdrawal symptoms. Addiction to technology is like this: we want the fix of that dopamine rush, and we'll waste hours upon hours of our days seeking it.

It just so happens that meditation and time spent in Nature are both very effective antidotes to the stress problem. When you put the two together, the transformation is outstanding. In this chapter, we'll explore the health benefits and cognitive boons that you can enjoy from meditating in Nature.

The Natural Healing Wisdom of the Animals

Animals have a natural healing wisdom that helps them to ditch their stress-load and return to full presence after a traumatic or stressful event. Following their example, we can turn to Nature for insight into the healing process. For me, one particularly memorable outdoor adventure especially highlights this transformational potential:

One afternoon I was walking in a meadow, when I heard a slough of frantic wingbeats coming towards me. Turning around to face the sound, a flock of American goldfinches suddenly whizzed by me at full speed, their tiny wingtips grazing my head in a hurry to flee... whatever was after them was a much greater threat than I might ever be.

The meadow suddenly became deathly quiet. All of the nearby birds stopped their songs and calls. Moments later, a hungry Cooper's hawk landed heavily on a low branch, just three feet off the ground. The branch swayed back and forth from the sudden weight and momentum of the bird, who gripped the branch with strong talons, flapping his agile wings a few times to stall his flight. The alert predator missed the goldfinches, but remained on the lookout for any nearby potential meals.

As the hawk scanned intensely left to right with keen red eyes, it was then that I noticed a small bird, directly positioned on the ground underneath him. There in the shadow of the branch, just three feet under the raptor and fully exposed on the short grass, stood a junco. The tiny songbird remained frozen and still. Would the hawk take notice and claim his lunch?

After a tense minute of scanning side to side, the hawk flew off. Not too long after, the sounds of tentative bird calls and even a whispered song or two emerged around us. The junco, though, remained frozen silently in place. I thought the diminutive songbird was just waiting for the "all clear" to get up and leave, but the junco had another, altogether different lesson in store for me.

After a minute or two, the small bird began violently shaking. It seemed as though every particle of the bird was vibrating, from foot to tail to beak. I could feel the intensity moving through the songbird as its body processed the traumatic run-in with the hawk. After 30 seconds or so of viscerally shedding the stress of the encounter, the bird simply took off and went back to its routine, having survived to live another day.

This incident opened a deep inquiry for me around what it means to soothe stress and resolve trauma. The encounter showed me how an animal can quickly transition from a full-fledged fight-or-flight response and back into the regular demands of feeding and foraging. The junco became a wiser bird on that day, yet continued forward in its life with full aliveness and presence. For me, the junco became a mascot for resiliency and flow in its finest sense.

To understand more about how we, too, can begin to shed stress and step into our full potential of flow and presence, we can turn to the body's nervous system and the powerful restorative effects of meditation upon it.

Relaxing the Nervous System with Meditation

Like a car, the nervous system has two basic pedals: one that speeds you up (sympathetic nervous system), and one that slows you down (parasympathetic nervous system).

The fight-or-flight response that we've discussed so far is connected to the accelerator. Stress hormones prepare you to get away from the danger, or fight it with all you've got. The question is, what about the brakes? How do we drop out of the 5th gear mode we use to meet a deadline at work, and get back down into a more comfortable second or third gear for time at home?

Harvard researcher Herbert Benson has spent much of his career studying how meditation can help us put the brakes on our flight-or-fight response. It turns out that how we use our mind can make all the difference.

Back in the early 70's, during the renaissance of meditation in the West, Benson's team hooked meditators up to EEG's and other equipment to find out what was happening in the body when they accessed altered states.

The Relaxation Response

Benson found that a number of repeatable physiological responses occur during meditation: electrical skin resistance drops, breathing rate lowers, oxygen consumption decreases, and cortisol levels also lower significantly. These effects kick in after 12 minutes or so of meditating and make up what Benson calls "the Relaxation Response."

But wait, there's more. Through his initial studies, Benson found that daily use of the Relaxation Response helps reduce headaches, normalizes cardiac rhythm irregularities, and reduces symptoms of PMS, anxiety, and both mild and moderate depression.

For its day, this was a landmark study. These early results provided exciting confirmation that the focus of the mind could directly affect the physiology of the body. The Cartesian "separation" between mind and body was beginning to break down. Further, the benefits were clear: the biochemical transformations that are awakened through meditation all support stress reduction and the overall health of the cardiovascular system.

In his popular book, *The Relaxation Response*, Benson shares that only four simple ingredients are needed to produce an effective stress-reducing meditation: a comfortable posture, a simple repetitive mental focus for 12-15 minutes (a mantra or simple phrase will do), a passive attitude (if you lose focus, simply shift back to your mantra when you remember), and a quiet environment. These simple and proven principles helped move meditation beyond the esoteric sphere and into a much larger audience that might never have embraced it before. As we move further into exploring various meditations later in this book, we will make use of these four key points to empower our awareness in Nature.

Later, Benson would find even more intriguing results. As the technology became more sophisticated, Benson's team began looking at the epigenetics of meditation. Each of the body's 54,000 genes can be switched on and off ('expressed') in different ways. How we use our bodies, what we eat, and what we encounter in our environment can all alter how these different genes are activated. This in turn can affect our health. Benson wanted to know what meditating would do to gene expression.

Benson gathered two groups together — a group of experienced meditators with over nine and a half years of experience, and a group of non-meditators. When his team measured the gene expression of both groups, it turns out that the meditators had over 2,200 genes that were expressed differently than the non-meditators, and that these changes support healthful living: the meditators enjoyed improved immune response, reduction of inflammation and premature aging, and diminished oxidative stress.

Benson then wondered how long it would take to awaken these positive changes in new meditators. A new group began meditating for twenty minutes a day, and were tested after eight weeks. This time, 1,561 gene changes were recorded, and 431 of these changes matched the signatures in the genes of the advanced meditation group.[2] A mere two months of daily meditation is enough time for you to begin reaping the benefits of the practice on a deep genetic level. *Daily meditation can positively change you — literally — from the inside out.*

Discussing these findings in his book, *The Relaxation Revolution*, Benson reflects that "our own current research at Harvard... shows conclusively that the mind can indeed influence the body down to the genetic level. Your mind can actually change the way that your body functions... you can consciously 'switch on' healthful genetic expression."

If meditating on a cushion isn't your cup of tea, you can also get many of the benefits of meditation out in Nature. Benson eventually realized that only two of his four elements are really needed to get in a good meditation: a simple repetitive mental focus, and a passive mindset. He found that with some practice, the meditative state could just as easily be achieved while walking or running, in a variety of environments. Basically, you can meditate anywhere if you develop the habit.

Later in this book, I'll be sharing simple practices you can use as focal points for your meditation in Nature. You'll get the benefits of meditation and at the same time expand your awareness to the flow of life around and within you. First, let's look at some of the benefits that you can receive simply from *being* in nature, whether you are meditating or not.

How Nature Soothes & De-Stresses Us

> *The temple bell stops but I still hear the sound coming out of the flowers."*
> - *Basho*

We've already touched on how the Relaxation Response lowers your body's cortisol levels. Out-of-control cortisol is implicated in all sorts of nasty stuff, from inflammation to weight gain and high levels of stress. When cortisol levels stay high, it's harder to lose weight, and it's also harder to de-stress. Walking is a great way to temper the body's cortisol release, and walking in Nature is especially powerful.

A 2010 study in Japan showed that compared to walking in the city, taking a walk in a forest will produce significantly lower cortisol levels, along with lower pulse rates and blood pressure, and generate more parasympathetic nervous system activity (meaning that forest walks help you press the "brake pedal" on your body's fight-or-flight response).[3]

The beneficial effects of connecting with Nature can reach

deeper into the immune system, too. In Japan, the practice of Shinrin-yoku or "forest bathing" (which means soaking in the atmosphere of the forest — nothing to do with rubber duckies and bath towels) is generating a number of studies demonstrating positive health benefits from time outdoors.

Most notably, it's been found that adults who took a three-day trip into a forest with daily walks boosted both their anti-cancer proteins and their natural killer (NK) cells.[4] NK cells are a type of white blood cell that supports immune response. With a boost in these cells, the body has an extra defense against viruses and tumors.

If you can't get outside right away, just getting a view of Nature will help. A study with office workers in South Korea found that simply having a window affording a view of the forest significantly reduced stress and boosted job satisfaction.[5] No office window? Even looking at photos of nature for ten minutes can help improve your cognitive performance.[6] In terms of what nature can do for the attention span, another study found that kids with ADHD who experience a natural environment for 20 minutes improve their scores on attention tests.[7] Taking a walk in Nature can improve your proofreading skills, too.[8]

Higher-level cognitive tasks benefit from time in Nature, too. Members of a four-day hiking trip study experienced drastic increases in their creative problem solving skills, averaging 50% gains. The authors suggested that in part, the cognitive gains came from time away from media and technology, which drain *directed attention* (the ability to manage the focus and direction of our thoughts). They also suspect the relaxed and emotionally positive stimuli of Nature contributed to the effect.[9]

Attention Restoration

What accounts for Nature's restorative effects? ART, or Attention Restoration Theory, suggests that Nature's patterns gently engage and "fascinate" our involuntary attention; we don't need to exert much consciously directed effort to appreciate our surroundings in Nature, so the higher-order attention systems of the brain can recharge.[10]

For example, think of when you're admiring a beautiful sunset... somehow, you are effortlessly aware of the tint in the sky, the bustle of end-of-the-day sounds around you, and the feeling carried by the last rays of the Sun... you don't have to exert a lot of energy to be in that moment, you're simply drawn into it.

Stephen Kaplan, one of the formulators of ART, wrote to this effect in his paper *Meditation, Restoration, and the Management of Mental Fatigue*. There, Kaplan comments that meditation and ART both promote "getting away" from your daily sources of mental fatigue - in one case through the unique mental focus of medita-tion, which often happens in a special meditation spot set apart from daily concerns, and in the other case, by getting into a natural area that is different from the usual home or work setting. These special settings allow the brain to draw upon different neural maps than the ones activated by day-to-day concerns, allowing the over-taxed areas of the brain to recoup.[11]

Since long-term meditation as a practice on its own has been shown through MRI scans to actually increase the thickness of the cortex in brain areas that support attention,[12] the combination of restorative walks in Nature complemented by outdoor meditation seems like a no brainer (or an "extra-brainer"?).

~ Practice: Taking a Restorative Nature Walk ~

Whether you have only one minute or an entire hour, you can gift yourself with a mental reset by taking a stroll and immersing in Nature's patterns. This particular walk brings together a sensory meditation with restorative wandering in Nature.

You can fold this process into an existing walking route, or seek out a special Nature trail or path in the park to enjoy. Walking a trail surrounded with greenery yields additional health benefits, as many studies have revealed that wellness is boosted by natural surroundings. A park is an ideal place for this practice. However, you can find Nature wherever you are, if you have a mind to look for it.

How is Nature present in your neighborhood today? Whether you encounter a single dandelion growing through the cracks of the urban sidewalk, or are surrounded by ancient trees in a remote wilderness grove, this simple question will attune your senses to what is around you. Eventually, you'll be able to keep your "Nature Mind" on wherever you go.

At first, stack the odds in your favor by limiting modern stressors; if possible, find a section of trail for this portion of your walk where you can avoid having to cross busy streets, look at crossing signals, or contend with traffic. Put your phone on Do Not Disturb mode, and keep it tucked away as you enjoy your restorative walk.

Wear comfortable clothes appropriate for the day's weather. As you get more deeply into your Nature meditations, you may find that wearing clothing patterned in basic earth tones helps you to blend into your surroundings, but don't let apparel hold you back from getting started.

Before you start your stroll, try out this little routine:

I. **Opening.** To open up your restorative session, simply take a few deep breaths. As you exhale, imagine releasing any stress out into a dark gray cloud that dissolves into the ground, where it is composted and transformed by the earth. Then take a few more deep breaths, drawing in the energy of Nature to replenish your creativity.

2. Expanding. Next, allow your senses to wander out across the landscape. Let your eyes be drawn where they will. Allow your hearing to spread out in all directions for a moment, soaking in the sounds. Sniff the air, and feel the breeze on your skin. Notice the taste in your mouth, and draw some air in over your tongue to observe any tastes on the wind. With all senses awakened, take a moment to simply be in your full sense of mindful embodiment.

3. Walking. Start your walk. Follow your senses. Allow them draw you across the land as you begin to walk. Let your curiosity gently guide you. Imagine with each step, or with each breath, that you are filling up with more of Nature's soothing energy. Be like water, flowing effortlessly wherever your path takes you.

4. Completion. When you are done with your walk, smile and place your palms over your navel. Take a deep breath, gathering in the good energy from your walk. Exhale slowly, simply sensing the feeling of peace and relaxation throughout your body. Enjoy this state for as long as you wish.

Creating a simple "opening and closing" sequence like we've done here helps your brain to establish a routine around relaxing. The deep breathing and visualization creates a positive trigger that anchors the relaxed state into your memory. Your brain learns what to expect, and with a bit of practice, you'll be able to slip into this restorative state quickly and easily.

What's Next

Over the course of this chapter, we've explored how Nature and meditation work synergistically to help reboot the mind and nourish your nervous system.

Whether you're enjoying the stress-reducing effects of the

Relaxation Response, benefiting from the immune-boosting powers of forest bathing, or restoring your attention with a jaunt in the natural environment, the path towards a new level of peace and well-being can be as simple as stepping out the door into your local park or favorite hiking trail.

In the next chapter, I'll share with you one of my favorite and most trusty outdoor mindfulness tools — the practice of the Meditation Spot.

4

FINDING A MEDITATION SPOT IN NATURE

> 66 *We talk of communing with Nature, but 'tis with ourselves we commune... Nature furnishes the conditions — the solitude — and the soul furnishes the entertainment."*
> — John Burroughs

I sat facing the game trail, positioned slightly uphill on an old stone wall that ran along the mountain's forested contour, as the sun sank low to my left at the end of a warm midsummer day. My mind, like my body, was quiet and still, veritably part of the stone that I rested upon. I was three days into a solo Survival Quest, having taken nothing with me save for the clothes on my back, seeking a deeper understanding of my connection with Nature and my Vision in life.

The activities of site exploration and shelter building demanded a tremendous energy expenditure in the first days, and now my body required recoup time. The high caloric expenditure and lack of food — for I was primarily fasting on this quest — led to a slowing of both body and mind to the point where it became easy to slip into the quiet murmur of the wind through the dry, drought-stricken beech leaves.

For large portions of each day I simply sat and listened, immersing in the varied sounds of the northwestern Connecticut forest. Each hour taught me something new about the citizens of the forest, as my senses expanded to encompass the mysteries of this place. Scarlet tanagers and ovenbirds lent their vibrant voices to the early morning chorus, though the soft hot breeze and buzz of cicadas filled most of the midday, with occasional up-slurred queries of hermit thrushes gracing the higher juniper-covered rocky slopes.

The game trail I kept sentinel on lay nestled amidst stands of third-growth beech trees and white oaks that had overtaken former pastures, the stone walls and overgrown graded roads now remnant reminders of pastoral scenes from long ago. No other humans were around, and few ever ventured to this area to begin with. My only companions were the animals whose trails criss-crossed the mountainside.

Each morning as I emerged from my debris shelter, I stretched and greeted the buck who slept just on the other side of the stone wall; the white-tail returned my greeting each day with wary curiosity at his new neighbor. We would often encounter each other at different places during the day, as my walking meditations led me along the deer trails and to a nearby spring where I found my drinking water.

Other creatures appeared, too. The first night in my shelter was warm enough that I crawled halfway out to watch the summer stars glimmer through the treetops, falling asleep right upon the oak leaf litter. Sometime in the night, when the moon had risen, I was woken from my sleep by quick footfalls circling around me in the debris.

Moments later, a chorus of coyotes sounded, just paces away. Their song filled my bones with electricity; I reveled in wild tones that seemed to reach all the way to the stars. The song-dogs never revealed themselves at this time, staying just out of sight in the shadowed forest. I wondered if we would meet again, if I might be allowed a view of their presence. But as soon as the coyotes had arrived, they were gone, and the mesmeric background of crickets lulled me again to sleep, still reposed half in and half out of my leaf hut on the warm summer night.

With all of these and many other experiences filling my being from the last few days, I now sat on the stone wall, contemplating my looming return to the everyday world of society. Certainly, I felt that the experience had changed me, and I knew that I would be returning with many gifts from the realm of Nature that would inform my life and my work for years to come.

My shelter, built with my own two hands from leaves and sticks and which kept me warm and dry even during a severe thunderstorm, showed me how Nature can provide us with a home even with the simplest materials. The spring's daily trickle of pure water showed me how the Earth gifts us with life itself, and the summer drought that surrounded the hills reminded me how precious a gift the water truly is.

Rough quartzite stones I had found buried in the hillside soil gave me sharp edges for crafting sticks into a fire-by-friction device, and various plants and trees offered material for rope and baskets. The necessities of survival had transported me back to the origins of human tool-use, to the primacy of meeting basic needs with raw ingenuity and vision.

Surrounded by the fusion of Earth and Sky, in the middle of which I walked, sat, and slept, I meditated constantly, attuning my senses. Nature provided me with an endless stream of awareness-expanding connections that stoked my curiosity.

During these timeless days and nights, I also remembered my family and the truly influential teachers in my life, and pondered the lineage of mentors who had passed these skills on since times long ago. I wondered what my own life would be like in the future, for I was only seventeen at the time, and considered what I could do to help keep these earth awareness skills alive for future generations.

As the day came to its end, I sat and released all these ruminations, relaxing into the stillness of the forest. All around me, the golden rays of the sinking sun illuminated the stones, bark, and leaves with an all-encompassing glow. Gazing forward at the scene with soft eyes, my peripheral vision suddenly alerted me — something was right next to me, just on the edge of my sight! Was it a snake that had come out of the rock wall to catch the last rays of the sun?

Slowly turning only my eyes down to the right, being careful not to move my head and cause a disturbance, I saw the true culprit — a chipmunk, whose cheeks were so stuffed with food that his face bulged like the sides of a rattler's head, was staring wild-eyed up at me just an inch from my hand. I was the last thing he expected to come across; probably, this chipmunk had never even seen a human before. Eventually the small rodent scurried off, and I returned to my sunset vigil.

After a few minutes, another movement caught my eye, this time a bit higher up. A downy woodpecker had come to forage, sloughing off bits of tree bark in his search for insects. The bird flitted from tree to tree, eventually coming so close I could have reached out and grabbed him, the red patch on the back of his head a bold compliment to the black and white patterns that covered the rest of his body. This visitor, too, eventually departed, leaving me again to immerse myself in my sunset reverie.

Just as I was preparing to get up and return to my shelter for a last night's sleep in the forest, a sound off to my left riveted my attention. A quick, even tempo of footsteps approached from the west, moving towards me on the game trail. These footfalls were faster and lighter than the crunching hoof-prints of the deer I had become accustomed to. I remained still and calm, not even moving my head, just my eyes, and keeping my vision soft and relaxed as I scanned for a glimpse of this new arrival. What I saw shocked my mind even further into silent awareness, for it seemed to defy any attempt to categorize this newfound apparition into a known quantity.

Bouncing along in a relaxed trot came a dog-like being, its fur a patchwork of earth-tones, grays and rust colors, with a bushy tail tucked oddly between his legs, each step providing a well-timed spring that propelled him further along the trail. The animal, which was moving deftly along the game run only ten feet ahead of me, did not pay me much heed, simply eyeballing me as he trotted past, giving me a mere glance over his shoulder as he continued along his way. Suddenly my thoughts came into focus — I had just seen my first eastern coyote! The visit left me in awe, and I remained silent and still in the vivid golden light.

Not too long after the coyote vanished in the forest, the sun set and I made my way back to my shelter for my final night on the mountain. With the appearance of Coyote I felt like my questions had been answered, my life trajectory confirmed by the voice of Nature in some mysterious way. I truly felt ready now to return from my meditations on the mountain, though I knew the person that was returning was not entirely the same one that had walked up the forested slope on the first day of the Quest; something essential had been opened out further within my consciousness, made possible through the journey of the Quest and the power of the long sit.

The Practice of Sitting in Nature

You don't need to go on a four-day marathon sit to benefit from meditating in Nature. The Meditation Spot is a simple practice then gives you a chance to refresh your awareness, reset your nervous system, and build personal connections with the earth, plants, animals, trees, and sky. It is a place to go and just *be*.

Immerse there in Nature's myriad patterns. Revel in sunrises and sunsets, duck under the cover of trees in the rain, splash through mud puddles, and listen to the wind whisper in the trees. Even cultivating ten minutes of embodied awareness while sitting on a park bench during your lunch break will greatly impact your day for the better.

As mentioned earlier, researcher Stephen Kaplan has explored how, when we spend time in nature, it restores the brain's capacity for *directed attention*: the kind of focus that gives us the crucial mental ability to successfully complete everyday tasks in learning, work, and daily life.

Kaplan's Attention Restoration Theory (ART) suggests that the mind needs breaks from its working state of intentionally directed focus, a mindset which it can only maintain for so long until fatigue sets in. Outdoor environments provide your mind with a "soft fascination" of interesting sensory experiences that effortlessly attract what's called *indirect attention*, allowing time for your brain to restore its power to focus.[1] If you're feeling stuck on a project, take a walk outside for a couple of minutes. The extra creativity you gain may save you hours of frustrated effort.

Natural settings also give you enough of a change in your surroundings to help you temporarily step away from the chain of your usual thoughts and demands, offering you a powerful restorative effect in a short time. By refreshing your attention through time in Nature, you can meet otherwise stressful tasks with greater ease and success.[2] In a *Psychological Science* report entitled "Cognitive Benefits of Interacting with Nature," Kaplan and colleagues noted that "simple and brief interactions with nature can produce marked increases in cognitive control."[3]

So, if you can just get to your Meditation Spot and simply *be there*, even without any specially directed focus, you will benefit tremendously.

Consistency and Resourcefulness

Consistency is the key to empowering your meditation practice. Get that ten minutes every day if you can, because each session will deepen and build on your previous experience.

If you sit at the same time every day, your brain and body becomes habituated (in a good way) and you'll more easily shift into a state of deeper inner resource and restorative attention. I've had clients make major breakthroughs in their well-being and sense of connection with Nature, just through developing a routine of consistent Meditation Spot sessions during their lunch breaks out in the office park.

When you can sit longer, go for it. Twenty to thirty minutes is a sweet spot for many people. A lot of folks I've coached like to get in deeper sits on the weekends, even for an hour or two, when they have time to visit a state park or other outdoor recreation area. During the week, they do what they can, sitting for a few minutes in the backyard garden before or after work, or on a park bench during lunch.

If it's bitterly cold or rainy and you can't bring yourself to get out, set up a bird feeder outside the window and station yourself in a comfortable chair nearby. There's always a way to succeed with this practice if you approach it in a resourceful manner.

So, your first Nature Jedi mission is to find a place outdoors where you can sit regularly. There are some great seated and moving meditations I'll be sharing with you in the chapters ahead, and I recommend adopting a special place now where you can work with them.

Actually, every technique in this book can be utilized at your spot, or in connection with it; the Meditation Spot is like the hub of a wheel, with spokes that connect to each of the various practices. Think of this special place as your "outdoor meditation studio."

The Qualities of an Ideal Meditation Spot

Ideally, your spot should be easy to get to, within a two to five-minute walk. The backyard, garden, or a bench in the local park will all work just fine. I've seen people delay their meditations because they get flustered about where to sit. Don't let this happen to you!

My own mentor, Jon Young, introduced this practice to me as the "Sit Spot," and it's really that simple.[4] Don't overthink this; it's a place to park your butt and just *be*. There are some features an "ideal" spot might have, but don't let these hold you back if you can't get to a spot like this. Work with what you've got. That said, here are some features that are great to have, when possible:

Trees. It's nice to lean back against a tree, or have a thicket behind you. This lets you feel a bit protected. Trees are great friends to have. There's an old Taoist saying, "The sage breathes the breath of the trees."

Recent forest bathing studies back this recommendation up. Research points towards the beneficial qualities of *phytoncides*, the antimicrobial essential oils emitted by trees. This natural aromatherapy source boosts your immune system, and the effects can last well beyond your stay with your tree friends; a group that stayed in a forest for three days in Japan showed enhanced immune function for an entire month afterwards.[5] Imagine what sitting with the trees every day can do for you!

A view. Beyond connecting with trees, I also recommend finding a spot with a bit of a view, so you can see somewhat into the distance to track what's going on. To maximize the diversity of birds and wildlife you might encounter, choose a spot that's near the edge of the woods where the trees meet a meadow. Having a water feature nearby is great, too. This is all optional, of course.

Urban or rural. Don't think you need a remote, wild setting to make this practice work. I've had urban coaching clients who've sat every day in the office park at work and had amazing experiences (it's often surprising for folks to discover the variety of wildlife that can utilize urban areas!).

But, if you're feeling a little more adventurous and you have some "wilder" options nearby, go for it. You could also get a second spot in an outdoor area for the weekends when you have more time to get out there. Just don't gloss over the handy backyard spot. That's the spot you'll be visiting the most, and the closer it is, the more likely you are to actually get out there.

Accessible. Consistency is what we're after here. If you get out to this place enough, you'll really get to know it. As a wildlife tracker, I always have fun walking with people through their yards and observing what they notice, and what they don't. It's amazing how many little details can go unseen that we just pass by every day — the muddy raccoon tracks climbing up the corner of the fence, the worn in patch in the grass that the fox trots over early in the morning, the alarm calls of the blue jay that can tell you about the cat hidden in the bushes...

Attuning to Place

When you get out to the same place over and over, and really take your time and pay attention, you'll not only learn about that place, but that place will learn about *you*, too. The birds and animals will gradually come to recognize that you are not a threat. You'll learn to blend into the natural pattern of the land. You'll get to see more of what really goes on in that place, because you won't be an "outsider" any more — you'll truly become a part of that place.

How often do you see people moving quietly in the forest, stepping quietly and pausing often to sense all around them? These days, in many places the animals are used to people noisily tromping through the woods, rushing from one place to the next. They expect hikers will just be passing through quickly; when people approach, the forest creatures simply duck for cover and wait until they've passed by.

People can get away with this kind of heedless behavior because we've removed most of the large, dangerous carnivores from the landscape (at least in the United States). We've become the apex predator, or at least the biggest and noisiest thing out there. But if you were to walk on foot through the Kalahari Desert in southern Africa, where the bush is filled with lions, leopards, black mambas, and other deadly animals, you'd be moving much differently.

Nature is Attuned to You

From a fox's perspective, a modern human being is one of the loudest, most obvious animals in the woods. A fox can hear a watch ticking from 60 yards away. Before your car is even parked, the animals know you are coming.

Any animal within earshot is listening intently as you open the car door — they are listening for anything they might need to avoid, like the sound of a dog jumping out of the backseat, or the speed and impact of your footsteps. Not to mention that the birds are keeping tabs on you, too. If you startle a bird from its feeding pattern, the moment it utters an alarm call, all the animals in the area will pause and zero in on your location.

This isn't all bad, though. As we learn the ancient art of decoding bird language, we begin to realize that the birds are a natural barometer for our own awareness.[6] Birds are Nature's teachers, and one of the lessons they impart is reminding us to be mindful. Instead of the Zen master hitting you on the head with a stick when you doze off in your meditation, you now have to contend with startled robins that make a racket when you bumble through their turf (getting whitewashed by sleepy owls beneath their cypress grove roosts is also quite enlivening).

If you get lost in your thoughts as you walk down the trail, you'll probably miss the soft calls of the juncos and other birds as they forage along the ground. You might also miss the sudden pause in their feeding as they glance at you, politely asking you to circle around them to give them some space. You might even miss the alarm calls they broadcast as you continue on, pushing them up into the branches as you plow along the trail. By then, every fox, deer, weasel, bobcat, and ninja knows you're coming, even if you're being fairly quiet.

But you're not going to do that. Because now, you know how the game works. You know that Nature is responding to your movements and is offering you feedback with every step you take.

You know that if you walk softly, take your time, and pause often to soak in the area with all of your senses, that you'll not only blend in with the flow of the woods, but you'll also access a deeper state of mindfulness in the process.

Awareness and mindfulness go hand in hand. *The more present you are, the more aware you become.* And as your awareness of your surroundings increases, the more reason you'll have to be mindful of the wild Nature you are part of.

~ Practice: Mapping Your Meditation Spot ~

When you get to know a place well, your brain creates its own inner map of the landscape. You can support this internalization by actually drawing a map.

Mapmaking is a useful art, because the process will force you to consider the land from a different perspective. You'll suddenly have to draw upon your memory to recall the features on the landscape and how they spatially relate to each other. This is also a great meditation that empowers your *inner sensory* skills.

After you've been to your Meditation Spot at least a few times, try this imaginal exercise:

TAKE A FEW DEEP BREATHS AND RELAX. CLOSE YOUR EYES. IMAGINE YOU are sitting there at your spot.

Then, fly straight up above your spot, looking down on it from high up in the air. Imagine as you look down that you can see yourself there, walking back home from your spot.

What does the path look like? How does it twist and turn? What landscape features do you see along the way — hills, forest, meadow, creeks? What man-made features are there — houses, roads, power lines, fences?

Once you feel that you've seen what there is to see from above, it's time to "come back." Simply sense your body, take a few deep breaths, feel your heartbeat for a moment, and open your eyes.

TAKE WHAT YOU'VE SEEN AND DRAW A MAP DEPICTING THE AREA

around your Meditation Spot. Include the four directions on your map (North, East, South, and West) to help you get oriented.

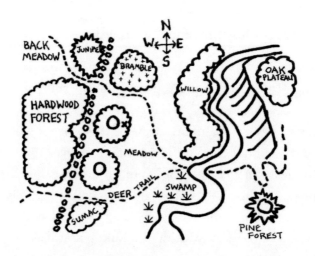

AFTER you've drawn your map, check out the satellite view on Google Maps and compare your drawing to the aerial photos.

I'll bet that the next time you get outside, you'll be looking closely to see how accurate your map was. And that's the whole point — to look deeper. Once you've soaked in some more details, try your hand again at making an updated map.

Now that we've covered finding a Meditation Spot and how to internalize its terrain through mapping, let's explore the topic of *when* to go there.

What Are the Best Times to Meditate?

The first answer to this question is: anytime you can. Life is busy, so any chance you get to de-stress and commune with Nature is awesome.

That said, there is power in routine, especially with meditation. You might have noticed that many traditions recommend meditating at the same time every day, and with good reason. Your body gets used to doing things at certain times.

If you have a dog, or have been around a friend's dog, you can see how important routine is. The dog gets used to being let out and then eating at certain times of the day. Before the owner's car rolls back into the driveway, the dog's ears have picked up the distant sounds of their car arriving. The instincts deep within the dog's body know that it is time to be let out, and then to eat! By the time the owner steps in the door, the dog is already up and ready.

We're not so different from the dog in this respect. Your body has a rhythm to what's it's doing. The "animal mind" part of you gets used to going to sleep and waking up at certain times, to exercising, and to eating meals at regular intervals. The power of routine is that once it is established, you don't have to think about it. A routine is something that you just *do*. When you make meditation a routine, at whatever time of day, your brain starts to realize there's a pattern to what you are doing. At that point, the power of routine steps in to help move you into action.

When you train your mind to meditate, the brain gets used to what this means. It thinks, "Oh, well, we're sitting in that special place again, and we're doing that deep breathing thing, and now we're being mindful. Guess it's time to settle in and pay attention." By having a regular time to meditate, you establish a *routine flow* that you can slip into.

Through quality repetition, you'll begin to establish a strong neural pathway that supports your meditation. Just like it takes a few consistent sessions to get used to exercising at the gym, it also takes a few sessions to establish a solid meditation practice. So, if you can, pick a time to meditate that's consistent.

Sunrise and Sunset

It should be said that there is a special magic to meditating in Nature at sunrise and sunset. The light reflects off of the entire landscape, filling everything with a spectacular hue. These are instinctive times to take a pause and settle into the shifting energy of the natural world.

Leading up to sunrise, you have a peak in birdsong. The birds' dawn chorus reaches around the world like the Wave at a baseball game, filling the air with warbles and trills of high frequency sound.

The combination of the rising light and the high vibes are a surefire way to start your day on a good foot. It's a great time to awaken your intentions for the day, and to feel Nature charging you up. The chorus is especially strong in the spring season when the birds are breeding, but you can catch snippets of it at other times of the year, too.

Listening to bird song is actually good for your brain. The pioneering French ear researcher Alfred Tomatis found that high frequency sounds like bird song can literally recharge your brain, just like plugging in an electric car recharges the car's battery.

The Corti cells are a linear arrangement of over 24,000 cells set in rows just beyond the cochlea in the inner ear. These unique cells respond to high frequencies. Their movement stimulates energy potential to flow to the central gray nuclei of the brain, which are essentially the "batteries" of the brain. Tomatis found that the *cortical recharging* provided by high-frequency sound stimulation supplements the nutrition already provided to the brain via the glucose and the oxygen that allows metabolism to occur.[7]

Sounds in the 5000 to 8000 Hertz range are most effective at recharging the brain (with 8000 Hertz being the most effective).[8] Birdsong happens to fall in the 5000 Hertz range, so time spent listening to the dawn chorus will naturally stimulate your inner ears and help generate energy for your day.[9]

You'll catch some bird song as the sun sets, too. The evening chorus isn't nearly as loud as the morning chorus, but it provides a fantastic end-cap to your day. Sunset is a sweet time to reflect on your day's accomplishments, and to ponder what's next. It's a time to let go of any stresses from the day, so that you can enjoy the evening and have clear dreams.

The Sacred Sunrise

When I was a teenager, a Wisdom Keeper shared an ancient song about the Sun with me. In the refrain the Sun says, *"I am coming to tell you something Sacred."* I often pondered the deeper meaning of these words. What was the Sun coming to tell us? What made the message so sacred?

One early morning at my Meditation Spot, part of the mystery was revealed. In the depths of a New England winter, I sat quietly on a log in the predawn darkness, waiting for the sun to rise. The ground was covered with a bone-chilling frost; the forest was still and silent. I was there because I wanted to feel the energy of the winter, seeking to understand the rhythm of life at that time of year at my spot.

The chill air eventually worked its way through my winter boots, through the many layers of thick wool clothing I had donned for the morning, and into my body. Like the maple trees around me whose life force had retreated down into their roots to survive the season, I could feel the cold pressing in on me, my body starting to shiver in order to conserve heat in my core.

Just at that instant when I felt I could take no more, a glorious light burst through the trees — the first rays of the rising Sun had appeared, touching the forest with warmth and the hope of a new day. *"I am coming to tell you something Sacred..."* A brief but glorious spatter of chickadee song erupted, a celebration of light and renewed life. Animals and humans would get up once more to live another day, to fly, walk, run and move across the earth and sky.

In that moment, I came to understand something more about the ancient song of the Sun, and about all the cycles of life tied to our closest star in the sky. The Sun is the activator of life. Through the Meditation Spot practice, we learn how its primal energy shapes and moves the patterns of the greater life force that we are all part of.

~ Practice: The Sunrise Sit ~

Get out to your Meditation Spot while it's still dark. Be in the stillness of the night air, quiet and still within. See if you can discover how to match your inner energy with the dynamic energy of the Nature around you as night turns to day. Allow some quiet time to soak fully into your senses; notice what the new day brings into your awareness.

As the light awakens, feel the life force of Nature activating within your own being as you prepare and gain energy for the day. Some questions and intentions you might consider bringing to your Sunrise Meditation could include:

WHAT AND WHO AM I FEELING GRATEFUL FOR IN MY LIFE TODAY?

Envision the supportive network of people, places, creativity, and aspects of Nature that are enhancing your life in various ways, from the farmers that grow your food, to the people that keep your Internet running smoothly. Picture your loved ones and friends, and the chain of ancestors both known and unknown reaching far back into time, most of whom have been connected intimately to the land and whose tenacity and creativity have enabled you to be here today.

Notice the life around you at your Meditation Spot, from the soil to the trees and sky, and all the beings playing a role in the web of Nature. As the light increases with each moment, feel the web of life pulsing stronger with each breath and heartbeat. Feel your place in the larger tapestry, and like the rising Sun, shine with the brilliance of gratitude for the chance to live another day and bring your best self forward into the world.

How do I want to show up today in my life?

Soaking in the morning atmosphere, feel yourself getting charged up with the energy of the new day. Hold in your mind and heart a living picture of how you want to be and be seen today: joyous, serene, energized, accomplished? Vivacious, attuned, knowledgeable?

Call in the attributes that speak to you and make you feel the most alive. Envision and *feel* yourself radiant and vibrating, as each atom and molecule becomes exuberant with these qualities. Know that as you hold this image it is being supported and energized by the new rising Sun.

What would I like to accomplish today?

After enjoying some inner stillness, consider the intentions you hold for this day. Take a moment to consider what needs to be done today, and sense everything flowing smoothly and easily. Imagine your goals coming to fruition, and experience the joy and sense of accomplishment this brings.

Bring these feelings to life within you now, as if these goals are already fulfilled. Feeling attuned to the needs of the day, sense the radiant energy of the Sun glowing in your heart. Smile to your heart and feel the energy of joyous accomplishment spreading throughout your being.

As the Sun rises and light spreads across the land, sense with each breath that your clear intentions are being energized. Feel your intention harmonizing with the larger patterns of Nature. Imagine how your desires help not only you, but others, too — including Nature.

After the Sun has climbed above the horizon, know that your intent has been energized. Let your intentions fly up on the morning breeze, and move forward with gratitude for the new day. Like the Sun, your enlivened heart now radiates the bright light of your peace and purpose with you wherever you go.

~ Practice: Sitting with the Sunset ~

Begin your sit at least twenty minutes before the Sun kisses the horizon. Settle into stillness as you connect with the land and sky. Feel the energy of the day winding down around you. Listen to the birds as they conclude their day's foraging, preparing to set up in their evening roosts.

Notice the shifting movements of the breeze that holds hands with the setting Sun. Realize that the trees are about to taper down their day's oxygen creation as the light fades; imagine and sense the shift that's happening internally within them at this time, from crown to roots.

Attuned to the land around you, now begin to sense what's moving within yourself. Feel the energy and accumulated lessons of the day gathering within you. Let the images of the day flit across your mental screen, and ask:

WHAT WERE MY BIGGEST ACCOMPLISHMENTS TODAY?

Bask in their energy for a moment. It's all too easy to skip over the things we've done well, to focus on the negative. Make it a point to celebrate your achievements regularly!

. . .

WHAT MIGHT I DO DIFFERENTLY TOMORROW?

Realize that tomorrow is a new day, with new opportunities to grow and learn. Let go of any disappointments or hurts. Imagine them dissolving and dissipating in the light of the setting Sun. Discover the learning inside the challenge. Form a picture of how you want to show up at your best for yourself and others tomorrow.

WHO AND WHAT AM I THANKFUL FOR IN MY LIFE?

Remember you're not alone. There is a vast web of life that supports you, human and beyond. Tune into that support network that gives you life, and send out a pulse of gratitude.

You've now gathered together the energy of your day and integrated its lessons. With this transition complete, feel the refreshing energy of the evening filling you up. After the Sun has fully set, step into your evening with balance and readiness for whatever the night brings you, ready to move tomorrow into a brand-new day.

Onward

In this chapter, you learned about the Meditation Spot practice, and how to pick a good spot for your meditations in Nature. We also explored the power of attuning with place, and some of the gifts that come with getting to know one place on the landscape well.

Hopefully by now, you've found your own Meditation Spot, and perhaps even tested your awareness by mapping your spot from memory. If you've visited your spot at sunrise and sunset, then no doubt you've experienced the amazing energy and nourishment that this simple practice can bring into your life.

In the next chapter, we'll discover some of the mysterious patterns that unfold within and around us when we sit and meditate in Nature.

5

THE NATURE OF ACTION & STILLNESS

I n the chapters to come, I'll be sharing a variety of engaging meditation practices that you can use in the great outdoors for more peace, awareness, and connection with Nature. But what actually happens in your brain when you meditate? For that matter, what happens around you as you find stillness within the "outer" realm of Nature?

We've already touched on the benefits of meditation and time spent outdoors. Now that you have a Meditation Spot of your own, let's dig a little deeper into the amazing transformations that occur, both in your brain and on the landscape as you sit and meditate.

My hope is that by understanding these patterns, you'll more clearly notice the changes that occur with each phase of meditation and have a more active sense of what's happening. This may encourage you to go deeper and enjoy more of the benefits that come with a regular practice. To complete this chapter, I will share a map of what takes place within you and around you as you meditate in Nature.

Before we get into the map, I need to give you a crash course in *brainwaves.* This knowledge will help you appreciate how the different practices can literally affect your brain activity, and why you might want to do so. Besides, haven't you ever wondered what was really going on in that noggin of yours? This is high geekery, but very cool.

In Appendix C at the end of the book, I've included a list for you of the different *Conscious Nature* practices and the dominant brain state that each routine supports. With this knowledge, you can tailor your meditations and awareness practices according to what you need, whether it's cultivating deeper relaxation, boosting creativity, or strengthening and balancing the attention.

Brainwave Basics

First of all, the cells in your brain are talking to each other constantly. Neurons communicate through chemical discharges that create tiny electrical waves. These waves ripple through the brain at speeds from less than one wave per second and all the way up to 100 waves or more per second, traveling across various networks and synchronizing areas that need to work together.

The older and more primitive areas of the brain emit slower waves; the fastest waves occur in the most evolutionarily recent addition to the brain, the neocortex.[1] Generally, the higher up you go in the brain from brainstem to neocortex, the faster the rate of the pulses will be.

The various systems in your brain interact to accomplish different things; electrical activity shifts around based on what you are doing in each moment, as neural areas "fire" or activate.

The brain is a pretty busy place — there's always something going on. As the different brain regions each do their own thing, there is often a cacophony of different waves moving all at once, with different neural systems firing at unique rates and intensities. This neural complexity is similar to what you would see if you were to study a global weather map, with various storm systems appearing around the world in different places. Through meditation, large regions of the brain can become synchronized and act (or relax) together in unison.

Brain researchers have identified eight different types of brainwaves, progressing from very slow to fast-moving, but I'll condense them into five major types for our purposes here. Each of the five types helps your brain and body function in different ways. I'll introduce you to each type and how they can help you. All five are at work in your brain in each moment, but usually only one or two are most dominant at any given time, depending on what you're doing.

Researchers are finding that optimal frequency levels exist within the spectrum for each type of brainwave. When certain systems in the brain become overactive or under active, these waves can get out of whack. Sometimes you get a brainwave occurring in a neural region where it shouldn't, creating a lack of attention, anxiety, or other perceptual challenge. In many situations, these off-kilter mental states have the potential to be retrained for more optimal functioning.

Meditation is one pathway that can help you to intentionally shift the activity of your brain waves towards a more desired state. *Understanding these waves is a hidden key to empowering your Nature Jedi skills!*

Each of the five brainwaves is generated by a unique zone (or multiple zones) of the brain, although the waves can ripple out to affect other areas, too. Slow waves from one region can couple with faster waves from another region to get different jobs done. Brain waves form the communication system that keeps these different areas working in harmony.

In our quick tour here, we'll start at the bottom of the brain where the slowest waves come from, and work our way up.

Delta Waves (𝛅)

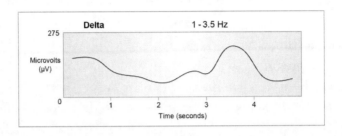

The most primitive part of your brain is the brainstem, which arouses your attention and manages the basic functions of your body. This area generates **delta waves**,[2] [3] which have a frequency between 1-3.5 Hz ("Hertz" are cycles per second).

Imagine the base of your brain pulsing with electricity one to three times every second, and you've got the idea. These are just about the slowest waves registered in the brain (there are also *infra-slow waves* that have been recorded,[4] but we won't get into those here). Any slower, and you'd be dead.

Delta waves are predominant in adults during deep sleep, but infants and children up to five years of age experience them in much of the waking state. These slow waves inhibit large sectors of brain cells from firing (which is good if you are sleeping, because you don't want to be walking around like a zombie – they keep most of us from acting out our dreams, getting out of bed, and making major movements while asleep). In particular, delta rhythms during deep sleep prevent the brain's sensory relay station, the thalamus, from communicating with the cortex.[5]

Even though you're usually tapped into delta when you're sprawled out and dead to the world, researchers have found that delta waves can also strengthen sporadically while you're awake, too. This is likely because the deep, primitive parts of the brain support your basic powers of alertness.

Delta activity spikes when you get surprised, and it also peaks when you are trying to match up the sounds around you with a sound you are expecting to hear.[6] So, if a sudden alarm cry from a nearby robin jolts you at your Meditation Spot, you may tap briefly into delta. Likewise, if you're trying to pick out a certain bird's song amidst the woodland chorus, these slow waves may momentarily enhance your perception.

Although delta waves aren't going to help you solve complicated math problems, they do replenish your energy each night. They can also offer a doorway to profound states of being. Even though most people are in unconscious sleep when their delta waves are rolling, Yoga Nidra practitioners and other advanced meditators can learn to maintain awareness in this deep state. Swami Sivananda once said, "We taste the nature of absolute bliss in dreamless sleep... you will feel oneness everywhere."[7]

Theta Waves (θ)

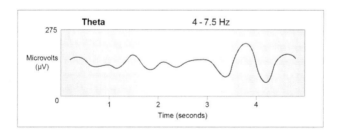

Theta waves (~4-7.5 Hz) are the next slowest type of wave. Theta waves pick up in power when you're forming new memories,[8] and they are also involved in the regulation of emotion.[9] Because memory is what allows learning to take place, theta waves are essential to your unfolding connection with the places (and states of consciousness) around and within you.

Since emotion is what motivates and drives the intensity of your experiences, this brain wave is a powerful contributor to your life journey. The goals, ambitions, and taboos that guide your behavior are all deeply embedded in your brain's inner recesses through these slow oscillations.

If there is anything that truly helps bring your dreams to life, it is the theta wave. These waves make a prominent appearance during daydreaming, REM sleep, and in transitions to wakefulness.[10] The dreamy state between wake and sleep is the realm of the shaman - if you find yourself immersed in a shamanic journey, you're in theta territory. Those vivid dreams that you find yourself in after you hit the snooze button count, too. In fact, the rapid drumming utilized in shamanic ceremonies entrains the brain's rhythms;[11] drumming at four to four and a half beats per seconds shifts the brain into theta states.[12]

There are two "loops" or systems in the brain that create these slow waves; the first is the brain's *hippocampal loop*.[13] I'm not talking about loopy hippopotamuses here. The hippocampus is a seahorse-shaped brain structure tucked deep in the limbic system that's especially involved with memory and navigation. The second loop sources from the hypothalamus. Both systems can synchronize together and help organize activity across all levels of the brain.[14]

Both a blessing and a curse at times, automatic behavior is also governed by theta waves.[15] When you go on autopilot, theta is there to keep things flowing. Whether you are driving your car during the early commute like a complete space cadet, or just groggily making your first morning coffee, thank your theta waves for orienting you in space and getting you where you need to be. These moments may not be shining examples of mindfulness in action, but they demonstrate how theta helps you get the job done.

Not all theta states are desirable. Sporadic bursts of intense theta are present during migraines in widespread areas of the brain,[16] and too much theta in the frontal lobes spells anxiety and overwhelm.[17] Neurofeedback training, in which participants learn to change the activity of brain waves, can help transform these patterns and bring healing.[18]

During meditation, theta waves are associated with bliss and experiences of positive emotion.[19] Because you can literally rewire your brain through meditation, these positively-directed theta states offer a tantalizing pathway towards healing stress or trauma and optimizing the mind.

Neural studies have also revealed that theta waves are present in the front of the brain during the *flow state*. Flow occurs when your awareness and actions merge seamlessly together.[20] The presence of theta is linked to the feeling of immersion that you get when you are fully involved in doing something you enjoy.[21]

Alpha Waves (α)

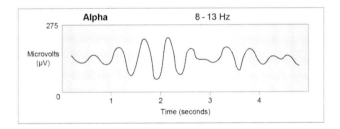

Next up are the famous **alpha waves.** Generated by the thalamus and moving between 8-13 Hz, these waves have been long-studied by neurofeedback researchers because of their prominent connection with meditative states.

Alpha was long thought of simply as the brain's "idling" or relaxed mode. However, more recent studies point towards alpha waves as an indicator of your readiness to perceive or take action; these waves synchronize large regions of the cortex, coordinating diverse areas to prepare for a fast response; at the same time, these waves also support continual mindfulness. Researchers have compared alpha activity to a "windshield wiper" that constantly clears away old sensory data, allowing your mind to be ready to receive new information.[22]

Meditators have long made use of these benefits. Traditionally, martial artists have trained themselves through meditation to be fully in the moment, ready to act at the drop of a dime. The alpha state helps them "be here now." You can quickly boost this brainwave for yourself simply by closing your eyes.[23] As soon as the visual cortex loses stimulation, it quickly goes into alpha mode.

However, you can also learn to powerfully experience the relaxed state of alpha with eyes open, through the Expanded Vision practice that I share in the next chapter. Add some deep breathing, and you'll get there quickly.

Alpha also picks up when you're immersed in natural scenery,[24] so getting out to your Meditation Spot regularly will effortlessly give you a daily dose of this peaceful mind state. No time to get outside today? At the least, drink some green tea. The amino acid theanine contained in the tea has been shown to promote the alpha state.[25]

Alpha and Theta

Alpha brain waves also couple with other brain frequencies to get certain jobs done. Alpha and theta waves like to work together — they make great dance partners! When you notice new things in your environment, these waves team up and increase in power; the theta waves allow your working memory to track what's happening, and the alpha waves "turn off" (inhibit) unneeded brain areas so you can remain focused on what's really essential.[26]

These neural partners also take turns dancing. Theta activity picks up when you form a memory, while alpha drops off. When you call up something stored away in your long-term memory, your alpha waves desynchronize into local spurts of activity. This happens as your brain shifts from a globally-connected state of relaxation into the smaller networks of activity needed to retrieve the memory.[27]

I think of this inner transformation as being similar to the way a reservoir stores water; the alpha state allows your brain's neurons to relax and remain ready for action, just like water gets stored up behind a dam. When an action is needed (such as recalling information), the relaxed state shifts to a burst of activity as a memory is activated, just like the way a dam opens and the reservoir can release its water to move and flow. The ability to make this shift is connected with optimal memory performance.[28]

Alpha waves are sometimes associated with a partner neuro-transmitter, *acetylcholine*.[29] This fat-based chemical coats the myelin sheaths around your nerves, helping information to travel more easily through the pathways of the brain and the body.[30] This chemical helps you integrate sensory information from your experience of the world.

By promoting acetylcholine release, your meditation and Nature practices bring you enhanced creativity and intuition, as your awareness clarifies and expands.

Beta Waves (β)

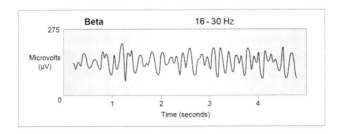

Focused tasks that require alertness and decision-making draw upon your **beta wave** resources. These fast waves ripple through localized areas in the cortex at 12.5-31 Hz. Beta activity enables you to ask good questions, solve those complicated engineering problems and Microsoft entrance exams that you love so much, and generally pay sharp attention to the world around you.

When you intentionally look around for something, whether it's a songbird in the treetops or your keychain that's "lost" right before you on the kitchen counter, the front of your brain ripples with beta waves that spread out to synchronize with the temporal lobes on the sides of the cortex.[31] This is an example of *top-down attention*, and it shows how beta waves are related to your power of intent; these waves start at the brain's executive command center and flow into its sensory and integrative areas, allowing you to direct your focus.

Beta waves are related to emotion in fascinating ways. Beta rhythms pick up during moments of negative emotion;[32] overactive beta in the right frontal lobe of the brain is associated with anxiety and depression.[33] Higher beta frequencies of 18-38 Hz appear when the mind is frantic and chattery.[34] Meanwhile, brain activity in the left prefrontal cortex helps you regulate emotion and appraise situations clearly.[35]

From these examples, we see that it's not just what *kind* of wave is present that impacts your mind state, but also *where* a certain kind of wave is happening that makes all the difference.

Beta activity can even rewire the brain when needed to increase mental acuity. Major depression can be accompanied by reduced levels of the theta and alpha waves that normally uphold optimal working memory and mental focus; beta comes to the rescue by increasing connections within the brain's frontal area and between the brain's two hemispheres, creating new makeshift neural circuits that support mental focus.[36] This adaptive rewiring provided by beta activity offers a helpful mental prop during rough times.

Beta appears not just in the cortex, but also in a deeper brain structure called the *basal ganglia*, associated with movement regulation and habit formation. This area forms a special feedback loop with the cortex; the beta waves flowing in this loop can inhibit your body's motion.

When you are about to intentionally move your body, beta levels in the motor cortex drop off; if you then have to check yourself and remain still, beta picks up again to help suppress the motion. Dopamine, a neurotransmitter associated with motivation, has the ability to suppress and regulate this beta activity.[37]

Sensory Motor Rhythm Waves

Within the larger spectrum of beta waves, a subset of slower ones moving at 12.5-15.5 Hz are called SMR (Sensory Motor Rhythm) waves. These gentler beta waves help coordinate your body's balance, movements, and even your digestion; when properly coordinated, these SMR waves allow you to feel present and calmly focused.[38]

Gamma Waves (γ)

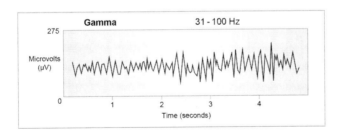

The most recently discovered frequencies at work in the brain are known as **gamma waves.** Oscillating quickly through the cortex at rates of 30-100 Hz or more, gamma waves can couple with other slower waves as the brain performs various functions, ranging from assembling perception to memory formation.

These fast waves are thought of by many neuroscientists as the "binding agent" of consciousness.

When you sit in your favorite place in Nature, you are immersed each second in endless sensations from all directions. How do you make sense of it all? How do you know where you are in the sea of infinity? What enables you to focus your attention on that which is truly important to you? How do you even maintain a continuous sense of self amidst the shifting tides of time and information?

Research is increasingly pointing towards the power of gamma waves for answers to these questions and beyond. Gamma waves bring together different aspects of sensory information into holistic perceptions.[39]

To get a grasp on this, imagine all of the distinct qualities that the eyes take in: shape, edges, shadows, contour, depth, color, and more. Different parts of the brain's visual system work to register these various qualities, but it is gamma action that rapidly synchronizes these diverse bits of information from each area into a meaningful whole.[40]

Gamma activity is closely linked with many other aspects of sensory perception and learning. In fact, these waves do so much, they are like the Swiss-army knife of brain frequencies!

Gamma power is connected with your ability to notice new aspects of your surroundings,[41] which is essential for tracking the changes around you in Nature. When you see a face in the distance, gamma waves surge as neural networks connect and allow you to recognize who it belongs to.[42] When you hear something, 40 Hz gamma waves help selectively focus your attention[43] and process the sound.[44] If you hear someone talking, these waves even help you remember the words that are spoken.[45]

Gamma picks up during emotional events, too, helping you

remember and learn from what is taking place.[46] The stronger the gamma synchronization is, the more accurate your perceptions are likely to be, and the more efficient your behavior will become.[47]

As with the other wave frequencies, gamma waves can be excess or deficient in certain regions of the brain. Individuals with severe depression have decreased resting rates of gamma in the anterior cingulate cortex, a key region associated with emotional regulation and decision making.[48]

Certain states of depression also show reduced amounts of gamma wave activity in the frontal cortex during emotionally-laden tasks (the frontal cortex is responsible for planning, communication, and social functioning); meanwhile, the temporal cortex, which assigns meaning to sensory information, displays increased power levels.[49]

Because gamma waves are connected to these various internal states, researchers are looking towards the intentional direction of gamma patterns as a way to regulate emotional disorders.[50]

Gamma & Meditation

Besides supporting sensory prowess and emotional resilience, gamma waves induce *plasticity*, which means they enable your neural networks to reform or create new pathways (which is essential to learning - it's why you *can* "teach an old dog new tricks").[51] When your brain has plasticity, your mind can better adapt to new situations. When life throws you a curveball, you'll be ready to meet the moment.

Meditation can help unlock this dynamic inner state. Back in 1992, the Dalai Lama nudged a neuroscientist named Richard Davidson to study the benefits of meditation. He arranged for a group of Buddhist monks to visit the lab and meditate while hooked up to an MRI machine.[52]

The monks performed a *pure compassion* meditation in which

they formlessly meditated upon the "unrestricted readiness and ability to help living beings." According to the study authors, for this type of meditation "the practitioner lets his feeling of loving-kindness and compassion permeate his mind without directing his attention toward a particular object."

With this ideal in mind, within 15 seconds the experienced meditators in the group were producing high-intensity gamma waves in their cortex. Further, they also showed a higher ratio of gamma waves before meditation than novice meditators. This means the monks' meditation practice had effectively transformed their brains over time, allowing them to respond with greater compassion and clarity throughout the day.[53]

The monks in the study had many years of meditation under their belts, but every quality meditation session can help you access further reaches of inner awareness. By becoming aware of the various brain waves and the mental and emotional patterns they relate to, you can more intentionally cultivate resourceful states of being that help you navigate life with peace and joy.

Brain Waves & Inner States Chart

This chart summarizes many of the internal states that we've discussed in this chapter, and shows how they are connected to each of the five major brain waves. The chart also shows the gifts offered by each brain state in its most balanced and optimized form, along with potential indicators of imbalance that are associ-ated with an excess or deficiency for each wave type.

Because brain waves are so complex, and there is still so much to discover about their functioning, this chart is only a simplified window into the amazing symphony of frequencies at play within the brain.

This chart is not meant to diagnose medical conditions or to propose any specific treatments, but rather to inspire wonder into the functionings of the neural systems that enable our connections with the Nature within and around us.

Brain Waves & Inner States

BRAIN WAVE	Yin (-) Deficient	Balanced (-/+)	Yang (+) Excess
Delta - δ	Lack of sleep; poor selected attention	Restful sleep; Discerning attention	Can't focus or think straight
Theta - θ	Weak memory encoding	Positive motivation; Creative	Daydreamy; Not present
Alpha - α	Reduced memory access; Impulsivity; Anxiety	Relaxed; Embodied	Spacy; Anxious; Overworked
Beta - β	Lack of focus; Reduced clarity in thought	Clear focus; Attentive; Firm decision-making	Anxious; Worried; Racing thoughts
Gamma - γ	Disjointed perception & thoughts; Depression	Well-integrated perceptions & thoughts	Depression; Peak Visionary states

The Inner & Outer Dynamics of a Meditation Session

Now that you have gone through this little crash course on brainwaves, let's take this knowledge and put it into action.

In the remainder of this chapter, I'll guide you through what's happening both inside your brain and in your greater surroundings when you sit and meditate in Nature.

Many of these changes are subtle and easily overlooked. As you learn to recognize each shift, you gain access to a new doorway of consciousness.

Through awareness of these hidden doors of perception, you can more intentionally walk through these thresholds towards a greater sense of connection and meaning in your meditations.

We'll now take a walkthrough of each phase in a twenty-

minute sit, exploring the transformations that open within and
around us as we consciously connect with Nature.

The following play-by-play outline shows what happens in
each of these phases, both internally and externally, as a meditation progresses.

With practice, you can learn to access many of the states
described here more rapidly, after you begin to embody the
routines shared in this book.

Beyond the shifts in brain wave patterns, you may also experience other transformations, including biochemical changes that
enhance well-being, and increased understanding of the language
of Nature that is communicating all around you.

In fact, through experience at your Meditation Spot, you'll
come to discover how these two "separate" aspects of Nature, the
inner and the outer, are in constant dialogue with one another.

Let's go on a "virtual sit" now to find out what happens...

———————

@ The First Five Minutes

Inner Nature:

During this time, your brain is "arriving" to your Meditation Spot.
As you sit down and settle in, your senses take in initial impressions of your surroundings.

Because your attention is transitioning from the day's to-do list
and into the consciously attended, felt presence of your body and
the natural patterns you are surrounded by, your dominant brain
waves still register in this phase as rapid *beta* patterns.

Beta waves may also strengthen if you are actively searching to
identify or locate something that you have in mind; the downside
is that a predominance of these waves may reduce your awareness

of new patterns.[54] This means that the beta state can keep you "focused-locked" on a problem or worry from your day, blinding you to other perspectives.

By dropping into your senses and gradually expanding into a larger field of awareness during your meditation, you begin to shift into a more encompassing field of possibility. Higher-frequency gamma waves may also activate in the visual cortex as you take in natural scenery;[55] these speedy brain waves help you selectively focus your attention.[56]

Within just five minutes of viewing a natural scene, significant changes begin to happen in your body; muscle tension and electrical skin resistance (both indicators of stress), as well as heart rate, can begin to diminish markedly.[57]

Outer Nature:

Animals may scatter if you rush to your spot. Move slowly and mindfully as you approach the place where you will sit, so that you can avoid disturbing nearby wildlife.

Once you sit down, it may take a few minutes to become present to the fullness of your senses, especially if you are transitioning from a busy day.

As the mind attunes to the natural environment, the more prominent patterns tend to catch the attention first: the louder bird calls, distinct wind or temperature changes, and even the comparative silence or stillness of the place may jump out at you. Movement from any especially obvious animals may also catch your attention during this phase. As you relax and enter stillness internally, the outer world responds as the animals gradually return to their normal behaviors.

As you settle in a bit, the bolder birds and animals may return quickly to their normal activities[58] — frogs resume singing, squirrels forage, and birds return to singing, calling, or feeding.

Through the calm state of being and the expanded awareness accessed in meditation, the outer world of Nature begins to reveal its secrets to you.

@ Ten to Fifteen Minutes

Inner Nature:

As you continue to sit and maintain mindful awareness upon a consistent internal or external focus, the *Relaxation Response* appears. Heart and breathing rates slow down, blood pressure is reduced, and cortisol levels decline.[59] Alpha brain waves increase significantly when viewing natural scenery,[60] indicating relaxed yet lucid awareness.

Gradually, you begin to notice greater nuances of activity within and around you, subtleties that were obscured earlier; spikes of gamma brain waves emerge with each fresh observation. Use of heart-centered meditations (see the *Radiance of the Inner Sun Meditation* in Chapter 12) at this time may generate an enhanced release of the "love peptide" oxytocin[61] along with increased heart coherence, and an increase in production of Immunoglobin A, which boosts immune system response.[62]

Outer Nature:

The "splash" caused by your arrival begins settling down as birds and mammals resume their foraging and usual behaviors nearby. Shyer birds gradually work their way back to their regular feeding zones or song posts, and the soundscape begins to fill in once more with songs and calls.

As your mind attunes to the environment, subtler aspects of

Nature now become apparent that were glossed over earlier; the various hues of leaves, delicate scents in the air, shadows on the landscape, and distant sounds come into sharper relief as your senses continue to expand.

@ Fifteen to Twenty Minutes and Longer

Inner Nature:

Through sitting still, your body's movement receptors quiet down and you may arrive at a *monolithic sensation* of your body as a unified entity.[63] With this paradoxic sensation, you might begin to feel like an ancient stone that is part of the landscape, even as your mind becomes expansive and free like the sky (realize it may take repeated practice to get to this deep state... but it is possible!).

At this point, the Relaxation Response fills your body with a pleasant sensation as blood lactate (associated with anxiety) continues to drop.[64] Activity in your brain's left frontal cortex, an area associated with the *internal dialogue*, a frequent companion of worry and distracted self-talk for many, slows down after 20 minutes of viewing a natural forest setting, indicating a relaxed state.[65] Experienced meditators may exhibit a mix of both alpha and deeper theta brain waves, often connected with enhanced creative flow and deep relaxation.

Outer Nature:

Animal behavior resumes a normal state as birds sing, preen, and feed; larger or more reclusive mammals begin to emerge from hiding.

By this time you'll have noticed previously hidden patterns

and trends related to the wind, clouds, bird activity, and other natural features that reveal themselves through careful observation. Through your stillness, you'll have begun to blend into the rhythms of the place, becoming a part of the landscape.

From Theory to Being

As you can see, there's a lot going on "under the hood" in your brain and body, even during the stillness of meditation. From the ripples of ever-shifting brain waves to the cascading chemical releases of neurotransmitters, numerous transformations are happening each moment.

Likewise, the patterns of Nature's symphony are constantly changing all around you, too. The animals dynamically respond to your actions and presence, mirroring on the outside through their behavior and voices that which is happening within you in the hidden realms of mind and emotion.

In the next chapter, let's step forward with this understanding and engage further in *being* with Nature. In the following chapters, we'll explore a set of practices that engage the senses, bringing a deeper awareness of the patterns moving around and within you.

Walk forward into these practices, knowing that meditating in Nature supports your overall health and cognitive functioning in amazing ways.

6

EMPOWERING YOUR SENSORY AWARENESS

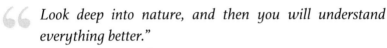

Look deep into nature, and then you will understand everything better."
-- Albert Einstein

As we've discovered, meditating in Nature is great for reducing stress and improving well-being. It's also an amazing way to deepen your connections with the Earth, the animals, the trees, and other elements of the natural world.

When you develop the kind of routines we are exploring in this book — routines that get you connecting regularly with your favorite outdoor areas — you have a golden opportunity to deepen your relationship with those places and the beings that live there. You'll begin to see and notice things that others pass by, because your awareness is open to the nuances of your environment.

Every visit becomes an opportunity to observe and learn something new about what's happening around you and within you, too. This is the kind of ever-growing awareness of place that's kept our ancestors alive in the past, and that allows hunter-gatherer cultures to continue thriving in remote areas today. Because of this in-born capacity, your brain is ready and waiting to connect with nature.

Wired for Awareness

Hidden in its inner recesses, your brain has neural receptors that make note of the places you go. The hippocampus creates memory maps of the routes and paths you take, and special "place cells" make an inner spatial representation of the spots you know well.

The cortex even has dedicated areas that catch and make sense of all the sights, sounds, textures, and other bits of data streaming in from your walks and wanders. These neural pathways get thicker and stronger for those patterns that you pay the most attention to.

If you observe the pine tree that you stroll by each day as you walk to your car, your brain starts to create a "pine tree" neural pathway. If you pause for a moment each day to connect with the tree, that neural web will start to grow and strengthen.

When you take time to study the clusters of pine needles, you notice how they grow in bundles of five needles each. This observation adds to your inner map of the tree. When you touch the bark and get the sticky sap on your hands, this connection adds a tactile layer to your neural map. As you take in a deep breath filled with the piney scent of the needles, your olfactory neurons come online. And if you were to take some pine needles and make tea with them, your taste buds will also register the pine in a whole other way.

Each moment like this is a chance to add to your growing inner map of Nature. Also, these moments of exploring Nature's mysteries provide a compelling "in the moment" invitation to practice mindfulness.

These little moments of mindful exploration really add up. Literally, the structure of your brain reflects your current personal connections with the Nature in your neighborhood. Over time, your neural circuitry will reflect the varied and complex patterns of your place.

The Power of Curiosity & Wandering

This ancient ancestral legacy is silently tugging at your senses still, cueing you into the sudden flutter of birds in your peripheral vision, and causing you to pause when you hear an unknown rustle in the bushes. It tugs at you with the nagging voice of curiosity when you come across a footprint in the mud — *who left this track? Is the animal around still? Could I see it?*

By taking time to be curious, to explore and wander, to poke around, or even to lie down and watch the clouds, you will greatly enrich your connection with the places you frequent. Approaching Nature with an open, exploratory attitude will reward you in leaps and bounds. Making space in this way creates an opening for your awareness to expand. By losing your agenda, your mind can tune into the present moment. That's when the magic happens.

You have probably enough structure already in all the demands of daily life. If you need exercise, get your hike or run in, but leave some time on the excursion for unstructured adventuring. By regularly giving yourself time to just wander and *be*, you learn to slow down to Nature's rhythm. This process is a helpful preparation for the meditations I'll be sharing with you in the later chapters. Wandering is a great way to get started in acquainting yourself with a restorative experience in Nature.

Wandering also helps you shift gears. If you are running fast in

5th gear all day at work, and you expect to suddenly drop into first gear in a Nature meditation, you might have some trouble getting the mind to slow down. With time and practice using the techniques in this book, you can learn to accomplish this shift very quickly, but I've found that it helps to drop down one gear at a time.

Before you sit, gently wander a bit first. Ease your brain into a relaxed state. Let Nature restore your attention and begin shifting you out of stress mode. Then, when you're ready, it's easier to go into a deeper meditative state.

Just Showing Up Is Half of the Journey

The first step to any cultivation of awareness is simply showing up. Whether you're indoors on your meditation cushion experiencing an Insight Meditation, or outside attuning your ears to the birds and the wind, "you have to go to know."

You have to get your body there in the right place to have the experience. If all you can do is show up in Nature regularly, you've already won half the game. Just by merit of plopping your body somewhere on the landscape, your senses are bound to notice something new. The colors of the sunset, the chirping of the crickets, or the feeling of the wind on your skin can be enough to shift you into a more relaxed state.

Of course, you could be in the most beautiful place in the world, but if your mind is elsewhere, you're missing a lot of what Nature has to offer you. Hence the second step, which is cultivating mindfulness and moment-to-moment presence. Mindful awareness helps you tune into all the amazing stuff that's happening *right now.* Your senses can help you with developing this habit.

Remember, the two cornerstones of the Relaxation Response include having a repetitive focus, and simply coming back to your focal point if you get distracted. This is similar to how mindfulness is achieved: sense what's happening *now*...and *now*...and *now*. That's the basic idea!

You can either turn your awareness inward and sense what's going on in your mind, body, and emotions, or you can turn it outwards and connect with the larger patterns around you. Eventually, these two aspects of inner and outer will fuse together as you realize the interplay that's constantly going on between the two.

A lot of people meditate with a mantra or a simple mentally-repeated phrase, but you can also meditate with your senses. There's a billion ways to do this. Sure, you'll get distracted, but simply come back to the moment when you realize your brain just hijacked you. We'll get into some very effective sensory practices in the Meditation chapters. For now, here's one of my favorites, just to whet your appetite.

~ Practice: Expanded Vision ~

Many of life's daily tasks require us to focus in on small details. Reading, writing, texting, and watching TV all require focus. If you stare at a word on this page, notice that you can see it clearly and sharply. But, if you start to move your gaze away from it, the text becomes less distinct.

This is because the eyes rely on the fovea, a small pit near the center of each retina, to pick up small details. Vision uses about 50% of your brain's processing resources, and 50% of that total is dedicated to the tremendous detail absorbed through the fovea.[1] This highlights how important foveal vision is for us as a species.

However, when you narrow your vision, you narrow your thinking to the task at hand. This focus helps you accomplish your goals, but it also limits creativity and can get you into a perceptual rut. When you expand your vision to a bigger picture, you also expand your awareness. *If you can change how you see the world, you can also change how you think about it.*

Beyond your foveal vision, you also have access to a much larger view of the world. Your peripheral vision is well-suited for taking in the big picture of a scene all at once. Peripheral vision also is adept at detecting movement, and it's adapted for helping you find your way in low-light situations such as dawn and dusk. We use peripheral vision most of the time without really thinking about it — we notice cars off to our side while we drive, or we use it to keep track of the defense when we're dribbling a basketball.

Peripheral vision draws upon different circuitry in the brain compared to foveal vision, and we can access it to discover some unique meditative states. We can learn to shift our perception to this bigger picture through a simple shift of intention. Here's a simple practice you can use to expand your vision, both indoors and outdoors:

Find a Visual Anchor

Look towards the horizon. Find a point in the distance to use as a visual anchor throughout this meditation. You'll be keeping the center of your gaze on this point as we proceed (of course, blink whenever you need to, and move your eyes around periodically so they remain comfortable).

Once you have your anchor point, lift your hands up in front of you at chest level, held out at arm's length. We're going do a little warm-up exercise that helps engage the entire field of your peripheral vision.

Awaken Your Peripheral Vision

Start to wiggle your fingers. Keep staring at your anchor, but notice you can also see your fingers wiggling without having to look directly at them.

Slowly move both hands out to the sides, continuing to wiggle your fingers. Notice that as you stare straight at your anchor, you can also track your fingers off to the sides in your peripheral vision.

Keep moving your hands out to the sides until they disappear in your horizontal field of view. You've just found how far your field of view extends to each side of your body!

Find the Vertical Peripheral Field

Now, bring your hand back in front of you. This time, raise one hand up and drop one hand slowly downwards. See if you can determine how far your vertical field of view extends.

Once you've done this, you can drop your hands down. Your peripheral vision is now "woken up." Simply look ahead to the horizon, and notice your entire field of view.

Expanding Your Vision

When you try this outside, notice that you can see the sky and the ground at the same time. Notice how your peripheral vision easily detects the movement of leaves, grasses, and birds or other animals.

Sit with this Expanded Vision for five to ten minutes, or however long it feels comfortable to do so. Because you may not be used to this way of seeing the world, start with shorter durations and work your way up to longer sessions.

Notice afterwards how this way of seeing impacts the way you think and feel. You may find that maintaining this Expanded Awareness allows you to quickly access the Relaxation Response. You may also notice that ideas and creative solutions to situations in your life bubble up into your conscious mind afterwards. Your dreams may also become more vivid and memorable. Now, let's take our journey into awareness a step further.

Active Awareness

There are two basic ways you can apply your awareness: actively, and passively. Both have an important role to play in meditation and Nature connection.

Every second, you are immersed in an endless sea of sensory information. You're basically a drop in the ocean of Infinity. Only a small portion of information from that big ocean actually reaches your conscious awareness at any one moment. There's a lot happening every second that you're simply not paying attention to. The two styles of awareness help you take in your environment in different ways.

In active awareness, your mind seeks to locate or identify specific things. If you were standing in the middle of a football field on a dark, moonless night, active awareness is the flashlight you are shining down at your feet to see the 50-yard line. The rest of the football field remains dark. Active awareness lets you direct your attention towards a small area in the vast sea of infinity.

Raspberries, Raspberries Everywhere

There's more to it, though. Imagine you're out on a hike. It's well into the afternoon, and you get hungry. Your hunger begins to drive your awareness. Food becomes a priority, and you start thinking of good things to eat. If you know how to identify raspberries, and if you've seen them in the area in the past, then your mind (being helpful), pulls up an image of a raspberry.

With this image, you suddenly get the desire to find some berries to eat. The memory of past raspberries you've eaten, and the sweet tangy taste you get when you bite into them, creates a vivid and compelling *search image.*

Perceptual researchers would say that you've now effectively "primed" your mind to find the raspberries. Now, all you have to do is match up the images around you with the image you are holding in your mind. As you scan through the thickets, you easily lock right onto the red forms of the ripe berries suspended amidst the greenery. This is a simple example of how you apply active awareness every day.

This story contains an important principle of awareness: what you notice is driven by what you need or intend to accomplish.[2] This is an effect of priming, and we experience this every day of our lives, whether we know it or not. Thinking about buying a new car? Your favorite car starts appearing everywhere you go. The vehicles have been there all this time; you just never had a pressing reason to notice them before.

Shifting Your Thinking

If you find yourself wanting to shift your thinking away from a repetitive worry or thought that's bothering you, active awareness could be just the ticket. Tackle a new challenge and give your brain's "worry circuits" time to settle down.

Shift away from your worries for a bit and learn to identify a robin — how can you tell its song apart from that of a rose-breasted grosbeak, or from a scarlet tanager? Setting up little sensory challenges like this for yourself is a great game that will connect you more deeply with your place. I like to keep a running list, so I always have something new to learn. It's kind of like "priming squared": priming myself to prime myself.

How to Prime Yourself by Learning to Identify Local Species

A good way to start the priming game is to pick up a few field guides. At the least, get a good bird guide, a tree guide, and an animal tracking guide to begin with, plus anything else you are curious about.

Priming your connections in these three particular categories will help to spread your awareness from the ground to the sky. Keep your guides handy around your house; put them in spots where you know you'll bump into them easily every day. There are some great field guide apps out there, but I personally like to have printed copies strewn about my home in key locations.

Make it a goal to learn one new species each week (that humble goal adds up 52 new connections in a year, accomplished in a relaxed pace!). After a few years you'll be an old pro at recognizing a couple hundred of your wild neighbors. If you like long-term projects, you're set to go.

Recommended Guides

I like the *Golden Books Guide to Birds of North America* by Robbins, Bruun, Zim & Singer, because each bird is listed by its family grouping with a representative sketch, a range map, a sonogram (a visual depiction of the voice), and other helpful information. I can find everything I want to know for a species quickly, without any page flipping.

The size of the bird, its posture and shape, the flight style, the beak shape, and any colorations or markings are key things to learn to tune into. Go on birding walks with your local Audubon group to get a running start on the top local birds to know. Cornell's AllAboutBirds.org is a great online resource, too.

For trees, Peterson's *Eastern Trees Guide* (or the *Western* version) is a great place to start. Learn to recognize trees by their leaves from spring to fall, and learn the buds and twigs in the winter for identification. Bark is available year-round to observe. The flower and fruit shapes are helpful not just to identify the tree, but they're also useful to know about because each species draws in a variety of birds and mammals as they ripen. You'll learn through observation who eats what.

For animal tracks, I recommend several favorite guides:

James Lowery's *The Tracker's Field Guide* includes fascinating behavioral information in addition to tips on identifying mammals through their tracks, movement patterns, and sign.

Paul Rezendes' *Tracking & the Art of Seeing* contains accessible color photos and detailed accounts for each species. I tend to recommend this book as an adjunct resource for many of my international clients who train with me remotely to learn wildlife tracking, too, because the patterns of sign tend to hold true for equivalent species in other areas of the world.

If you want the ultimate tracking tome for North America (but a bit daunting for newbies), the serious naturalist will also require a copy of Mark Elbroch's *Mammal Tracks & Sign*, which encyclopedically lists almost every track, scratch & nibble that a mammal can leave in the woods.

Grounded Awareness

Active awareness is extremely helpful for learning about Nature. If you want to learn how to identify animal footprints, or tell apart poisonous plants from edible ones, begin by using *active awareness*.

Practice asking questions, comparing and contrasting, and switching between the big picture and the little details. These are all powerful aspects of active awareness. This mode of perception is very intentional and clearly directed. If you pay attention in this way as you get outside, you'll naturally start to wonder about the things you regularly encounter:

What kind of tree am I always leaning against? What is that bird that's always singing to the east of my Meditation Spot in the morning? These questions will start to add up. You might find yourself doing some research when you get home, or carrying binoculars around to get a better view.

You can prime yourself to notice more in Nature by looking through field guides regularly, which reinforces these observations, or simply by exploring what's around you at your Meditation Spot. Even if you don't know what a tree or a bird is "officially" called, you can make up your own names for things.

As you start to look deeper, you'll start to notice distinctions that would have passed you by earlier — that pitch pines, for instance, have bundles of three needles, while white pines have bundles of five, or that red oak leaves have jagged edges, while white oak leaves have rounded edges.

When you prime yourself with these kinds of bits of information, you are building up new neural circuits that hold these forms in your mind. The dendrites in your brain cells literally branch out, cued and waiting to match up with sensory information from your environment.

Active awareness comes with a cost, though — it uses the higher-order areas of your brain's prefrontal cortex, which help you maintain focus, ask questions, and achieve goals. Hopefully, the berries you identified will replace this expended energy!

A Mental Workout

I think of active awareness as a mental workout. There's some effort involved. The rewards are great, but it can leave you a little tired. After all, you've got a roadcrew of neurons making new highways in your brain.

Some days you may want to get outside and just *be* (we'll get to that with the *passive awareness* section next), but consider gifting yourself at least one active awareness session each week. You'll learn something new every time. It'll rewire your brain, literally. Even five minutes can do the trick.

Once you internalize a new bit of sensory know-how, though, you won't need to engage the same degree of active awareness to identify and recognize details in the environment. After you've built up the proper inner search imagery to recognize something (and you've reinforced that neural circuitry with experience), you'll just effortlessly notice it when you pass it by. This level of recognition draws on the sensory cortex and the memory centers of the brain, and it happens automatically.

Making Connections

When you notice something, the areas of the cortex related to the senses you are using in that moment are activated. So, if you come across a mysterious animal track and look at it, your visual cortex lights up. If you touch the track and feel the moist muddy soil, your tactile networks get engaged, too.

Almost instantly, the brain matches up what you are sensing with any similar memories. If you see four toes and claw marks registered in the track, you might get an image in your mind of your dog's footprint that you saw on the beach last month, or of your dog running on the sand.

As a match forms, the language areas of the cortex link up with words that describe whatever you are noticing — you might think, "That looks like my dog's footprint a little bit."

The image and concept of your observation works its way to the frontal cortex (the "chalkboard" of the brain), where you can make a strategy, ask deeper questions, or contemplate the connections that are arising. "Hmm, is that really a dog track? Could it be a mountain lion track? Don't they register four toes in their footprints, too?"

Based on your reflection, you can create an action plan. "Maybe I should pay extra attention when I come through here. If it is a lion track, perhaps there are other signs I might watch for."

Finally, your responses are set into gear in the motor cortex. As you walk forward, you keep your eyes out for other indicators of mountain lion sign, such as additional tracks, scat filled with fur and bones, or the small mounds of leaf litter scraped up by the cat's feet for scent marking.

By taking action and making additional observations, you get feedback on your idea. "Oh, there's a long scrape in the dirt, with a pile of pine needles mounded up on one side... maybe this is a mountain lion's territory!"

These basic steps are how your brain connects with the world and makes sense of it.[3] Active awareness helps you immerse in your senses and fully engage this cycle of learning.

By getting out to your Meditation Spot and experiencing these steps many times and in many different ways, you'll eventually come to internalize the patterns of Nature around you at your Meditation Spot. Then, you'll carry that place and what you've learned there around with you wherever you go — the unique sensory patterns of your place will literally be "hard-wired" into your brain!

Once you know what you're looking for and where to find it, the brain can predict where things "should" be. At that point, passive awareness naturally takes over a larger portion of your observation, and you can notice a tremendous amount of detail without much effort.

~ Practice: Priming with Active Awareness ~

Try this little priming exercise, and notice how active awareness can support your connection with your environment. Close your eyes and picture the color red. Imagine a red apple in your hands. Then imagine a red stop sign. Really see and sense the color red. Now, open your eyes and take in the scene in front of you. Notice any red?

When you prime a color this way, it really tends to jump out at you. This is a classic psychological thought experiment. Try it with a few other colors, too. The same idea works with shapes (leaves, tracks, bird silhouettes), sounds (bird calls, learning a foreign language), and really any other pattern.

Blended & Passive Awareness

Priming, by the way, also happens when you observe your inner landscape. If you are focusing on your breathing in a meditation, you've effectively primed yourself to notice your breath. If you're focusing on a mantra or internal mental phrase, you've primed yourself to activate that particular circuit in your brain.

Setting an Intention

This level of priming is to do with setting your intention and focus (though others can prime you without you even knowing it, too — that's what commercials do!). Many meditation traditions begin with an invocation, prayer, or statement of intention for the session. This is a way of directing one's awareness towards a certain purpose or frequency of experience.

Here's where we get to the fine line between active and passive awareness. Once you've set your intention and primed your mental circuits by using active awareness, you have an interesting choice available: you can keep actively *pushing* your awareness towards a goal, or you can simply relax and be, allowing your intent to *pull* what's needed towards you at the right moment.

This blended active-passive style is more of a "set it and forget it" approach. Once you've primed and activated the neural circuits that will help you notice whatever it is you're seeking, you can just sit back and enjoy the moment until your sensory system finds a match.

For example, if you want to find some raspberries today, actively prime them in your mind before you set out the door. Then just slip into mindfulness, letting Nature fascinate you as you walk. If you come across some raspberries, trust that they will jump out into your awareness.

Making Space

The next level is to use a purely passive awareness approach. Here, you're not priming anything other than the desire to be aware. You're not inputting any particular imagery into your brain to match your senses up to. You're simply making a space within your awareness to expand and be present to the discovery of what's there around and within you.

I call this "sponge awareness," because in this state you're just soaking up the environment with your senses. There's no agenda, there's just the moment and what it offers.

Now, you can go "broad spectrum" with this sponge state, and simply attend to everything in all directions, within and around you. This is a good mindfulness practice — it invites you to discover how truly present you can be, and links the attentional circuits in your brain with the input of the entirety of your senses. Such a state is entirely passive in nature. Fifteen minutes of pure awareness combined with periodic deep breathing should get you to the Relaxation Response.

You might also choose to actively create a "zone" in which your passive awareness can rest. This is what happens when you decide to rest within the awareness of your breath, or within the sensations of your body. The same is true if you are listening to the bird sounds in a particular direction around your Meditation Spot. You actively set up the zone, and then you just passively sense what is there.

There are many ways to play with the dynamics of the passive and the active, the yin and the yang. As you experiment with these different states, you can learn the combinations that will serve you best at different times.

~ Practice: Soaking It In ~

Try this practice outside at your Meditation Spot, or even at the kitchen table. Simply settle into your senses, noticing what's around you. *What's different here compared to the last time you visited this spot? What haven't you noticed before?* The differences may be subtle, but they are waiting there to be discovered.

Let your senses go where they will, scanning near and far, up and down, and all around you. Let your curiosity out to play, and simply relax into the place as you absorb what's there.

You might find that your inner dialogue distracts you at some point. When you catch this happening, just smile and return to your senses. It's just the brain's habitual pathways activating.

Give yourself a good ten minutes to soak it all in. When you do this in a beautiful natural place, let yourself take in the good energy there, too. You'll leave your meditation refreshed and with a new appreciation of what's there around you.

Learning to just be and to "take it all in" is helpful because the brain has a tendency to make up its reality. Neuroscientists have found that 80% of what we call "seeing" is actually the brain making predictions of what it expects to be there; only 20% of sight is about noticing what's really there![4] That's why it pays to look, *and then look again.*

To compensate for this tendency, in Zen meditation, practitioners learn to achieve the state of Beginner's Mind. A beginner doesn't know what to expect, so her awareness is more open to what's really there. The expert knows what "should" be there, and the trap is that because of this, she may not look closely enough. Expertise is a double-edged sword. This is one reason that Yoda said, "You must unlearn what you have learned."

~ Practice: Write Your Story Down! ~

Keeping a Nature & Meditation journal is a great way to track your experiences at your Meditation Spot.

When you get back from your Meditation Spot, take a few minutes to mentally relive your time there. Then, write down the story of your experience, including any especially memorable observations.

Include any key sensory details that are needed to help bring your story to life:

If you were going to re-read this journal in ten years (which you very well may do), what specific moments would you want to remember about this day? If you were sharing your story with a friend, what essential sensory impressions and feelings would you evoke to transport the listener there with you into your story?

Approach journaling in this way to make the most of your reflection process; reliving a story with vivid sensory detail in mind helps reactivate and reinforce the neural circuits that were involved at the time, greatly increasing your odds of turning fleeting impressions into long-lasting memories.

For an added memory boost, gently hold any favorite nature exploration moments in your mind as you fall asleep. When you do this, you might even find yourself at your Meditation Spot in your dreams...

Sensing Forward...

Mindful curiosity is the key to discovering the "hidden" world that surrounds you in Nature.

The sensory awareness tools in this chapter offer you an accessible vehicle for slipping more fully into the moment; the arrival into this eternal *Now* is the first major threshold on the journey into Nature.

Whether you are enjoying active or passive awareness, or some combination of the two, it is your intent that guides your way. *Intend* to be present, and then settle into your awareness. Through quality repetition of these practices, you'll establish neural pathways that allow you to notice more of your surroundings, while attuning to the moment.

Remember that each sense offers a potent access point into a meditative perception of your environment, when approached with this spirit of mindful curiosity. Every outing is a chance to discover the gifts your natural senses have to offer you.

Writing your story down helps reinforce your observations, and builds lasting long-term memories of your experiences; the next step is to ask some deeper questions.

7

FLEX YOUR QUESTION MUSCLE

> *It's the question that drives us. It's the question that brought you here. You know the question..."*
> — *Trinity, in The Matrix*

Once you've written down the story of what you experienced during your Meditation Spot session, you can go even further by flexing your "question muscle." Get into the routine of writing a few questions in your journal every day.

You may or may not know the answers; the most important thing is to ask. Your questions can be about the things you encounter at your Meditation Spot, and they can also be about Life, the Universe, and Everything.

The Art of Inquiry

Asking good questions is a simple way to prime your perception. This practice will increase your awareness of the Nature around your place, and it will also help you look more deeply within yourself into your inner world.

The power of asking questions is not to be underrated. Questions can help you examine a situation and experience it from different angles that you may not have originally thought about. The art of questioning can expand your thinking to take in a larger view, revealing possible interconnections that were previously hidden.

Questions change your brain, too. When you ask a question, you naturally extend your brain's neural web to reach towards an answer. By posing a question, you're drawing upon the conceptual power of the brain's prefrontal cortex to reappraise your experience. When this part of this brain is activated, it can actually help you regulate your emotional state.[1]

So, learning the art of inquiry not only empowers your senses to notice more of what's around you, but it gives you a way to challenge your own thinking. Through questioning, you can add more intention to your own frame of mind. You can coach yourself towards adopting a more solution-oriented point of view, and optimize how you approach different situations.

Mentors understand that questions add up over time. Taking time to ask good questions is a powerful routine to build into any ongoing learning endeavor. Sharing about her experience in a nine-month outdoor mentoring program, I heard one teenager reflect, "I now realize that questions aren't just something that come before answers; they are a doorway to a deeper awareness."

When & Why to Journal

For our purposes here, I recommend to do your more reflective journaling at home, after you return from your Nature excursions. By writing in your journal later at home, rather than in the field, you are simulating the role a mentor or elder would play in a traditional culture. The mentor's responsibility is to help integrate what you experience each day, asking you questions that test your memory and draw out your learning into new dimensions.

Imagine Yoda is grilling you with questions about your morning walk through the Dagobah swamp... what did you see? Hear? Smell? Feel? What did you encounter? What did you learn? The mentor wants to know, and so does your journal.

But, you have to have an experience first to integrate. The sensory practices in this book can serve as springboards for those experiences; make space to fully *be* in each experience, rather than constantly jotting notes while you're outdoors. Of course, there are times when using a journaling or sketching process in the field can help you to be attuned in the moment, and that's great. Just don't let your journal become a screen that distracts you from your direct, raw experience of Nature.

The processes of writing down your story and then asking questions are two ways to engage your sensory-memory, and then to look deeper at what you've noticed. This also creates a need to pay attention when you are in the field, to be truly mindful. Knowing that you will be writing about your observations later gives you a reason to pay attention more deeply in each moment, and then to train your capacity to recall this information on demand. What unique sensory details and stories are waiting for you today?

The Field Journal & the Home Journal

Acquire a small pocket notebook for taking any key notes in the field. Later, when you look back on your day and journal in more depth, you can refer back to these notes. Use this field notebook to jot down interesting sensory details, sketch your observations, take measurements of animal tracks, and catch inspirations on the fly.

Moleskin journals (available at your local bookstore) are great for this, though I often just use a cheap pocket spiral pad. Your field journal will probably get pretty beat up and dirty, and over time you'll go through quite a few. Also set yourself up with a nice, inspiring Nature journal to use at home that is a joy to write in and catch all your stories with.

Make journaling a ritual that you can look forward to each day, knowing that reflecting deeply will add some real juice to your growing Nature Jedi awareness skills.

The Questions

There are two basic questions that are a perfect starting point to springboard your own journaling routine:

1. *What happened around me in "Outer Nature" that stood out today?*
2. *What happened within me during my sit, in the realm of "Inner Nature"?*

You can keep it simple and just work with these two basic questions. See where they take you. For those of you who want to go further down the rabbit hole, let's dive into each of these inquiries a bit more.

Part 1: Outer Nature Reflections

What happened around me in "Outer Nature" that stood out today?

With this first major question, you are invited to consider your observations of the entire ecosystem: the weather, any special encounters with animals, the plants and trees, the earth and stones, the water, the wind and sky, and anything else that jumps out at you.

This question trains you to pay attention to Nature's signals and happenings. Half of a conversation is being able to listen effectively. *Nature is always speaking to us, but do we know how to hear what's being said?*

As you write in your journal, imagine you are sitting at your Meditation Spot, observing once more all that surrounded you on your last visit. Let your awareness gradually work its way up from the ground to the sky, lightly connecting with each layer of Nature. Just notice any impressions and memories that come through. Get an overall sense of what you remember from your recent visit, and then jot down some notes in your journal.

~Practice: Sensing From Earth to Sky~

Here are some further questions to help guide your observations to a deeper level as you gain skill with your Outer Nature awareness:

- **First, sense into the ground layer** — what do you observe happening in the soil and stones today? Is the soil more sandy, loamy, or clay-based, and what color is it? Does the ground feel wet or dry? What is the scent of the forest loam? Are there mushrooms out? How full

are the creeks and water sources, and what sounds are
they making? Is there frost, ice, or snow?

- **What's going on with the plants, shrubs, and trees —**
  what is their stage of growth? How are the growing
  things responding to the current weather conditions? Is
  the grass covered with dew in the morning, or is the
  ground dry?

- **What animal tracks have been left in the night?** What
  animal sign have you come across — scat, feeding
  signs, beds? Who's on the move in the area now? Why
  are these animals here right now — what's drawing
  them into the area?

- **Now begin to turn your awareness towards the sky.**
  What are the birds up to? What sounds do you hear
  them making? What are they eating now? What are
  they focused upon? What are they telling you?

- **What direction is the wind coming from?** How strong
  is it? Is the air moist or dry? What kind of clouds, if any,
  are in the sky? What are the clouds and wind telling
  you about the weather in the coming days? Is there any
  rain or snow falling now, or on the way?

- **Where is the Moon in the sky right now,** and what
  phase is it in? When is it rising and setting? Can you
  point to where it rises? How high up in the sky does it
  get in this season?

- **Where does the Sun rise and set right now,** and at
  what times? How high up does the Sun get at midday
  right now?

- **What are the Stars doing this week?** Where is the
  North Star and the Big Dipper (or the Southern Cross
  in the southern hemisphere)? What Zodiac
  constellations are visible just after sunset right now?
  What planets are visible?

Though it sounds like a lot, remember — you're just scanning from the ground on up. I've simply offered you some ways to dive deeper into each layer.

This exercise is quite revealing. Perhaps you can remember some of these details from your time at your Meditation Spot. Likely, some of these categories will draw a blank in your memory. That's to be expected, and it's just part of the connection process. As my friend Jon Young has often reminded me, "it's the gaps in your awareness that have the most to teach you." Journaling is one way to begin identifying these gaps.

When you take time to reflect on what you've just experienced, you are reinforcing the sensory pathways and short-term memory areas in your brain that were activated in the field; through remembering, you are helping to consolidate these perceptions into lasting long-term memories. You're also priming yourself to connect further with these patterns the next time you get out.

At first, it may take some concerted effort to direct your attention towards noticing all of these aspects of Nature. This is because you're forming new neural pathways. You're teaching your brain to add importance to sensory information that you might never have intentionally noticed before! To do this, your brain literally has to create proteins and forge new synaptic connections.

It's well worth the relatively small amount of effort involved. Do this complete journaling process once a week; after a month or so, you'll find yourself enjoying a new level of awareness in the out-of-doors. You will have stepped further on the journey of re-awakening your attunement to Nature's cycles, in the way that our ancestors all once lived and breathed.

When you step out the door, Nature will begin to speak to you and enrich your day with many rewarding observations. Your friends will wonder why you've become obsessed with the alarm calls of the local squirrels and become mystified by your knowledge of the portents of the clouds and wind. Every walk down the street will suddenly be an adventure filled with mysteries worthy of a Sherlock Holmes novel.

Don't let getting bogged down in details stop you. A 30-second version of this practice is to stand outside your door, sweeping your senses from the ground to the sky (or vice versa), asking, "What do I notice now?" Then, close your eyes and imagine everything that you just sensed, as vividly as you can. This can also be done on the horizontal plane, from near to far. I promise you, there's always something new to notice.

Part 2: Inner Nature Reflections

What happened within me during my sit, in the realm of "Inner Nature"?

LET'S LOOK NEXT AT THE SECOND QUESTION, WHICH TURNS THE attention around and invites you to look within, to "Know Thy Self." It's time for some Deep Thoughts, people.

Reflection for Self-Knowledge

Now, you are shining the light of your attention on your inner landscape, tracking the ecology of the imagination.

There's just as much complexity to track on this inwards level as there is in the workings of the larger world around you. Just as the Milky Way galaxy holds about 100 billion stars, each human brain contains around 100 billion neurons. Each of these neurons can have links with up to 10,000 other neurons. In fact, the web of neurons that make up your brain contains a possible *thousand trillion* connections![2]

By getting to know the places within yourself and the various "animals" on the move there, you will gain insights that help you to be more effective in all levels of your life. To get more specific with this inquiry, you might ask yourself, *"How did I feel before my meditation, compared to afterwards?"*

When you make it a habit to assess your state of being before and after meditation, you'll consciously feel the positive impact. Through direct knowledge, you'll quickly come to realize meditation's true value. Then, you'll be more likely to keep up your practice. You'll also get into the positive habit of self-awareness, which is an opportunity for cultivating mindfulness.

~ Practice: Exploring the Gratitude Mindset ~

A particularly important pair of questions that I recommend asking regularly is: *What inspired me today? What and who am I thankful for in my life?*

As we are more inundated with negativity in the news and other media outlets every day, we need to consciously flip on some positivity channels for the health of our mental well-being. The old saying "garbage in, garbage out" is all too true. Psychologists observe that the brain is more easily impacted by the negative things that happen in life than the positives.[3-4] People tend to more easily pass by the positive events, but mull over negative moments.

Have you ever caught yourself thinking about an interaction that didn't go as well as you would have liked, perhaps days or weeks after the fact? This is an adaptation that helps you remember dangers, so you can avoid them in the future. Still, you can balance this natural tendency by actively cultivating a positive mindset. Make positivity part of your daily routine.

How can you get started with all this good stuff? A daily gratitude practice is a simple way to boost optimism and mood.[5] You can make space for gratitude at the beginning or end of your day by writing in your journal. Or, do this after you arrive at your Meditation Spot. Just ask the question, "What and who am I grateful for right now?" Let the images of your day flit through your mind.

Who can you think of that helped you out or inspired you in some way today, however great or small? Who do you hold in your heart with deep care and love? Who is helping you in your life that perhaps you don't even know, and have never met?

Start first by thinking about your family, friends, teachers, and the people you know well who enhance your life. Imagine you are sending them each a big smile, and that they in turn are smiling back to you. Feel this smile travel back and forth like a big glowing hug of goodness.

Then, consider the people that provide your food, electricity, water, and clothing... and all of the fabric of Nature supporting your existence each day. Let your wave of gratitude ripple out, and imagine the entire Earth receiving your smile, and smiling back at you.

In case any of that sounds silly, well, maybe it is. But here's why you should still do it: You'll start to feel damn good. When you smile, you are accessing an awesomely simple "bio hack" that quickly reduces your heart rate, lightens your mood, and lowers your stress response.[6]

There are actually over 50 types of smiles (!!), but the most powerful smile researchers have identified occurs when the muscles around the eye get involved;[7] if you feel your cheeks raise up and crow's feet forming in the corners of your eyes, you've got it! With that in mind, smile as you go through your gratitude meditation. If you need to, fake it 'till you make it. Beneficial physiological changes are happening immediately, even if ye are of little faith. *Trust in the Force, Luke.*

For my geeky friends in the audience, you'll appreciate knowing that this kind of beatific smile increases activity in the left hemisphere's anterior temporal zone, a state which is associated with a good mood.[8] When you smile, your facial muscles contract, minutely shifting the structure of the underlying bones;[9] this in turn increases blood flow to the brain's frontal lobes.[10]

But you don't need to know all that neuroscience and physiology to benefit from a good smile. Taoist meditators have long known the power of smiling, making it a routine to smile to each part of the body. This simple practice opens the energy flow in the body and blissfully prepares you for deeper meditation.[11] Try it - it feels great!

Empower Your Motivation & Curiosity

"What's that? Why does it do that? Why? Why? What's that mean?"

These are the kinds of endless questions that a typical five-year-old child loves to ask any hapless adult within earshot. Try as you might, you can't really quench the questions, and any explanation that's subject to this barrage will end up going in circles until you finally say, "I don't know — because that's the way it is!"

The young child is in the process of forming their impressions of the world and how it works, and their main tool for getting this crucial information comes through the ability to ask questions and be curious about the grand world around them.

This force of mind is a formidable gift, warming us with the light of knowledge. Curiosity has the power to bring you deeper into the moment as it offers new links to the Nature within and around you. As the flame of curiosity grows, it becomes a potent impetus for expanding the light of your awareness. If we can tend its flame and carry the light of curiosity forward with us into our adult years, we have a mighty tool at our disposal indeed.

The curiosity-driven mind is present and alert. Like a raven, it scans for novel items or "hidden" patterns, seeking out the gems scattered across the usual scenes of daily life. Curiosity has led humankind to explore the world, seek adventure, and reach to the Moon and beyond. Each foray into the unknown expands our understanding and leads us to a deeper appreciation for the world and its mysteries.

~ Practice: Asking the Deep Questions ~

Like the raven that fades into the twilight sky as it flies to its mountain roost, curiosity merges with the deeper waters of creativity that flow within your inmost self. Simply getting in the habit of asking questions will gradually awaken this natural power. A set of particularly helpful questions to regularly investigate include:

- **What thoughts and dreams have appeared in my mind lately?**

- **What messages from Nature have I been receiving? What feelings do these evoke? What is this telling me?**

- **What are my goals? Do I feel aligned in my thoughts and actions towards these goals? How will I work to achieve these desires?**

These kinds of questions will help you access your deepest dreams and bring them to life. Your dreams are driven by your core values and your deep-seated feelings about what you wish to experience. These feelings are what give you the power to generate action and transform your life. When you have clear goals in mind, you can then create a series of small action steps that you can take to achieve them.

Having this clear sequence of steps in place allows you to harness your brain's natural motivational system. Every time you complete a step and relish the success, your brain releases *dopamine*, a powerful neurotransmitter that builds intrinsic motivation (this is one reason why video games are so compelling[12] — every small action your character takes, and each level you beat, builds your motivation to continue playing).

When you have something to look forward to, you are already setting yourself up to achieve your goals. Simply anticipating a success can trigger the dopamine release;[13-14] the more dopamine you have available in your prefrontal cortex, the more likely you will be to take action and work to achieve the results you want to enjoy.[15] The small steps of your action plan create a "dopamine ladder" that motivates you to climb towards the achievement of your larger vision.

Curiosity itself is thought to boost dopamine in areas of the brain that support memory. By building up your curiosity, you are setting the stage both to lock in your learning for the long-term, and to recall a broader range of details (including contextual things you weren't even trying to remember).[16] By journaling regularly and writing down your questions, you are learning to flex your curiosity muscle.

How Questions Changed My Life

The first time I truly realized the value of this routine was during my teenage years, and it literally changed my life.

I had signed up for a week-long wilderness skills class in New York state. Our small group became immersed in earth living skills, timelessly connecting with the rhythms of Nature. My "tent" was a debris shelter I had constructed with my own two hands, and the fire that warmed us each night was made through fire-by-friction, as we ate from bowls and spoons that we burned out of solid wood using the coals of our fire. Each day we relied less and less on the items we had brought with us, until most of our core needs were provided for by the gifts of the Nature around us.

Most impactfully, the *learning culture* of the class was designed around a mentoring approach. Mark Morey, a long-time Outward Bound trainer and connoisseur of human potential, had just completed a residency at the Wilderness Awareness School. There, he had travelled to observe a unique set of nature mentoring strategies that were generating massive transformations in participants' lives.[17] Having told me that he had never seen such an impactful learning environment before, Mark was now excitedly implementing all that he had absorbed, to my benefit!

Mark co-led the workshop with Steve Young, an experienced naturalist, and together they recruited a number of volunteers who would appear at various opportune times to add their perspectives to the learning culture.

Want to learn how to stalk through the woods silently? Well, here's someone who can show you how. Want to learn how to tan deer hides? Yes, and here's a couple more people who know exactly what to do (and yes, every animal does have enough brains to tan its own hide). As if by magic, a small "primitive village" had suddenly formed for a week in the woods at the edge of the Berkshires, sprouting up like a mushroom after a rain.

The mentoring approach in our little village beneficially uprooted all of my previous notions of learning. Instead of teachers filling my head with information for a test that I didn't care about, I was inspired with potent stories that built a meaningful context and a real desire to learn. Then, after the teachers demonstrated their techniques, they gave me the a chance to do it, too, so I could learn experientially. Throughout these lessons, we were taught the art of questioning, which provided a bedrock for driving home what we were learning.

During the week, the teachers peppered me with questions that prompted me to pay attention to my environment, and to reflect on what I was experiencing. The responsibility was on *me* to find answers, and to take charge of my own learning. This is an old way of passing earth skills across the generations, and in response to it, I thrived.

Before the modern educational system was developed, traditional mentors in Wisdom Cultures around the world relied upon this ancient combination of stories, role modeling, and questions to inspire learners and propel their growth. From my own experience, and having mentored many others, I see that our brains naturally recognize this ancestral approach and respond amazingly to it. Learning in this dynamic context quickly takes on an exciting life of its own.

After a week of breathing life into my own questions and curiosities, I arrived back home feeling different somehow. I had engaged a whole set of neural circuits that had been sitting there in my brain, just waiting to wake up!

From then on, it was full steam ahead. The ball was now in my court. My life would forever move forward in a new way, carried by the power and drive of the questions that burned within me (Mark, by the way, would go on to inspire a whole generation of nature connection mentors).

Gaining Orbit

Since that foundational experience over twenty years ago, I've had the chance to mentor many other individuals from around the world in these skills. As a mentor, I love to ask questions. I know that by doing so, I am helping my clients to cultivate their own relationship with this positive habit. As the questions gain momentum and take root, their sense of the world grows.

It's endlessly fascinating to watch the power of questions

unfold over time. After experiencing several months of nature awareness mentoring, one of my clients recently reported:

> *Mentoring opened my eyes to an entirely new way of seeing the landscape... for some reason, I am finding that my memory of strange but important information is better. It's almost like I can revisit something and see other details that I didn't remember the first time around...*
>
> *"When I make statements or take an opposing position with someone, I have a new personal strength that helps others to see my position clearer, and I see their position clearer. I feel more confident in making decisions that have a bigger impact, because I can better understand the whole picture — not just my view point."*

By developing questions and curiosities about life, and then exploring and seeking answers, you are setting up an action pathway in your brain that will gather momentum with each adventure.

By making it a routine to intentionally consider these two aspects of Nature, the inner and the outer, you'll develop your awareness in a balanced manner. This balanced approach creates a strong foundation upon which your Nature meditations can continue to deepen over time.

8

MOVING MINDFULLY IN NATURE

66 *In every walk with nature, one receives far more than he seeks."*

— *John Muir*

Your meditation doesn't start when you sit down; it starts the moment you decide you are going to meditate.

In that moment, the deep parts of your mind realize there will be a transition coming, implying a switch between whatever mental state you are in now, and the meditative state you will be diving into when you arrive at your Meditation Spot.

Whether you realize it or not, your intention has already started to transform your awareness. There are some specific things you can do next to support this shift.

In this chapter, we'll explore some tools you can use throughout your day to maintain and deepen your awareness skills. We'll also explore the power of mindfulness in motion, and how you can blend and flow with Nature as you walk to and from your Meditation Spot.

These tools will help you build momentum from one meditation session to the next, and make the most of your time when you do get out to your spot.

Finding Opportunities to Cultivate Awareness

There's a saying that "meditation is practice for the rest of your life."

In meditation, you certainly learn things like mindfulness, stepping into a larger field of view, and tempering your reactions with a skillful response. These are all incredibly useful skills that can apply immediately in every other area of your life. However, I would also add that *all of life is practice for meditation.*

Rather than living in a whirlwind of thoughts throughout the day, and then plunking down on the meditation seat for a complete 180° turn into mindfulness, what if throughout the day, you could make space for cultivating small moments of awareness? A minute here, and five minutes of mindfulness there can really start to add up and change your experience of the day.

Remember, you don't need to go to a remote Himalayan cave to get in a few minutes of mindful awareness. You can find small moments throughout your day to fit in this practice. Set your phone to remind you every hour to take one minute for this. Transition times are also effective moments for cultivating this awareness — when you leave or enter your house or car; in between meetings or calls at work; on your lunch break.

Take a moment right now and list out five times during your day when you can pause for even a minute to get centered. Use the lines below to list out what you'll do and when.

Early Morning:

_____

_____

_____

Mid-Morning:

_____

_____

_____

Lunch:

_____

_____

_____

Afternoon:

_____

_____

_____

Evening:

_____

_____

_____

~ Practice: Walking Mindfully to Your Car ~

Here's a simple practice you can use to cultivate mindful aware-ness each day, whether you are going to your Meditation Spot or simply headed out the door for work.

Before you open the door, pause and take a deep breath. Slow down for a minute. Realize that by pausing this way, you are changing the type of energy you project out to the world around you. Now, you can choose what to project rather than being caught up in your own momentum.

Peek out the curtain for a moment. Take stock of what's there — is there a robin feeding on the lawn? A squirrel? If you had just stormed right out, you never would have known, unless you saw the animals fleeing into the distance. Just this one moment of awareness is already shifting how you might experience the short walk to your car.

Slowly open the door. Be aware of the sensation of your posture and the feeling of your hand gripping the knob. Use each motion as an invitation to truly experience the world.

Step gradually out the door and onto the doorstep. After you close the door, stand still for a moment and take in the world around you. Go into Expanded Vision.

Notice any animals on the ground or in the trees. Notice the sky, any clouds, and feel the breeze move across you face. Sniff the air.

Make sure there are no animals in your path. If there are, and you have the time, either circle around them or wait for them to move before you continue along. If you simply have to keep moving, *c'est la vie*. Life goes on.

Savor each footstep as you walk to your car. Feel the ground supporting you beneath your feet. Smile to the Earth in recogni-tion of this support.

Take a deep breath before you open your car door, and feel the vastness of the sky filling you with the breath of life. Smile to the sky in recognition.

Sense your heartbeat for a moment and smile to the creativity that dwells within you. Then, start your car and get on your way.

Note how a simple shift in awareness like this can impact the rest of your morning. This meditation can be done in as little as a minute, though you might give yourself as much as five minutes when time allows. It's worth it.

Ditching the City Walk

Do you know Bob? That's not really his name, but that's what the animals call him. Here's why.

Bob lives in the city, but he likes to get out into Nature when he can. Being a spiritual dude, he also meditates a lot. Bob really wants to feel "at home" in the woods, like he's one with everything there.

Bob surely get a lot out of his visits to the forest, but he feels like he's missing something.

Certainly, these hikes energize him, and the woods are relaxing, but he feels like he's just passing through; he never gets to see what the animals are really up to, besides running away from him.

Bob wonders if there is some kind of secret code for blending into the forest that he doesn't know yet. Actually, he's right — there is.

Slowing Down

Thing is, when animals sense Bob in his "city walk" careening along the trail, they observe a cacophony of movement and sound.

As Bob energetically hikes through, the animals see his head bob up and down (hence the name); his arms are flailing, and he's often looking either right down at his feet, or into the camera for a selfie.

If you were to put your ear to the ground like in the old Western movies, or if you were a critter living beneath the soil, you'd hear and feel the pounding vibrations of Bob's city shuffle moving through the ground like a freight train. Bob's style of walking simply doesn't lend itself to blend into the slower, quieter rhythms of the forest.

The animals just don't get it. Why would Bob come into their home and cause such a ruckus? The juncos chip and fly away when he comes down the trail, and even the squirrel chatters nervously when he passes. Forget about the fox and the bobcat; they're well-hidden and out of the way long before he gets anywhere near.

If only Bob could realize what's happening...then he might have a chance to adjust his movement to match the flow of the woods. He'd see so much more, and sense how he's part of the story of the land. Part of Nature, all that good stuff. After all, his presence is impacting the animals and all the rest of it.

It's not really Bob's fault, though. He's just walking the same way everyone else in the city does, too. Moving this way is normal for him, though at some point in the past, his ancestors knew differently. He's got a few other things going that aren't helping, either.

Ditch the Expectations

There's one major impediment that's not helping Bob to really connect at the fullest level with Nature on his hike (and with his capacity for mindful awareness), and it's a simple fix. This has to do with *expectation*.

Bob is *expecting* to finish his hike by 6:30, and he's *expecting* to do the entire red trail in that time. That's fine, there's nothing wrong with that. Hiking is fun, and there's a time to cruise and get the miles in. It's great exercise, and I do this myself all the time.

But, if your goal is to cover miles, you're going to have to move fast. This means you're going to make a splash as you stir up birds and other animals. That's score one against mindful awareness.

It's a conflict of intentions that's causing the issue here. Bob has clear expectations around the parameters of his hike, but nothing very clear around what it means to make space for a deeper connection to happen.

If Bob really wants to tune into the rhythm of the place and blend in, slowing down can really help his cause. Bob might sometimes set aside special trips to the woods where he can go "timeless."

Sure, he still only has an hour to play. But during that hour, he tunes to the feedback from the animals and the place, and discovers a natural pace that allows him to flow with the land.

On these special trips, Bob explores and wanders, maybe sits meditatively for a bit, and doesn't worry so much about getting from Point A to Point B.

Mindful and Barefoot

Ditching the shoes can help, too. The shape of modern footwear greatly impacts the way we walk. Thick rubber soles tend to create a heel-first step onto the ground. The robins feeding on the trail can probably feel the impact from that heel strike. I'd bet the worms can, anyway.

Protective hiking boots also grant us the luxury of tromping quickly through the brush, somewhat heedless of what we are stepping on. This modern footwear gives Bob the ability *not to pay attention.* Score two against mindfulness right there. Again, an easy fix.

Experimenting in Nature's laboratory, let's see if we can find a solution for Bob's dismay. What happens if you take your shoes off and walk on a pebbly trail? You'll naturally find yourself taking shorter steps, gingerly feeling the ground with your feet before committing your weight.

You will also slow down. You'll have to shift your weight smoothly from one leg to the other to maintain your balance on the uneven ground. Your movement instantly becomes more intentional and mindful, because it's necessary. And when the animals watch you, they notice your head isn't bobbing. It's gliding along like a fox in the morning mist.

What the Fox Can Teach Us

Foxes know what's up. The fox's big pointy ears can take in the quiet rustling of a mouse from half a football field away. The fox's nose catches a myriad of faint scents drifting on the wind, decoding stories about dogs, squirrels, and a thousand Google searches worth of other information we can only guess at.

If we want to study mindful movement in Nature, we can't ask for a better teacher. These bushy-tailed, reclusive four-leggeds are tuned to their surroundings, and they know how to move.

Nestled with my camera at the edge of a meadow one fine late April day, I observed the antics of some young fox kits playing at their den entrance.

The giant throw-mound of dirt that was excavated months before during the burrow construction was still there, piled up and spilling out of the spine-filled hawthorn thicket that protected the den entrance.

The kits perched and tumbled against each other atop this

mound, their nervous motions reminding me of an antsy pitcher's shifty moves during a high-stakes World Series game.

Suddenly the kits got still. A distant song sparrow that must have been pushed off of its feeding spot let out a mild "sweep sweep" alarm, and the mother fox came gliding into view. She strode confidently but with awareness towards her kits, ready for feeding time.

The vixen's smooth trot blended seamlessly into the meadow, a horizontal blur that seemed perfectly streamlined with the breeze and the flowing of the meadow grasses. Her movement truly seemed an expression of that place, paws and fur a dynamic extension of the earth itself. In that brief moment, I saw and understood why foxes have long been emulated as masters of motion.

When we move like the fox, we conserve our energy. Instead of bobbing up and down with extraneous motion, we focus on achieving a smoothness of step, tempered by balance and poise.[1] Instead of striking with the heel and issuing vibrations into the ground, we gently feel the ground with the foot before placing the weight.

Pro Tip: Keep your arms close by your sides when you wish to avoid disturbing animals. This makes you look more like a tree than a human.

~ Practice: Fox Walking ~

The Practice Area. Learn to Fox Walk barefoot on a flat, grassy area that's free of broken glass or other sharp goodies (or, you can learn like I did, in pitch darkness in the middle of a moonless night deep in the forest, but that's another story). Practice gradually and pay attention to your body; only move in ways that feel good to you. Find what works for *you* in your Nature explorations.

You'll quickly get up to snuff and can take this practice onto, or off of, the trail. Fox Walking works great with Vibram five-toes and other minimalist shoes, too, and you can even learn to adapt it for use with any shoe, and at any speed — even running.

Placing the Feet. The mechanics of Fox Walking sound a bit complex, but really aren't. The foot is gently lifted, and a short step allows the outer ball of the foot to lightly sense the ground. If there is nothing sharp or troubling, the inside ball of the foot is allowed to lightly touch down to sense further. Then, the toes, followed by the heel.

Once a sure step is certain, the weight smoothly transfers from the back foot to the front foot as the body shifts forward. The effect internally is somewhat like a slinky pouring its mass from one side of the coil to the other, effortless and flowing.

Body Posture. The Fox Walk is similar to a relaxed Tai Chi stance. The chin is slightly tucked, and the head is kept level throughout the walk. The spine is full, and the pelvis is allowed to "drop" towards the earth, tucking slightly in — but this tucking comes only through the relaxed dropping and pull of gravity, not by force. The tucked pelvis helps fill in the lower back, and it allows the pelvic bowl to better support the internal organs.

FYI — if the "drop and tuck" is hard for you, it could mean you have some *anterior pelvic tilt*. This may come from tight hip flexors combined with other areas that need attention (often the abs and glutes need strengthening, as well). This is a very common condition for those who sit at a desk all day. It's recognized by a "swayback" or concavity of the lower back — a physical therapist or skilled bodyworker may be able to help you correct this through exercise and stretching, if needed. Everyone's different though, so seek professional advice.

If All Else Fails. Don't worry if you can't get the posture or how the footsteps work exactly. At the least, just slow down your walk, and move as quietly as possible — you'll be sure to see more animals and cause less disturbance to the Force, young Nature Jedi.

~ Practice: Meditation in Motion ~

Once you get the Fox Walk down, you can now use your feet to feel the ground. This frees your eyes to look up more often. Practice allowing your eyes to look into the distance, at or just above the horizon; with this zone as your visual anchor, slip into Expanded Vision.

Notice how walking with a larger field of view changes your experience of the environment. Your awareness is now freed up and can spread further out to notice birds, animals, and more. Take your time, and build skill by practicing in increasingly challenging places. But, start simple on a flat, open area.

Vary Your Vision. You can also let your eyes dart around to focus towards items of interest, such as a cool warbler or that precariously wobbly rock you want to avoid tripping on. Take in what detail you need to, and then when you feel satisfied (and safe) allow your gaze to expand all around you again.

The tracker, Tom Brown, calls this back-and-forth toggling from the big picture to the little details "varying your vision;" it's a great way to alternate between peripheral and foveal points of view, to get the best of both.

Choosing a Speed. You can use different speeds of Fox Walking for different purposes. Really, you can learn to do this at any speed, even running.

If I have a ways to go before I reach a spot that I want to really check out, I might jog for a bit, and then slow down before approaching the area. This way I have more time to really check out my favorite zones, but I slow down enough before I get there that I don't startle anything. If you track a coyote that's scouting hunting zones, you might sometimes notice a similar behavior.

The general principle is that the slower you go, the more information your senses will be able to take in, and so the more aware you will be of your surroundings and how you can flow with them. But, you can still run and be aware, too.

The One-Second Step. At one second per step, you can relaxedly move through an area with a pretty good awareness of what's going on, and still get somewhere without causing a huge ruckus amongst the animals. If your used to through-hiking, this speed will probably feel pretty slow at first. Note your brain's reaction to different tempos: *boredom just means you're not really paying attention yet.*

If you want to get to your Meditation Spot and have a chance to actually see some animals, and also enter the meditative state before you even sit down, you might use this speed to "cover some ground" on a trail (everything's relative), slowing down further if you encounter an animal you don't want to alarm.

The Five-Second Step. To get into a nice deep moving meditation zone, I personally like to get into an even slower walk with a smooth rhythm, about five or six seconds per step. If you do this for even five minutes as you connect with the environment through your senses, you'll start to shift into a very relaxed yet aware state. Remember, the Relaxation Response can be accessed even while moving. The rhythm of your footsteps and the sustained attention on your senses can be a doorway to this state.

~ **Practice: Mindfulness In Slow Motion** ~

What do you do when you encounter an animal and you want to either move by it, or get closer without startling it? Slow down even more!

Moving extremely slowly while observing wildlife is a powerful way to slip into the moment. You'll need to pay attention to your balance, the wind direction (so your scent doesn't startle the animal), the sounds your feet make with each step, and so much more. The refined mindfulness that comes with very slow motion also amplifies your senses and heightens every aspect of your awareness.

If you move slowly and smoothly enough, and your clothing blends in enough to the background to break up your outline, it's as if you're not even there. The animals may begin to let you into their secret world. I've had a lot of magical encounters with all kinds of animals through this practice. You can, too.

Here's a favorite story of a time this practice came alive for me:

One year, the last of the late winter snows was thawing, leaving patches of exposed leaf litter in my local forest. I had a couple of hours at my disposal to wander that day, and was able to move around fairly slowly, savoring the remaining tracks in the snow that I knew would be the last of the season. On this day, I was particularly interested in following the deer tracks and seeing what they were up to. No one else was out there on this overcast, cold day.

Up ahead I heard the sound of something scraping through the leaves. A bunch of somethings. I shifted into a slow fox walk, and discovered what it was. A large group of American robins was foraging on the ground, turning over the fallen leaves. The males had not yet split off to form their own territories, though they would soon.

The understory was very thick in this part of the forest, full of catbriar and multiflora rose. The robin flock effectively blocked the trail up ahead, leaving me with few options. I waited a bit to see if they would move on, but they were happy to keep foraging. It was a cold, wet day in a tough season, and I really didn't want to scare them up and force them to waste energy just so I could pass by. On the other hand, I actually did need to eventually get to the other side of the park to meet someone a bit later.

Taking a few deep breaths to relax even more fully, I dropped into a very slow 20 seconds per step, holding my arms close to my sides. As I neared the robins, I slowed even further, into a roughly one minute per step walk.

This kind of incredibly slow speed takes a good amount of precision and awareness to execute smoothly. It also renders you close to invisible, at least in terms of reducing motions that draw attention. At a minute per step, even the human eye cannot discern any visible motion — it's just too slow, and it looks like the person is just standing there![2]

Absorbed in the moment, time seemed to disappear. Step by mindful step, I found myself suddenly amidst the flock, with birds feeding all around me. The sounds of active foraging filled my ears. Slowly I worked my way through the feeding zone, and emerged out onto the path, free to go my way. Though it took some time, the birds had allowed me to move through their midst. In that moment I truly felt at one with the rhythm of the forest. This is one of the gifts that comes with moving slowly and mindfully.

~ Practice: Creating Your Own Mindful Walking Circuit (or, Mindfulness for Dog Walkers) ~

Not everybody likes to sit in the woods. Some people just can't sit still, and others just feel a need to move after sitting in an office all day. I get it.

Sitting is a bit of a learned practice, and I do hope you give it a try. Take a 30-day challenge to sit every day and just be in your senses for ten minutes. It could be right on your back porch, or during your lunch break.

But I know that some of you reading this will think, "No way! I'm not sitting in the woods, ever!" Or, "I just don't have time, I'm too busy even to sit in my yard. All I can do is walk my dog, and that's all the Nature time I can give myself."

Fortunately, you can still get many of the benefits of meditating in Nature even if you can't sit. Your dog is already in the mindful zone, and you can join along. Because mindfulness is a state of mind, you can use this awareness practice on any route you choose, even in the city.

If you have a route that you walk already, or you are going to establish one, I invite you to start thinking about it as an opportunity for connecting with Nature through mindful awareness. Those of who you do have an outdoor Meditation Spot can use this practice as part of your routine on the way there and back, too.

Set Your Start & End Points. You don't even have to spend the entire walk in meditation. What I'd like you to do is to choose a section of your regular circuit that will be dedicated each time you walk there to being fully in your senses. A two to five-minute section of trail can be a good starting point.

Later, you may expand the markers to include more of the circuit, until you achieve a full fifteen minutes of mindfulness (which is plenty of time to get you into the Relaxation Response). Think right now of the places you pass by; pick a start point and an end point as "triggers" for your meditation.

Prepare Your Mind. Now, imagine yourself walking by your starting point; imagine that as you arrive there, you remember to slip into your Expanded Vision. You pause for a moment to listen all around you. What birds and other sounds do you hear? What scents do you smell? Where is the breeze coming from, and where is the sun in the sky? What signs of Nature do you see?

Then, imagine yourself continuing along to the end marker, wrapped in mindful awareness. Imagine that with each step, you are transforming stress into peaceful, rejuvenating energy. This envisioning process is training your mind in advance to begin paying attention in a deep way the next time that you walk past this spot.

Put It To Practice. Be sure when you get to your starting point in real life that you pause to go through the same sensory routine, too. Then, stay in your expanded sensory awareness until you reach the end marker.

At the end marker, take a few deep breaths and let your awareness reach all through your body. Carry the peace and relaxation with you through the rest of your walk. If friends come with you on your walk, you may invite them to join you for the mindful meditation, too.

~ Practice: Advanced Walking Circuit - The Mind Walk ~

Once you've established your mindfulness walking routine, here's a way to deep the routine on those days when it's just too rainy or you don't feel like going out. Even if you can't get out for your walking circuit, you can take a "Mind Walk" there in your imagination. Just like we did a moment ago, use all of your imaginal senses to envision the walk, and in particular, the aspects of Nature that you encounter there.

The brain responds to such envisioned activity almost as if you've really gone on the actual walk.[3] [4] Olympic athletes,[5] virtuoso musicians,[6] and other high-performers mentally rehearse with full-sensory imagery to improve their skills, in addition to regular physical practice.

The Mind Walk is also a great way to test your awareness: what details do you remember along your route? Double-check your memory the next time you get out there. Here are some questions you can try your hand at. You might come to enjoy these brain teasers even more than Sudoku.

Ten Nature Awareness Questions For Your Walk:

1. Which way is north? How do I know?
2. Where's the sun right now? (or, the moon, or the wind)
3. Where's the closest water? (stream, pond, ocean, drainage...)
4. What are five different birds I hear in my neighborhood? (make up names as you start to get used to their unique songs)
5. What animal footprints can I find today? (urban critters include squirrels, raccoon, fox, opossum, mice, and sparrows, just to name a few)
6. What color flowers/leaves/fruits/buds do I see today? (pick a color to find)
7. What clothes was the first person I encountered on my walk wearing? (if any :)
8. What are some unique scents I notice on my walk? (check out the leaf litter under different trees)
9. What's a place an animal could sneak through? (gaps in fences, holes...)
10. What inspires me on my walk?

Put It Into Action

Phew. In this chapter you've gained a whole toolkit of awareness skills that you can enjoy while you cruise around your Meditation Spot. Now, your mindfulness practice can kick into gear not just while you sit, but anywhere you go through these moving meditations.

Try the practices out. If Yoda was here with you, he'd make you carry him around on your back as you try to levitate stones in mid-air, all the while saying, "Focus your mind. Be one with the Force."

In his honor, pick a couple of the practices from this chapter that you want to do this week, and put them on your calendar. Go do this, right now!

In the next chapter, we're joining in the Great Dance of Nature. But, you have to walk before you can dance, so go for a stroll around your neighborhood and put these mindful movement techniques into practice. I'll be waiting for you in the next chapter.

9

THE GREAT DANCE & TRICKSTER'S CAVE

I f you were to sit around a campfire with the hunter-gatherers of the Kalahari Desert, known collectively as the San people, there is an ancient story you might hear:

Long ago, people could turn into animals, and animals could turn into people...

At that time, all beings could understand one another, unified in the ceaseless turnings and transformations of the Great Dance. This was the realm of the First Creation. In this wordless ecstatic flux, there was no sickness or death, only true creativity and joy. Beings could transform themselves into whatever form they wanted.

Then, one day, the first word was uttered and the world stopped. Language had appeared. From these words, the Trickster was born. Using words, Trickster whispered to each animal, telling each one of their current appearance. Suddenly, these descriptions hypnotized the animals. They could no longer remember how to transform.

The power of these words locked the beings into a false belief about what they each were or could be. Unable to transform as they once had before, the beings of the Dance were forced to remain as whatever character they happened to be in that moment. Giraffes were stuck as giraffes, hippos were stuck as hippos, and people were stuck as people. The Great Dance was halted; suffering, sickness, and death appeared as a result of this stagnation. The Second Creation had begun.[1]

The anthropologist Bradford Keeney, who shares this story in his book, *The Bushman Way of Tracking God*, was initiated as a *n|om-kxaosi* healer by the traditional San Wisdom Keepers. Keeney writes there that:

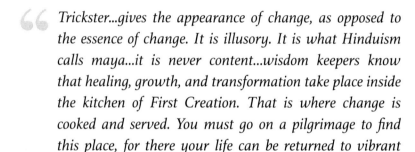

> *Trickster...gives the appearance of change, as opposed to the essence of change. It is illusory. It is what Hinduism calls maya...it is never content...wisdom keepers know that healing, growth, and transformation take place inside the kitchen of First Creation. That is where change is cooked and served. You must go on a pilgrimage to find this place, for there your life can be returned to vibrant living."[2]

N|om is the vibration of life. San healers raise this primal energy up through their dancing and song and pure love of life, allowing the energy to move and quake their bodies; through the ecstatic shaking, they transmit the healing energy to those in need. San Wisdom Keepers recognize that a person must be made ready to receive this potent transmission; the heart must first be softened, and the mind must be freed from its shackles of worry and comparisons.[3]

Healing Vibrations

The study of Nature is integral to healing traditions the world over. *Prana*, *qi*, and *n|om* are just a few of the names given to the universal vitalizing power of Nature as it is worked with in different cultures. In the Taoist healing practices, *Qi* (pronounced "chee") is the energy or life force that moves through the breath. *Gong* (pronounced "gung") is skill that develops through refined practice. *Qi Gong* literally means "skill with the life force."

As one of my Qi Gong mentors often reminds me, "The body knows what to do to heal itself. We just need to help the mind relax and give the body the space to do what it needs to do. The *qi* knows where to go." When the path is open, the life force flows and vibrates through, bringing change and healing. By simply being present and feeling what's happening, we open the path for the *qi* to go where it will.

All of Nature is composed of vibrations. The life force manifests itself through the Great Dance, forming the endless shapes and patterns of the natural world. Peering into the fabric of Reality, quantum physicists speculate that the world is composed of strings of vibrating light. Shamans and mystics have long reported visions of this scintillating grid. The power of life dances through the lines of this web, connecting all of Nature. The song of this dance is broadcasting to us day and night, if we are tuned to hear it and catch the melody.

When we expand our senses and tune into the Great Dance, we are remembering our connections with a larger share of this dynamic web of life. When we tune into the power of the moment, we step out of the eggshell of the ego's worries and to-do lists; we slip away from Trickster's grasp. Our hearts open to the true, essential vibrations of the Nature within and around us, and healing occurs.

First Creation is still here, waiting for you to come to your senses and join in the Dance. When you do, each moment is an opportunity to grow and transform. What will you become next?

Joining Nature's Great Dance

Because the Great Dance of Nature is in motion at all times, all that's needed to join in is to get yourself into the moment. Anything that spontaneously engages your senses, your body, and a spirit of play will do the trick.

Still not sure what to do? The story of the Great Dance offers us some tantalizing breadcrumbs to follow:

A long time ago, animals could turn into people, people could turn into animals, and they could understand one another without words.

One of the most ancient creative skills that our ancestors learned was how to put themselves in another's shoes, imagining the world from a new perspective. Today, psychologists call this crucial ability the "Theory of Mind," and many would argue that it's one of the major traits that makes our species so successful.

Shamans and trackers have long known this skill as the art of "becoming,"[4] using this ability to become the animal they are tracking, or to mentally merge with an animal or element of nature in support of the shamanic healing process.

Long before we could look at a piece of paper and make sense of the abstract letters and symbols written there, our ancestors gained the mental hardware needed for this skill through tracking.[5] The hunter needed to look at a set of footprints and "see" the animal moving within them, connecting the dots between the marks on the ground and the living being that made them. This ancient skill opened the door to the symbolic under-standing that we rely today on for reading, writing, the arts, and the sciences.[6]

The Art of Becoming

San hunters still practice this ancestral skill of *becoming* the animal.

During the persistence hunt, the tracker follows a kudu or other large herbivore's tracks all day, literally chasing the animal until it becomes exhausted. The tracker knows he must become attuned to the animal, so that he can tease out which tracks to follow, which route to take. His own family's life is depending on the outcome. Step by step, the tracker comes closer in his mind to the mind of the animal, until he feels at one with this mysterious being he is tracking.

In the documentary film *The Great Dance: A Hunter's Story*, a group of San Bushman trackers gather around the campfire after a day of hunting and reflect: "When you follow the prints, you see in your mind how the porcupine thinks. Every animal is like this — you jump when the track shows it jumps!"

Another tracker adds, "When you track an animal, you must become the animal. You feel a tingling...when the animal is close. When tracking is like dancing, then it is the Great Dance... when the springbok heart beats in your ribs, you see through its eyes, you feel its stripe dark on your cheek."[7]

When you track in this way, you are giving your brain an amazing workout. Your senses are peaked, taking in the complex patterns of Nature. Your ears are attuned to the voices of the birds, scanning for alarms that indicate the animal's passage in the distance. Your skin feels the breeze, tracking how your scent is being carried off by the air current. Your feet feel your way across the ground as your eyes scan into the distance, predicting where the animal could duck through a gap in the brush, or where the tracks turn and veer onto a new pathway. In this dance, there is no room not to pay attention; there is only pure spontaneous engagement with the moment.

Tracking further, your imaginal capacity kicks in, and you feel yourself *becoming*... your hands and body grow furry... hooves or claws appear in the corner of your eyes... your ears become pointed, and your nose long... the feeling of having a tail appears, and your senses take on a new quality as they scan the environment... your body itself moves in synchrony with the tracks, as if you had left them there yourself.

Through such an experience, you soon arrive at points of insight, and open to entire new vistas of understanding. You are left feeling *more* than you were before you started on the trail. Now, you are connected with that place through the thread of that animal, realizing something essential about the way its life uniquely fits into the tapestry of Nature.

Tracking teaches you that you can become anything. The only limits are formed by what you can imagine. When you *become* something, you begin to stretch beyond the limitations of your daily thought.

Becoming creates a crack in the armor of "business as usual" and the story we tell ourselves about how the world is, and how we are in it. New possibilities emerge, and the Dance goes on.

Fools Crow, a renowned traditional Lakota healer, recommended the practice of *becoming* as a way to expand our relationship with all of the rest of Nature. His mentor showed him that he could hold an item in his hand and *become* it, or if it was too big, to hold it in his heart. Once this heart connection was established, Fools Crow would then ask questions and hold a conversation just as if he were talking with another person.[8]

For instance, if he was holding a rock in his hand, Fools Crow said he would ask the rock "...where it comes from, what it has seen, what it has heard, and what it feels. We become friends. Doing this expands the way I behave towards rocks and toward other things, and my mind grows. The more I do 'becoming,' the wiser I become about everything."[9]

Becoming isn't just a practice that shamans and trackers can enjoy. Kids do this all time. What did you like to become as a kid — a superhero, a princess, a dinosaur? What will you become today?

~ Practice: The Art of Becoming ~

Visit your Meditation Spot today and find something to *become*. Don't think too hard about this whole thing, you'll just screw it up. Like Yoda says, "Do or do not, there is no try."

Does a child *try* to become Spiderman on the playground? No way! A kid just jumps right into play mode and *becomes* Spiderman. That's all there is to it. There's no effort involved. It's not rocket science.

Become the fox. *Become* the oak tree. *Become* the wind and the creek, the soil and the stone. It's all fair game. Just play at it, and let it be whatever it is. Each being you *become* will invite you to stretch your senses in new ways. As Fools Crow said, you'll learn something every time.

If you need a little more than that to get you going, here are a few ideas:

For a peaceful experience, become a tree. Observe a particular tree and become it. Study how the tree grows, and consider what makes its form and essence unique. Let your arms twist and reach upwards like the branches, and root your feet into the ground. Experience the wind in your leaves, your roots in the soil. Or, just find your inner "treeness" and sit quietly, feeling yourself as part of the landscape.

Some good questions can take this journey a bit further. What's different about being a pine tree compared to an oak, or a cottonwood? How do you feel as each of these? Which one leaves you feeling more energized, or more relaxed? What kind of soil and slope are you drawn towards as each type of tree? What other trees do you want to have around you, if any? Who might roost in your branches? What does it feel like when animals move nearby?

If you want some action, become a predatory mammal. Pick one that you think might be around — bobcat, coyote, weasel, otter, or fox are all fun options. How fast do you like to move? What do you pay attention to? Where are you drawn to pause, or to hunt? What would you eat? How can you sense a person coming, yet remain unseen? How does becoming this animal affect your senses, and your energy?

To understand the predators in an area, become the herbivores that they prey upon. Try on being a deer. What leaves or twigs look tasty right now? Where do you feel safe enough to bed down for the day? Where could you plop down at night for a bit to chew your cud? What trails can safely get you from your bed to your food? What will you do if dogs or people come through?

If you want to really get out of the box, become an underground animal like an earthworm or a mole. How does it feel when people walk over your domain? Or when a robin is poking around on the surface? What do you do when it rains? Where do you go to the bathroom?!

WHEN YOU'RE IN THE FIELD *BECOMING*, GIVE YOURSELF FREE REIGN TO be completely creative. There's no right or wrong. It's a judgement-free zone. You can analyze all you want later. For now, just *be*, and allow yourself to enjoy the flow of Nature.

When you get home, you might write in your journal afterwards. What did you experience? What did you learn? How did this particular *becoming* affect your sensory awareness? What do you want to research about this animal? What would you ask the animal if it could tell you one thing you really wanted to know about its life?

Remembering How to Play - Or, Into the Cave

This "playing" thing is actually a stumbling block for many adults these days, especially if you ever got into trouble for daydreaming as a kid. You might have had the "play" taken out of you by The Man. If so, you're not alone. A lot of people have, no doubt about it.

Daydreaming doesn't get that spreadsheet filled in, or get that big project done (although ironically, the most impactful inventions and life-changing innovations come about through the creativity of the imagination, but that's another story for another time). So, The Man teaches you not to play. You gotta focus, that's the new game.

For a lot of us, this all happens when we're so young that we don't even realize it. Until later, when you read some book about meditating in Nature, and then you bump into a funny practice that asks you to play and imagine. Suddenly, hmmmphhh... brick wall.

Well, if you find that the feeling of "play" or "imagining" seems as elusive as the fox that you know is around your Meditation Spot, Nature's here to help you get your mojo back. It's your birthright, dammit. Maybe you just need a little dusting off, you know, get your Spiderman or Princess costume out of the attic. We'll get you right as rain again.

Reclaiming the Joy of Play

If you think back, what did you love to do as a child? What games did you play, what or who did you pretend to be, what songs did you sing? What trees did you climb, and where did you play hide and seek? Nature is your most amazing ally in this quest. Go to your Meditation Spot with the intention simply to remember. Ask Nature to help you get inspired. Then, go do some of these things.

I used to love climbing to the top of the refrigerator and waiting to grab adult's hats off their heads as they walked through the kitchen. I'd perch up there and arrange a wall of cereal boxes to hide behind, waiting for the perfect moment to strike. That was my version of being Batman. Down at floor level, the kitchen cabinets were also perfect to hide in and wait for unsuspecting passersby.

Outside, there was a thicket of catbriars that made a great fort in one of the local parks. Anything climbable was of interest, especially if we weren't supposed to climb it. There was also a rock ledge full of poison ivy where we liked to set things on fire (not a good combination, really — that's why kids need mentors).

Ninja whiffle ball (the bats doubled as swords, and the game took place on rooftops), BMX bike races, and neighborhood hide-and-seek were all popular suburban games of choice. Drawing comic book characters, hunting for cool rocks, throwing ninja stars... that's my list. What's yours?

If you find that no ideas appear, just pretend you have one. Seriously, run with it. Play at the idea of playing. Eventually, it just happens.

If you get a fun impulse (like singing to the trees) but you feel oddly inhibited, take stock of yourself. Look around — are you all alone sitting under a tree? Who's really going to judge you, except yourself? Crack a smile and realize that's just the remnant voice of The Man. This is a golden opportunity to step into the Great Dance, even if it's a bit uncomfortable.

Encounters with "The Man"

For many of us, that particular voice goes way back, passed down like a broken record through the generations, propagated like a virus from land to land. Many attribute it to the days of ancient Rome and other conquering nations of long-ago. Armies swept into places and warlords took over, telling people how to live and even what to believe. Divide and conquer was the strategy, and then control and maintenance was the ongoing agenda.

That's where the old ticker-tape voice of the Man was codified into existence (though some say it goes back even further, like an ancient shadow inside of us, giving us a choice each moment for how we want to show up in life. I dunno...mysteries...).

However, I do know one thing: you get to run the show now. Imagine you can delete that old file. That's all it is. Notice the voice of judgement, however it comes up. Maybe it's a little whisper — *"You can't do that!"* Or, maybe it's a feeling of utter dread or mortification. It shows up differently for each of us.

Entering the Cave

Remember how I told you the story of the Cave at the beginning of the book? I said we'd be returning to it. Well, here we are. This is the stuff of the Cave. We're at the entrance, and Yoda is sending us in.

The Cave's actually not here to scare us. Its real function is to reveal that which is unresolved, to irrefutably show you (as the Hero or Heroine of your own life story) that which you need to face and let go of. *Only then will you be a real Nature Jedi.* No, scratch that. You already are a Nature Jedi — you just need to own it.

So, this doubt, this worry, this shame... whatever it is, it shows up. Maybe you're feeling awkward or embarrassed about sitting in Nature against a tree, wondering what people think. Or it could be some old wound that's seemingly come up out of nowhere as you tuned into the presence of your *Being*.

Feel it, be present to it, and just breathe. Realize it's a program, and it doesn't need to run your life. Smile at it lovingly. It's got nothing on you. Feel its power diminish as your pure awareness simply acknowledges and gently embraces it. Hear its voice get quieter and quieter as you realize you are the one in control of the volume.

You might need to cry it out. That's good! Let the tears flow. Smile, and let this old energy pattern dissolve down your roots into the Earth.

Ask Nature to gently help you with this. Put your hands on a tree or rest them upon the soil, and ask for help to release and transform the energy. Nature's great at transformation, that's what the Great Dance is all about. The Cave is actually the back-alley kitchen of First Creation, and this is where you come to get cooked.

Facing Your Shadows

I've known people who've simply had to go their Meditation Spot and cry every day for a month or longer. Sometimes they didn't even know why, they just had to. But then, they felt amazingly lighter. Their meditations suddenly opened to a new level, and their life smoothed out in many ways. Something was healed that they didn't even know they were carrying around. That's what Nature does. Trees are great listeners. Stones, too.

Now, know that these kinds of judgmental, inhibiting voices that come up are just frozen pieces of the Dance, pure energy that has been tricked into a stagnating pattern by limiting beliefs and fears. These little voices convince you into thinking "I can't do this, because ___ (fill in the blank with whatever fear or worry you prefer)."

For instance, imagine you are settling into your Meditation Spot, leaning against your favorite tree. Your senses are tuning into the peace of the birds and the wind. Suddenly, a person walks by in the distance and the dialogue appears in your mind, "I *shouldn't* be sitting here... what if I look silly leaning against this tree? I really *should* be getting ready for tonight's party."

In this case, the appearance of a person has triggered an old fear around being perceived as different, or not fitting into a certain social expectation. For instance, you might believe that if someone observes you on the trail, just sitting against a tree with your eyes closed, they'll think you're weird. That thought might fill you with anxiety because you fear social rejection, or because when you were a kid, other kids teased you. The old dialogue of 'if I'm weird, they'll tease me' might still be operating, even though now, as an adult, most other adults won't care one bit about what you're doing sitting against a tree. They might even envy you!

If something like this comes up, it's a chance to become aware of what's moving within the waters of your Inner Nature, and then to be present and allow some degree of resolution. In fact, these voices are waiting for a moment just like this, so that they can finally be healed! In just a moment, I'll share a few simple tools that can really make a difference in transforming these old patterns. Before that, let's dig a little deeper into the mechanism that's at play.

Notice that the words these little stinkers operate with often include things like can't, should, have to, because, and after. *"I shouldn't do that, because _____. I can't do that, because _____. I'll do that after I do _____, because _____. I have to _____ because _____."*

Do you really need to listen to these old beliefs? I'm not suggesting that you go against your better judgement here. Not by a long stretch. The rules of common sense still apply. But there's a difference between common sense and the imaginative blockages that get programmed in us by culture, whether intentionally or just by accident.

If you've watched *Empire Strikes Back* (and I hope you have by now, having gotten this far into the book — otherwise, major spoiler alert coming up, 38+ years after the fact), you'll vividly remember who Luke ended up facing in the Cave: it wasn't really Darth Vader — rather, it was Luke's own face was waiting there to greet him inside the mask.

The Cave was showing Luke his own insecurities that he had acquired somewhere along the way. These wounds actually shaped the vector of Luke's life, driving him to become the hero he was turning into. But still, he would not find real peace in himself until he came to a reckoning with these inner shadows. You, too, must face the Vader within; *"Only then a Jedi will you be!"*

Your Brain, the Protector

The good news is that even in the depths of the Cave, you are amongst friends. These little worries that Nature is bringing to light have a place to land, ironically, because your brain is adapted to help you. You're facing yourself in the end. Whatever happened in the past is long gone. It's your own brain patterns that are now at play here.

Shamans have long noted how people get themselves into great trouble through over-identification with their mind's internal dialogue. Remember, the Second Creation began when language was created, and that's when Trickster appeared on the scene. Although words give us the power to name and codify the world around us, they are a double-edged sword.

The Hazard-Detection Loop, Gone Awry...

There's a part of the brain that runs with this inner dialogue, and its function is to bring your attention to things that are hazardous. One of the jobs of the amygdala is to scan for danger; when it senses trouble, it can jump the body into fight-or-flight mode.

A feedback loop of anxiety and worry can then begin, with all the uncomfortable emotion and thoughts that go with this state.

Memory circuits from old uncomfortable moments spark to life, and rapid beta waves fire over and over in the areas of the brain where the negative internal dialogue goes on repeat.

So, if you are made fun of as a child for being "different," your brain remembers and makes a special note; to avoid the pain in the future, anytime you get into a similar situation, the old warning signals come on: "Hey — you don't want to experience that again! Don't sit here in the woods and be *weird*... just get in line with everyone else, and you'll be fine!"

The brain tries to pull up some nugget of memory that can guide your action, some pearl of wisdom, but what it sometimes comes up with is an outdated cautionary tale, or a moment of embarrassment or trauma from when you were a kid, or from some other time in your life.

Maybe the idea you had absorbed was useful at the time, or perhaps it was the only input you were getting, but it's what you were programmed with, and you've been carrying it with you every since, tucked away for just the "right" occasion.

The old belief that's coming up might have never even been useful to begin with — simply someone else's misinformed opinion — or it could have been a protective response that your child mind used to stay safe as best as possible in the moment. Your brain kept it to try to help you, should the need arise again.

Although this brain function is biologically intended to keep you safe, it may be running amok, needlessly limiting your experiences. You're not a kid anymore; you can sit against a tree in the woods whenever you want to! Yet, the amygdala system can get stuck in this "on" mode, especially as stress and unattended small or large traumas pile up through the fast pace of modern life.

The Dog Chases Its Tail...

The other problem is, once this dialogue starts to run automatically on repeat, if you hear it enough times, you might start to believe that's how things really are. "Oh yeah, I guess I *am* weird..." In effect, through repetition, you'll seamlessly buy into your own inner propaganda!

This is an example of the mind running out of control, wearing itself out like a dog chasing its own tail. Don't limit yourself to these inner labels. You are much more than any of their limiting definitions. Like Morpheus said to Neo in *The Matrix*, "Let it all go... fear, doubt, and disbelief. Free your mind."

You are greater and vaster than the activity of any inner chatter... when you discover this, you can step back from the activity of the dialogue, into the space of the pure awareness that surrounds it.

It's Time For An Update...

A final observation: your hazard avoidance system may not always be giving you accurate information. It does it's best, but it has limitations. 80% of what you see and hear is actually your brain's projection, as it takes old data and maps it against the moment.

If the data that's running your awareness system is partial or obsolete, you might be missing out on a lot of life's magic.

This is why cultivating mindfulness is a core aspect of the Meditation Spot and all the other Conscious Nature practices — each time you can return to the moment, you have a chance to reach beyond these old filters to what is really there now.

When you can access the moment, you have a greater degree of choice as to how you wish to respond. Instead of just reacting to the old wound and leaving your Meditation Spot ("I don't want to be seen as weird, I'm getting out of here!"), with mindful presence, you can choose to stay put and attend to the old pattern.

In traditional wisdom cultures, village life often has a number of failsafes built in to account for the human tendency to accumulate stress and trauma. The shamans, healers, and village elders work together to monitor and oversee the health of the community.[10] Grieving rituals, meditations, ceremonial dances, and healing ceremonies are all designed to account for the regular wear and tear of life, helping to release and soothe the stress.

Today, without the support of village life, we need to take the responsibility to create our own self-maintenance rituals and routine ways of caring for our highest well-being. If you don't do this for yourself, who will?

Just as Luke had to face himself, we each must face these little (or big) "Negative Nelly's" that we've collected on our trips around the Sun. Whatever caused it, when it comes up, there is an opportunity for healing to occur.

~ Practice: Letting Go of Old Limiting Beliefs ~

So, you notice there's an old belief or limiting emotional pattern coming up. Here's an opportunity to remember the Great Dance of Nature and step into a state of positive transformation!

Here are two extremely helpful tools that you can explore to support this intention. Each can be used on their own, or combined as described below.

Finding the Center of the Head

The center of the head, called by Taoists the Upper Dan Tien ("elixir field"), is an exceptional place to position oneself while processing old beliefs and emotions. This meditation can be practiced on its own for many benefits, including feeling more grounded and centered.

To find this spot, imagine a line going from the tip of one ear and through the head to the tip of the other ear; then, imagine a line stretching back from the area between the eyebrows and deep into the head; finally, sense the crown of the head and a line dropping straight down from that point. The junction of these three lines is the center point of the head.[11]

With your eyes open or closed, go into Expanded Vision. Once this state is engaged, imagine that you can "sink backwards" through your eyes to the center of the head. Now, you are looking out from a deeper place within yourself. Imagine this point of consciousness glowing brightly. Sense the entirety of your body now as you inhabit this central point. Smile as you perceive your body glowing and filled with light, getting brighter with each breath. You may close your eyes if you wish, or keep them open.

You may find that shifting to this point of inner awareness is enough in itself to release the activity of the inner dialogue. Savor this experience for as long as you wish. If you like, once you are established in the center of the head, you can then move on to the next meditation, continuing to sense what's happening from this point of inner awareness.

The Inner Waters Meditation

Pick a place where you will not be disturbed, and a time when you have 10-20 minutes to just sit and be present. This might be at your Meditation Spot, but it could also be at a quiet indoor space.

First, notice what's moving in your mind and heart. Just become present to what you are thinking and feeling.

Next, disengage from identifying with the activity of the inner dialogue. Imagine yourself stepping back from the mind's chatter; allow yourself to expand into the much larger space of pure awareness that is available to you. Imagine that you are part of a river of Pure Awareness, and that these thoughts are simply floating on its surface.

Sense the spaciousness of your Pure Awareness. Realize the true depths of the waters of your Inner Nature... and sense now that you are, indeed, much more than the limited confines of the mind's dialogue.

From this larger perspective, again sense the movement of the mind's chatter and emotions, perceiving them like fleeting ripples across the water's surface. Allow the surface thoughts and the deeper emotions beneath them simply to flow and pass, without getting caught in their wake.

Without attachment, *feel* the currents of emotions moving beneath the thoughts; by *feeling* them, you allow them to flow and transform. If you need to cry, cry. If you need to shake and tremble, let it happen. Just keep feeling and sensing into what's happening, without labeling or judging it.

These are the old crystallized emotions caught by the Second Creation, waiting for a chance to flow and be released in the river of awareness. Breath, feel, and be. The important thing is to know that *by feeling the emotion and inviting it to release, you are allowing the needed transformation to occur.*

Allow any old thoughts and emotions simply to expend themselves as they drift away; remain anchored in the flowing peace of the waters.

When you are done, sense and imagine the clear, refreshing water filling you up with peace and vitality. Thank the waters, knowing you can easily return to their healing presence anytime you need. Work with this process as needed.

Growing with Nature

Now you have some perspectives on the mind's internal dialogue, and the way it sometimes generates mischief in its Trickster role. You've also gained some tools that can help you relate creatively with the energy of old belief patterns as you invite fresh change into your experience.

Don't buy into the mind's limitations of belief. You're more than that, much more. You are a force of Nature. As you release these old patterns, you are letting that much more of your light shine forth.

Often life is just so busy that when we bump into these old discomforts, we just as quickly brush them back under the carpet. When you meditate in Nature, you finally get to slow down. You start to get in touch with these internal odds and ends, and it becomes a season of change.

Nature doesn't hold onto things. The leaves serve their purpose in the spring and summer, but come autumn, it's time to shed them to the ground. Be like a tree, my friend, and leaf. Let go of those outdated beliefs that no longer serve you.

Grow into a bigger tree: a more bad-ass, fun-loving, relaxed, truly alive and loving-it tree. Climb out of that Cave with the certainty that you are now a full-fledged Nature Jedi, remembering that you are one with the Force, and that truly, you always have been. Sing to the trees, become a wild fox bathed in the moon-light, and walk forward with presence and love as you join once again in the Great Dance of Nature.

GETTING GROUNDED

> *Forget not that the earth delights to feel your bare feet and the winds long to play with your hair."*
> — *Kahlil Gibran*

"Feel the earth here for a moment!"

We paused digging, and I turned my head quizzically towards Grandpa as he spoke.

"It's good to put your hands in the soil," he continued. "Take your shoes off and walk barefoot, too. Some people say that when you touch the earth, it gives you a mysterious energy. What do you think, hmmm?"

When I was growing up, my grandfather would often say this to me, spoken with a smile and a curious raised eyebrow as we worked together out in the garden. Certainly mysterious!

Over the years, I've often remembered his question as I've sat close to the earth at my Meditation Spot, or while walking barefoot through the forest. What unseen energies are at play, inspiring my meditations and enlivening my senses?

Fortunately, researchers have been busy finding ways to quantify this intriguing idea. It turns out that when you ditch the shoes and directly contact the earth, you'll literally change your body's electrical voltage. As we'll get into, this has some potentially huge health implications.

WARNING: NERD ALERT. This is perhaps the geekiest chapter in the entire book. Just sayin'. :)

The Earth Electric

The earth is conductive. The water molecules and minerals that weave through the soil and stone provide a channel for electrical currents to flow within. The soil beneath your feet works as part of a much bigger electrical circuit, with the other end connected to the sky.

Just as the atmosphere is filled with radio, television, and wi-fi signals that you cannot detect without the proper equipment, the air and the ground are also imbued with a sea of invisible natural energies that are constantly in motion. We are literally immersed in a mulligatawny soup of electromagnetic activity.

Having heard all my life about how good it is to connect with the earth, I started to wonder about the science behind it all. How does this big circuit of the earth and the sky work? How much energy is really on the move? How might we be adapted to fit into this natural energetic cycle, and what are the health implications? I began to dig into the research, and in this section I'll share what I've found.

This knowledge has given me a new layer of appreciation for what's happening when we walk barefoot in the woods or at the beach. It's also convinced me of the many benefits of "earthing" that come when we get in touch with the ground. Perhaps it will convince you, too.

In the next few pages, you'll find the scoop on the mechanics of the sky-to-earth electrical system. Then, you'll learn how "earthing" affects your body and your health. If you just want something you can try right away, you can skip ahead to the practice at the end of the chapter; this won't hurt my feelings, I promise. For the nerds in the audience (the Force is strong with you), here's how it works.

Electricity in the Sky

Let's start with the atmosphere's portion of the equation. The sky is crazy electrical. As you go straight up, every additional meter of air up from the ground increases its electrical potential by 100 volts.[1]

This potential really adds up. At 110 kilometers off the ground (in the high-latitude auroral zones), a million ampere electrical current flows across the rarefied upper atmosphere; through electromagnetic induction, changes in these high strata energies cause a flow of *telluric currents*, which are low-frequency currents that ripple within the earth and oceans.[2]

So, we know there's all kinds of electrical activity up there in the sky. But what mechanisms get all this energy from the sky and down into the earth? Well, several neat things actually set it all in motion, and it begins 93 million miles away at the Sun.

The 3 Big Players in the Sky. First, we have *solar wind* entering the magnetosphere and charging things up (non-nerd speak: energy from the Sun is coming towards the Earth and hitting the earth's magnetic field WAY up high in space). Next, we have *ionospheric wind* (the ionosphere starts at 40 miles up, also way up there, and it conducts electricity through the weakly ionized air that flows there). Finally, we have this energy moving through the 50-100 lightning strikes hitting the ground *each second* around the world. That's a lot of lightning!

All three of these forces contribute to the constant energetic flow between the earth and sky.[3] So, basically there's a big movement of energy that starts all the way at the Sun, hits the atmosphere, and works its way down to the ground through lightning. These forces cause the upper atmosphere to maintain a net positive electrical charge, while the surface of the earth maintains an overall negative balance.

The Global Current. All of the energy up in the sky is constantly on the move. There's actually waves of this electricity above us, pulsing invisibly through the ocean of the sky. Check this out: at 50 kilometers up (in the ionosphere mentioned earlier), the atmosphere becomes especially conductive. It's like a reservoir of energy, hidden up above. From there, the electricity dips down to the earth in great unseen waterfalls of current.

This invisible Global Electrical Current (GEC), whose fluctuation is called the Carnegie Curve, ebbs and flows like a giant electrical tide each day, shifting in voltage by up to 15%. The curve was discovered by the Carnegie Institution of Washington's ocean-going research vessel in the early 20th century,[4] a wooden yacht that sailed around the world to measure global atmospheric electrical currents.[5]

Like many cycles in Nature, there is a daily rhythm to the flow of this mysterious electrical current. The great GEC "tide" peaks every day around the world at 7PM Greenwich Mean Time, with a daily low at 4 AM Greenwich Mean Time.

Why is this? It all comes back to the patterns of lightning activity. It turns out that global thunderstorm activity peaks at 7PM Greenwich time each day. According to Richard Feynman's famous *Lectures on Physics*:

Lightning storms carry negative charges to the earth. When a lightning bolt strikes, nine times out of ten it brings down negative charges to the earth in large amounts. It is the thunder-

storms throughout the world that are charging the earth with
an average of 1800 amperes, which is then being discharged
through regions of fair weather.[6]

Charged Clouds. Energy isn't just moved through the atmosphere by lightning, though. Clouds have a role to play, too. About half of the Global Electrical Current does come from overland thunderstorms, and a third from ocean thunderstorms; however, another sixth of the energy stems from *electrified shower clouds* over the ocean (ESC's are charged clouds without any lightning, rather than something you see when you drop your iPhone in the bathtub), and the remainder source from ESC's over the land.[7]

Scientists have been trying to figure out exactly how much energy these "electric clouds" churn up. With satellite analysis, we can now peer into the composition of these clouds, allowing us a glimpse into the electrical fields that are at work above us in the skies. A 2017 study suggests there's an average 1.4 to 1.6 kilo-ampere "generator current" created by global storm activity.[8] So, both the land and the ocean are getting charged by the sky's electricity, and the world's storms act as a giant pump that keeps all the energy moving.[9]

Grounding into the Earth

Now I know (and you know, too) what's going on up there in the sky. But, what's happening on the ground? And how does this energy affect you?

Besides all that tremendous energy that gets stirred up from the cosmic rays, solar wind, and other forces from above, scientists have discovered at least 17 different ways the earth itself produces electricity, and 4 ways that groundwater constantly churns up electric power.[10]

All kinds of mysterious stuff is going on, right under our feet. Because certain metals are magnetic, as they move around each other in the earth, electrical fields are created. Electromagnetic (EM) signals are emitted from volcanic and seismic activity.

EM effects even arise from charged water flowing through porous rock, from extreme pressure on rocks and stress on underground crystal deposits (if you squish topaz it creates electricity), and even through the temperature gradient that reaches across a large body of ore.

Getting Grounded. Because of the ground's negative charge, free electrons can easily flow to a human body in direct contact with the earth's surface. When we touch the earth with bare skin, we effectively "ground" ourselves, no pun intended.

Regular contact with the earth keeps the human body at an electrical potential even with that of the earth. The human body is adapted biologically to "expect" this grounding. My Grandpa was right: we need contact with the soil.

Earthing (aka "grounding") has become a popular trend in recent years, thanks especially to a pioneering book by that name written by Clinton Ober, Stephen Sinatra, M.D., and Martin Zucker.[11]

Noticing how people insulate themselves from the ground with rubber soles, and remembering how old rabbit-ear TV sets produced a clearer image when a viewer grabbed hold of the antennae, Ober wondered how the body conducts electricity, and whether this conduction has any impact on health.

Ober hooked his voltmeter to the ground via a long wire tied to a metal stake. Then, he proceeded to walk around his house to see what readings he could pick up as his body interacted with the indoor environment. When Ober approached his home's electrical wiring and devices, the meter showed a noticeable change is his own ungrounded body's voltage reading, compared to the earth's voltage.

Out of curiosity, Ober made a grid from some metallic duct tape, hooking it up with a copper wire run out the window to a metal stake set in the ground. Direct contact with the wire would ensure his body was electrically connected to the earth's grounding effect.

Laying down on the grid, Ober checked the voltmeter again and found his electrical reading had returned to close to zero! The wire was successfully conducting his body's excess voltage down into the ground, just as if he was standing barefoot on the soil. He also quickly fell asleep and slept better than he had in years.

Ober proceeded to test his home-made "earthing" contraption and found anecdotally that it helped others to feel better and get much better rest.

Eventually, Ober's persistent inquiry led to a growing body of research studies demonstrating a measurable physiological impact from earthing. In fact, a 2006 research project found that grounding to the earth reduced body voltage from 3.27 volts down to 7 millivolts, an average 467-fold decrease in voltage![12]

The health benefits of getting grounded, which we'll get to in a moment, might be enough to convince you of how important this is. But why do we need to bother with "earthing" ourselves in the first place?

Blocking the Flow

Modern footwear and building materials can get in the way of our connection with the earth's energy. Skin-to-earth contact is now unusual rather than the norm, as people rarely go barefoot or sit on the ground.

Instead of packed-earth floors, we have wood, tile, or other manufactured materials underfoot that insulate us from the earth's healing electrons. Our homes are also filled with electrical devices emitting various frequencies of energy. The wiring systems in our walls surround us with ambient electrical stimulation, too. All of these features of modern life subtly impact the body's bioelectric system.

Even when we stand on the earth itself, not all patches of ground can conduct the same amount of electricity. The earth's conductivity varies depends on many factors. Soil moisture, water table height, mineral content, and the weather are just a few major variables. Damp soil conducts better than dry soil. Plain concrete conducts well, especially if moistened, whereas painted concrete or asphalt does not.

So, go stand on some damp dirt, or on some wet concrete. Doesn't sound appealing? Soak the lawn with a sprinkler, or wait until after it's rained; then sit in a lawn chair while you read a book, and let your feet touch the earth. Walk barefoot outside every day that it's warm enough to do so, ideally for at least 20 minutes. A forest trail will nicely do the trick. Or, do what my Grandpa recommended, and get your hands in the soil as your tend your garden.

What Happens When You're Not Grounded?

Insulation cuts off your electrical connection to the earth and builds up your body's electrical charge. When you stand outdoors wearing modern insulated shoes, cut off from the grounding effect, your body equilibrates with the positive potential of the atmosphere, increasing your net voltage.[13]

Whereas since the dawn of humanity our ancestors have maintained regular sensual contact with the earth, thus naturally regulating the body's bioelectric organism, today our modern experience prevents such daily regulation.

Instead, we're left walking around with an accumulated charge that may be impacting our health and well-being. To restore our natural electrical balance, all we have to do is connect with the earth.

The Health Benefits of Earthing

So, we've seen how the vast energy exchange between the earth and the sky works, and you've learned that your body's electrical charge "evens out" when you comes into contact with the soil.

But what are the health impacts that come from grounding yourself on the earth? A burgeoning number of small but interesting studies are pointing towards numerous health benefits associated with earthing.

Reducing Cortisol Levels. Cortisol's got a reputation like the bully in the school cafeteria. An arousal hormone, chronically elevated cortisol is a diagnostic biomarker that indicates stress; the body benefits from lower levels of the hormone at night. Excessive cortisol levels are also implicated in connection with depression.[14]

Reducing and regulating cortisol is therefore essential for stress reduction and wellness on multiple levels. Besides taking a daily walk, earthing can help with this. Taking a barefoot walk is a great way to combine the two!

An initial 2004 study (ironically run by a skeptical Dr. Maurice Ghaly as a way to disprove Ober's claim!)[15] found that sleeping while grounded significantly re-synchronized cortisol release with the natural 24 hour circadian rhythm, and reduced nighttime cortisol levels; participants reported improved sleep and reduced levels of pain and stress.

Reducing Inflammation. Inflammation is also thought to be connected with raised cortisol levels. Again, earthing to the rescue! The sea of free electrons available to the body from the earth can also help reduce this condition.

In a review of earthing research entitled "Can Electrons Act as Antioxidants?," researcher James Oschman notes that the mechanism of inflammation relates to a buildup of positively charged free radicals that wreak havoc in the body, and posits that earthing provides a solution:

> *Free electrons from the earth neutralize the positively charged*
> *free radicals that are the hallmark of chronic inflammation...*
> *The evidence suggests that free (mobile) electrons from the earth*
> *are natural antioxidants...loss of direct contact with the earth*
> *appears to introduce another kind of adaptive stress, an "electron*
> *deficiency," which compromises the immune system by slowing*
> *the resolution of inflammatory responses.* [16]

Using medical infrared imaging in two clinical trials, Oschman scanned patients for inflammation before and after treatment with earthing, finding a significant reduction in both pain and inflammation, with patients additionally experiencing marked improvement in sleep and overall health.

Lifting Your Mood. Earthing changes your mood for the better, too. A 2015 double-blind pilot study on 40 adults found that mood significantly improved for those who were grounded on conductive mats and pillows compared those who were "sham-grounded" with similar devices that did not actually ground to the earth. [17]

Supporting Cardiovascular Health. In fact, more and more studies are surfacing that point towards a diversity of real health benefits that can be gained through this simple practice. Earthing impacts the workings of the blood, and even the heart.

A 2012 study by Karol and Pawel Sokal found that earthing rapidly drops voltage down to levels of -200 millivolts in the venous blood, showing once again that the connection with the earth affects not just the electrostatic surface potential of the skin, but also that of the internal body environment. [18]

Grounding positively supports heart rate variability, [19] a measurement used to detect cardiovascular stress (a low variability rate predicts the advancement of coronary artery disease[20]). Blood viscosity, an important component of cardiovascular disease, responds quickly to earthing treatment.[21]

A 2013 study found that after just two hours of grounding, the *zeta potential* — surface charge of red blood cells — increases, reducing both blood viscosity and clumping. Summarizing their findings in a *Journal of Alternative and Complementary Medicine* article, Gaétan Chevalier and colleagues wrote, "Grounding appears to be one of the simplest and yet most profound interventions for helping reduce cardiovascular risk and cardiovascular events."

Relaxing Your Brain. An earlier study by Chevalier, Mori, and Oschman found that earthing even impacts brain function. Within a single second of being grounded, electroencephalograph (EEG) recordings revealed that the frontal lobe activity of the left hemisphere immediately changed, suggesting to the study authors that "earthing may have influenced rational and parasympathetic aspects of brain functioning."[22]

Remember that the parasympathetic system is what generates the Relaxation Response, allowing the body's typically overburdened fight-or-flight systems to reset. The study results also showed that blood volume pulse (BVP) decreased, another indicator of parasympathetic activation. Here was further tangible evidence that earthing helps reduce stress.

Adding to this finding, readings of muscular tone in participants' trapezius muscles quickly shifted when earthed, with the muscles relaxing for stressed individuals and normalizing in tone for excessively relaxed participants. This led the authors to posit a "normalization or balancing" systemic effect on the body's physiology from the earthing procedure.

Summary. In a nutshell, there is plenty of tantalizing evidence that our tactile connection with the Earth improves our well-being on many fronts: cardiovascular health, brain function, reduced inflammation and cortisol levels, and mood improvement have all been demonstrated.

Hopefully, even more studies will continue to add to this growing body of research. In the meantime, take your shoes off and enjoy a stroll outdoors.

~ Practice: Getting Your Earth On ~

Take your shoes off and walk gently for twenty minutes on the earth. Find a spot with moist soil where the conductivity is more active. A muddy trail will do just fine, as will a barefoot stroll in the surf at the water's edge.

If you're in more of a sitting mood, no problem. You might set up a folding chair in the woods and turn over a patch of leaf litter to reveal the cool soil hidden below. With your bare feet in the soil, enjoy a nice woodland meditation. Or, bring a good novel and a thermos of some wild-crafted tea, and settle in for a bit as your feet soak in the good vibes.

~ Practice: Grounding Your Qi ~

Even if you can't get your feet on the soil, you can still ground yourself on a certain level through using your body's *qi* or life force (pronounced "chee" and also known as *prana* in Yoga, and by many other names around the world).

Western science is just beginning to learn about the mechanisms and potential of qi,[23] [24] [25] but the body's bioelectricity system has been studied in traditional Wisdom Cultures for thousands of years. Martial arts practitioners, Qi Gong healers, shamans, and advanced meditators have all used variations of this technique to strongly connect themselves to the Earth's nourishing energy. You can, too.

The sensation and effect of qi grounding varies from person to person, yet this simple technique can potently shift how you feel. Tingling, sensations of warmth or coolness, and feelings of relaxation or relaxed alertness are all possible indicators of qi flow.

You can use this practice to center yourself and gain a new level of clarity, or to release built-up energy that wants to move. It works great at the beginning and end of a meditation session, first to gain presence, and then later to solidify your awareness.

I've even helped my clients to access this state right in the office to de-stress and ground before important meetings (you can pretend to be looking at your computer or reading a book, if you have to).

BASIC MEDITATION POSTURE

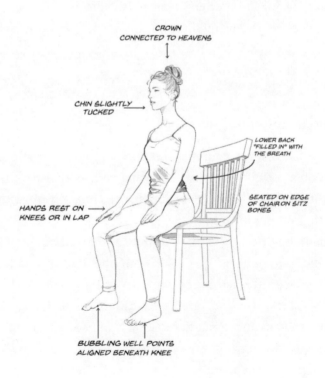

CROWN
CONNECTED TO HEAVENS

CHIN SLIGHTLY TUCKED

LOWER BACK "FILLED IN" WITH THE BREATH

HANDS REST ON KNEES OR IN LAP

SEATED ON EDGE OF CHAIR ON SITZ BONES

BUBBLING WELL POINTS ALIGNED BENEATH KNEE

Body Alignment. If you are sitting on a chair, sit as far towards the edge of the chair as possible, right on your sitz bones. Sitting this way frees up your perineum from getting squished; this spot is called the *hui yin* or "Meeting Place of Yin" in acupuncture, and it's the spot where the earth energy rises up from your legs and into your torso.

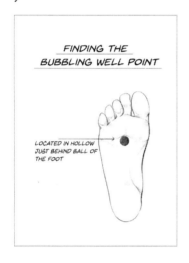

FINDING THE
BUBBLING WELL POINT

LOCATED IN HOLLOW
JUST BEHIND BALL OF
THE FOOT

Also, sit on a chair that allows your thighs to be parallel to the ground. Position your feet so that each knee is directly above the foot's "Bubbling Well." This is the Kidney 1 acupuncture point; you can find it by pressing into the hollow just behind the ball of the foot. It's a great place to knead and massage. This point is a major route for earth qi to work its way up your feet.

Now, tuck your chin in *slightly*; this action aligns the crown of your head with the upwards axis, facilitating Heavenly qi from above to flow into your system. Finally, take a deep belly breath and feel your diaphragm moving downwards as the air fills your lungs, gently expanding your abdomen in all directions and "filling in" your lower back. As you exhale, relax your muscles and sink into your structure, allowing your bones to hold you up.

What's the point of all this? By adopting an aligned posture and releasing muscular tension, we are setting you in position to receive the most benefit from the qi that's about to flow through your system. Though it sounds complicated, you'll quickly get the hang of it. Practice makes better.

Now that you're aligned and relaxed, let's go deeper.

The Meditation.

As you relax into your bones, sense them as an extension of the Earth's structure. They are, after all, made of the Earth's minerals. Starting at the top of your head, begin sinking into the sensations of your spine, your pelvis, your knees, and your Bubbling Well points. Imagine your feet are melting into the floor as you relax more and more.

Now, envision a soft, glowing light that is sinking downwards from your feet — down through the floor, down through the foundations of the building, and down into the bedrock. Sense this light flowing downwards as it becomes a taproot that sinks deep into the earth. Feel your personal taproot as it sends runners out in all directions, anchoring you to the energy of the Earth.

Notice the feelings and sensations that arise through this grounding process. Feel the vastness of the Earth extending out in all directions across the horizon, and sense yourself root like a tree in the midst of this expanse, held between the Earth and the Sky. You can sit with this feeling as long as you like.

If you feel the need to release any "stuck" or "nervous" energy, simply take a deep breath and as you exhale, allow it to travel down the roots and into the Earth; see it dissolve and transform it into fresh energy. You may also choose to notice any invigorating energy from the Earth moving up into your system. Smile throughout the process, letting the Earth engage its potent Inner Alchemy.

This process can be worked with on its own, or as part of a larger meditation cycle. If you're continuing on to other parts of your meditation, you can simply keep your roots extended. When you're done, smile with appreciation to the Earth, and to your roots. Then, gradually allow your roots of light to withdraw back to your feet, knowing that you are always connected to the Earth, but that you can also achieve this deeper level of connection whenever you need to.

By the way, an alternative method is to grow the roots down directly from your tailbone to the earth. This works well especially when you are sitting right on the ground, but you can also do it seated in a chair. Experiment and notice how each method works for you.

SECTION II

THE MEDITATION CYCLE

Here, we bring together the foundational skills of Inner and Outer Awareness into a complete four-part Meditation Cycle. Explore:

- **Further techniques** for honing Inner Awareness & refining your intention

- **Tools for clearing stress** & blending into Nature's patterns at your Meditation Spot

- **How to attune to Nature's language** through your instinct and intuition

Learn step-by-step, and discover a new level of participation in the outdoors...

11

"I'M HERE..." ARRIVING TO MEDITATE

We're in this life, and if you're not available, the sort of ordinary time goes past and you didn't live it. But if you're available, life gets huge. You're really living it."
— *Bill Murray*

I n the earlier chapters, I shared some essential awareness skills that will enhance your practice of meditating in Nature. The Meditation Spot, Expanded Vision, Walking with Awareness, and the other practices are foundations that awaken your senses and enliven your days.

Hopefully, you've put these skills into action. From my own experience, and from having mentored many others, I know that when you integrate these simple tools into your day, your personal connection with the Nature within and around you will deepen.

Beginning now and continuing in the following chapters, we will bring all of these foundational skills together into a cohesive practice that can serve you for many years to come.

We'll break down the awareness skills into four key steps that you can implement during your meditations: arrival, turning within, expanding around you, and gathering together what you've experienced.

In this chapter, we're going to dive deep into what it means to really arrive at your Meditation Spot, and explore tools to help you realize a deep and abiding presence. By taking the time to examine what you need to prepare within yourself in order to fully "be here now," your meditation sessions can become that much more enjoyable and supportive.

Arriving Into Your Mind & Heart: A Self-Awareness Pre-Check

Have you ever tried to focus on reading a book, or moving forward on some creative task, only to have your mind drawn away from what you are doing and pulled into a worry or concern?

The mind naturally seeks resolution to worries. When the waters of the deeper layers of the mind are troubled, the currents cause ripples on the surface. The unconscious wants to get the conscious awareness' attention, so that something can be done. Part of arriving into awareness of one's Nature includes becoming present to any pressing needs or concerns.

If it's freezing cold and you just fell into a lake, the only transcendent experience your body wants you to focus on is getting a fire started. Any meditating you do in that moment will be in service of getting your limbs to function enough to get the body warmed. Any other focus will be a misalignment of purpose, and you'll end up as a frozen TV dinner with a label that reads "Distracted." In other words, there's a time and a place for everything.

Meditation hones the spotlight of your attention. This clarified acuity increases your awareness of what's moving within your mind, heart, body, and senses. Any issues that have been pushed into the background now have a chance to surface and face resolution. This clearing of your "old stuff" allows the light of awareness to shine even more brightly, just like polishing the mirrors and cleaning the glass of a lighthouse enables the beacon to send its rays far out to the distant sea.

I have found it helps immensely before meditating to make a brief check on all the major things I have going in my life, and just to recognize how I am feeling about each of them. Simply doing this enables a stronger connection between the vast ocean of feelings and sensations moving within the unconscious, and the comparatively limited awareness of the conscious mind.

This internal communication pathway between the conscious and unconscious is a key to your connection with Nature on all levels.

The more you practice engaging this pathway and intentionally recognizing what's moving deep within, the more clearly you will experience the depths of your mysterious connections with Nature.

~ Practice: The Current Needs Inventory ~

As you sit and prepare to meditate, simply ask yourself:

What are the major things happening in my life right now? How do I feel about each of these aspects?

This doesn't have to be a long process. About a minute or two will do. Simply become aware of the big projects you have going, the major relationships you hold with others in your life, and any goals you are working towards. Cycle through these one at a time and notice what comes up.

Just allow each aspect to come into your mind, and sense the feeling in your heart and body as you hold the image. Do you feel tense or relaxed, open or closed? What's the emotion connected with the feeling? Allow a simple word or phrase to appear that describes how you feel about each image. Simply sense and recognize how you feel in this moment about each one.

Spend five to ten seconds on each item, and just cruise down your list. Trust that your unconscious will help you become aware of those things that need immediate attention. Don't ruminate or think too hard; it's just taking stock with a quick gut check on the major areas of your life. Once you are done and feel complete, say to yourself "I'm here!"

Here's an example...

PROJECTS THAT NEED TENDING:

- Buy present for Aunt Sally's birthday: feeling is relaxed, emotion is joyful.
- Getting bills paid: feeling is mild tightness, emotion is annoyance at the extra charge the Internet company sent me. > Yellow flag this as action item.
- Mow the big back lawn this afternoon: feeling is open, emotion is resolve. Get it done.

RELATIONSHIP TENDING:

- Wife & anniversary coming up: feeling is relaxed but fluttery, emotion is excitement > *Remember to get flowers!!*
- Parents' recent visit: feeling is open, emotion is appreciation for help they gave.
- Co-worker incident: feeling is closed & tense, emotion

is confusion > Red flag to examine! Why did Bill say that at the office party? *Will circle back to this later.*

PERSONAL GOALS:

- Run two miles tomorrow: feeling is open and strong, emotion is determination.
- Meditate 20 minutes today: feeling is relaxed, emotion is certainty.
- Learn to juggle 7 machetes and a bowling ball by next month: feeling is TIGHT, emotion is exasperation — *6 machetes is enough, dangit!*

OVERALL CHECK-IN:
"My list feels complete for now... OK, I'm here!!!"

REMEMBER, EACH ITEM ONLY GETS A FEW SECONDS OF ATTENTION. The goal is simply to become aware of any major items that might be currently drawing on your inner resources. By doing this, several important things will happen.

First, you'll get in the habit of reviewing your life and simply being aware of its many facets from one big vantage point. With awareness comes a greater degree of choice in how you can meet each need.

Secondly, by taking a moment to imagine, to sense, and to feel, you are attuning to what your mind, body, and heart has to say about each item. This allows you to become more aware of just how much your body can tell you about a situation, and how emotion interacts with the body and the mind. This awareness will pay off in great dividends, not only through the growth of your internal awareness, but also as you connect with the language of Nature around you.

Lastly, by simply presencing each current need, you can note anything that truly needs attention and flag it. I sometimes carry a small pocket notebook for this purpose. By writing down action steps (or just becoming aware of them), you can free up your attention to be more present for your meditation session.

You now know what the action steps are, and that they will be waiting for you when you get back home. Now, you can attune to the rhythms of the land and to your deeper self, knowing that your day-to-day needs are being properly tended to.

Saying to yourself "I'm here!" helps you transition from your inventory process and into the recognition that you have taken stock of whatever needs attention, and that you are now fully here and available in the moment.

When you mentally say this phrase, pay attention to the sensation and feeling of inner congruence that ripples throughout your mind, heart, and body. This simple phrase helps to anchor you to the moment. Own it. Be it. Say it a few times inwardly, if you like.

~ Practice: Setting Your Intention ~

Now that you've briefly scanned through the larger field of your life with the Current Needs Inventory, it's time to hone in on what you need for this particular meditation session. *Realize that your intention focuses your attention.*

Intention is like a valve that directs and attunes the vast field of the attention. As we discussed earlier in the book, when you set an intention, you are priming your mind by activating neural pathways related to your goal. Your intention stems from the need you are seeking to meet.

Do you want to relax after a hard day's work? Then your intention might be to enjoy the experience of *peaceful relaxation*. Say to yourself in your mind, "My intention is to experience peaceful relaxation in this meditation."

Next, conjure up the feeling of being "peacefully relaxed" for a moment. What does that feel like? What do you see, hear, and sense when you envision yourself in this state? Hold your intention in this way for a moment.

Then, smile into your heart as you inhale with a deep breath. Hold the intention in your heart for a moment. In Qi Gong, the heart is considered an amplifier that empowers whatever intention you are holding. As you exhale, feel your heart "smiling out" in all directions as your intention is released.

The unconscious mind thinks in pictures, feelings, and sensations. When you imagine yourself experiencing the intended state, you are priming your brain to set the intent into motion. By using internal language to describe the state, you are also activating the neural networks connected to those words.

Through this combination, you are intentionally turning the power of your internal resources towards your goal. Now you have primed your system with your intention, and you can move into the next phase of your meditation.

~ Practice: Presencing Through the Complete Breath ~

So far, you have taken a quick inventory of any pressing needs, and you've set a clear intention for your meditation session. This has involved some active thinking. Now, it's time to release the activity of the day-to-day mind and reach towards a deeper awareness. It's time to arrive even more deeply into the presence of your body.

The ancient yogis realized that the activity of the mind is directly linked to the activity of the breath. As the breath slows, the mind stills and becomes one-pointed. As the fluctuations of the mind settle down, the awareness expands into a clearer perception of *being*. Therefore, we will begin arriving into the body through the vehicle of the breath.

We will use a simple yogic technique called *Deergah Swasam*, the Complete Breath. Place one hand on the navel, and the other on the chest. By putting your hands on these points, you can really feel the expansion and contraction of the breath as it pushes and pulls on the body.

As you slowly inhale, notice how the lungs press the diaphragm downwards, which pushes your belly out. As you breathe in further, the air continues to fill up the lungs, expanding the solar plexus and then the chest. Briefly pause once you've filled up with air, and imagine your lungs fully absorbing all of the fresh oxygen. Then, breathe out slowly, first allowing the chest to release, then the solar plexus, and then the belly. To fully exhale, contract the navel towards the spine to help push out the last bits of air. Then, repeat the whole sequence three to five times.

If you're not up on anatomy, the diaphragm is the band of muscle that separates your heart and lungs from the other organs that lie below it. Shaped like an upside down plate stretched between the ribs and spine, the diaphragm gets pressed downwards towards the lower organs as the lungs fill with air, and then releases upwards as the lungs exhale.

The diaphragm's movement not only powers your breath, but it also pumps a large amount of lymphatic fluid through your system, which empowers your immune system to fight off gnarly invaders. The action also massages the organs and promotes digestion. The oxygen drawn into the body through the Complete Breath pattern helps clear stress and enliven the awareness. Not bad for three big breaths.

After you've enjoyed three to five Complete Breaths, allow the breathing to return to normal. Allow your awareness to settle into your body, savoring the stillness that's been opened through these deep breaths. Sense your body connecting to the Nature of your place, supported between the earth and the sky.

~ Practice: Arriving Into Your Body ~

The final step of the arrival sequence is simply dropping into the sensations in your body. There is an ancient Taoist practice called "Ice to Water to Steam," and it's a great way to relax into your body and let go of tension.[1]

When you hold an ice cube in your hand, the warmth of your body melts its and transforms the ice into water. As the water spills to the ground, the warmth of the sun evaporates it and refines the water into steam. Think of your attention as a warming, healing power that transforms stress, just like the warmth that dissolves the ice. Simply by lightly placing your attention onto a spot and breathing into the place with awareness, the tension can begin transforming and releasing.

Start at the crown of your head, noticing the subtle feeling of the air moving across your scalp. Work your way down your forehead and temples, and then down the back of the head, feeling these points opening and relaxing. Next, sense the muscles around the eyes and allow these spots to relax. Let a smile form on your face, imagining your whole face, head and neck deeply relaxing as you sense into these areas.

Gradually work your way down your body, through your shoulders, chest, back, torso and down the legs and feet. Spend more time on areas that are tight, "breathing into them" and simply being with the sensation in these places, allowing your awareness to transform them. At the end, grow your roots down into the earth and allow any remaining stress to travel down and dissolve in the Earth's vast healing power.

Arrival Sequence Summary

Once you've practiced each phase of the Arrival Sequence, you can easily flow from one section to another as you prepare yourself for a deeper meditation. With a week or two of regular practice, you will have these skills down pat. Plan to devote about 10 minutes for arriving, or longer if you wish to go deeper into the body relaxation practice.

1. Current Needs Inventory (2 minutes)
2. Setting Your Intention (1 minute)
3. Three to Five Complete Breaths (1-2 minutes)
4. Arriving Into Your Body (5-15 minutes or longer, as desired)

12

TUNING IN

> *The goal of life is to make your heartbeat match the beat of the universe, to match your nature with Nature."*
> — *Joseph Campbell*

N ow that you've truly arrived, your meditation can begin. Shamans and mystics the world over have long looked to the trees as a powerful role model and teacher of awareness. The trees stand between the earth and the sky, just as humankind does. Rooted in the nourishing depths of the earth, a tree's trunk and limbs reach up to the endless sky.

To paraphrase the mythologist Michael Meade, "the soul needs deep roots in order for the spirit to climb up into the verticality of the heavens."

Meditation without grounding creates a dreamy, disembodied awareness. Our goal as we meditate in Nature is to increase our presence through fully embodied sensory awareness, while also accessing new heights of creativity and vision, informed by Nature's patterns. This means we are connecting with the body, heart, mind, and with the deeper levels of creative energy that drive our awareness. The process is holistic and interwoven.

Through the arrival process, you have already connected intentionally with your body sensation and with the emotional self that communicates through the body's muscular tension and relaxation. You've also connected the visionary center of the mind's eye with these feelings and sensations during your inventory process and intention setting. Like the tree, you have settled into your being, allowing your roots to ground you to the very earth that is supporting you.

Next we will explore the "heart" of the tree, the mid-point between earth and sky. Just as the trunk of a tree carries nutrients through its xylem and phloem, the heart pumps the blood and the life force through your system. Attuning to the place of the heart reveals an access point of deep intuitive connection to the Nature within and around you.

The Mysterious Power of the Heart

Returning to the Heart. Now that your attention is fully present, I invite you to return again to your heart center, to the same place we visited during your intention setting. The "energetic" heart center is found in the middle of the chest. Mystics of many traditions have discovered that as we turn within through our meditations, some of the greatest mysteries are to be found in the vast expanse of the heart.

In many Qi Gong traditions, the heart center is considered a major way-station and amplifier of life force, capable of imbuing the energy moving through your system with great intention and healing power.

On a biological level, the heart is known to contain 40,000

neurons, similar to the cells of the brain yet adapted to work in the unique conditions of the heart. This area is sometimes called the "heart-brain" for this reason. The heart not only pumps blood but also serves as a biochemical factory, creating the "love peptide" oxytocin, as well as adrenaline and other hormones that alter the body's physiology.

Here in the realm of the heart, we can unlock a very special meditative state that clears stress and enhances health. Although the Relaxation Response can lower your overall heart rate and reduce stress, it does not change the quality of the rhythms *between* the beats of the heart. There is a another unique physiological response that can be gained specifically by meditating on the heart itself, called *coherence*.

Heart Coherence

Research has found that by simply being present to the sensation of the physical heart or to the center of the chest, within a short time the rhythm of the heart itself changes. Holding a positive emotion such as appreciation or love adds to this effect.[1] This internal shift creates profoundly positive effects on the body, mind, and emotions.[2]

Although the heart has an average number of times it beats per minute, the exact timing between each beat varies a bit depending on what you are doing. If you think of something stressful for a few seconds, it may speed up the heart rate for a moment, whereas if you take a deep breath, the heart rate suddenly slows down.

This alternation is the result of the inner accelerator pedal and the brakes of the nervous system at work, helping adapt your body for whatever it needs to deal with. It's actually healthful to have this variability, because it demonstrates that your body is ready and able to cope with life's changes.

However, the rhythm of the beats can either be chaotic, or coherent. Chaotic beats are all over the place, and are prone to occur along with negative emotions such as frustration and anger.[3] By meditating on the sensation in the center of the chest, and also through a focus on positive emotions such as appreciation, the heart's rhythm becomes "coherent," with a smoother distribution of variability between the beats.[4] Coherence brings you important benefits, including increased immune system function,[5] lowered stress levels,[6] and enhanced cognitive function.[7]

Health Benefits of Coherence. It's been discovered that coherence directly impacts your levels of Immunoglobulin A (IgA), an essential defender against viruses, bacteria, and fungi. By simply recalling a positive memory and enjoying several minutes of coherence, you can boost your IgA levels for up to six hours afterwards.[8] By deepening the practice with a daily 30 minute session for five days out of the week, within a month's time it is possible to significantly enhance the body's hormone balance; one study showed a doubling of DHEA, and a 23% drop in cortisol.[9]

The Heart as a Connector. There is growing evidence that the electromagnetic field generated by the coherent heart is not only detected by other cells in the body,[10] but also affects the function of vital processes such as enzyme activity.[11] Amazingly, researchers have observed how the electromagnetic effects of the coherent heart extend through touch and even through space to affect others nearby.[12]

~ Practice: The Radiance of the Inner Sun ~

Though the sky may appear drab and gray on a rainy day, if you were to fly up above the clouds, you would be greeted with a great expanse of bright blue horizon. The light and warmth of the Sun shines down upon even the thickest, most opaque clouds, undaunted and ever radiant.

The brightness of the Sun connects us with the vibrant power that fuels life, and with the clarifying energy of fire that lights even the darkest night. These qualities dwell inside your Inner Nature, too. Through awakening to the Radiance of your Inner Sun, hidden in the depths of the heart, you can access a state of coherence and expansion that fuels your highest creativity and well-being.

The Meditation: After you have tuned into your breath and body sensation through the Arrival practices, become aware now of the center of your chest. Notice the sensations there; perhaps you might feel your heart beating, or sense the tide of each breath as the chest rises and falls; or, you may simply notice the warmth and energy of this vital area.

Greet your heart center with a smile. Imagine that your heart is smiling back at you like a dear friend that you are excited to see. Bask in this feeling of joy and recognition for a moment.

Now, begin to see and feel a bright glowing sun, right there in the center of your chest. Feel the warmth of this sun pulsing and filling your body with light as you continue to smile. Enjoy this sensation for a moment before going any further in the meditation.

Maintaining your connection with your Inner Sun, now allow your awareness to sense the vastness of the Earth beneath you, stretching out to the horizons in all directions. Let your awareness drop into the ground, sensing the depth and mass of the living Earth.

If you are sitting close to the Earth, if you wish, you may also place your palms on the ground to support this awareness. Feel the texture of the soil, and note its temperature and moisture level. Realize as you touch the soil that the earth's free electrons are literally filling you up, balancing your body's electrical potential.

As you peer downwards with your inner senses, you become aware next of a soothing, radiant glow emerging from the depths.

This is the light and energy reaching up to you from the Earth's dynamic core, the life force within the Earth.

Allow the light of your heart to recognize and connect with this dynamic force, feeling the pure energy from the depths of the Earth moving through your being... transforming, purifying, and enlivening your entire system.

With palms facing down, lift your hands slowly out to your sides, allowing the energy of the Earth to fill your being and float your hands upwards; when the hands reach chest level, rotate the palms up to connect with the energy of the Sky, as they continue lifting up above your head towards the Sun. Now, hold your arms straight up, your palms facing each other with fingertips pointing up. Imagine that you can reach up to the Sun, holding it between your upraised palms.

For a moment, imagine and internally sense the physical Sun in the sky above. Realize how this great radiant force is streaming light down upon the Earth, causing the winds to move, water to flow, and life itself to thrive. Feel the energy between your palms growing, filled with the energies of Earth and Sky. Now, bring your palms together as you lower your hands down into a prayer posture,[13] at the same time feeling your heart's connection with the Sun awakening.

Notice now that your Inner Sun is mysteriously connected to the Sun in the sky above. Sense and feel the connection between the two. As you immerse in this connection, notice that your Inner Sun increases its radiance and strength, empowered by the Sun above.

Now, become aware of your own heart interwoven together with both the luminous Sun above and with the radiant core of the Earth below. Sense yourself at the meeting point of the Earth and Sky, immersed in the healing powers that sustain life. Now, the energies of Earth and and Sky have become one within you. Feel and see your heart center glowing with the supportive energies of both the Sun and the Earth's core, an unstoppable beacon of light.

Feel the life-giving pulse of light and warmth moving across this unified solar system of energies, empowering and clarifying the energies of your own heart. Feel your body, heart, and mind relaxing and nourishing as your Inner Sun emanates a warm radiance in all directions. Enjoy the presence of this radiance for as long as you like.

When you are ready, allow your perception of the Sun above and the core of the Earth below to return to their "usual" positions. As always, you yourself remain poised between the two, rooted between Earth and Sky. Offer appreciation and thanks as the energies settle and harmonize within you. Place your hands in your lap, palms up, with one hand over the other.

Feel the energy move where it will throughout your system, allowing the life force to heal and nurture you. Give some time for this settling process to occur, and make space now to just be, enjoying your unique position in the Universe — as a human being immersed in the mysteries of Nature.

From Inner to Outer Awareness

In this chapter, we turned our awareness inwards. There, we discovered the realm of the heart, and the gifts that come with cultivating the state of internal coherence.

In the next section, we will continue building on our growing meditation routine. We'll explore how we can open our senses to the world of Nature around us, and you'll learn to begin reading the language of the birds and animals that you encounter at your Meditation Spot.

13

EXPANDING THROUGH THE SENSES

 " *The sage is one with the world, and lives in harmony with it."*
— *Lao Tzu, in the Tao Te Ching*

In the last two chapters, we began building the foundations of an awareness routine that you can use at your Meditation Spot.

We explored the art of truly Arriving into mindful presence, and tools for turning to the Inner Nature. Through inward meditation, we began calming the waters within through the power of heart coherence. If you've put these tools to practice, it's likely you've now tasted the peace and clarity that comes with a rooted presence.

Now, we are in a good position to expand outwards once more. Like the still point in the middle of a hurricane, your inner cultivation of deep relaxation opens a doorway to sensing the patterns of the Outer Nature moving around you.

In this chapter and the next, we will explore practices that expand your senses so that you can detect and decode these patterns. When you learn Nature's language, you gain a powerful access point into mindful awareness. The voices of the birds and the wind become a mantra that connects you with the flow of life.

Discovering Nature's Language

There is a language in Nature that is shared amongst the animals. People once commonly knew this language, too. Today there are still some who understand. It's not that the language isn't spoken anymore; actually, every bird and squirrel in your backyard uses this ancient code; it's just that people forgot how to listen. Learning the building blocks of Nature's language is easy (because you're part of Nature, remember?); it just takes some time.

Because you're going out to your Meditation Spot regularly, I figured you might want to learn some of this language, since you're there and all... at least, enough to know what the birds are saying about you, and about the fox that's always sneaking past you. Tuning into Nature's language is actually a simple and dynamic way to meditate, while at the same time realizing your connection with the land and animals around you.

I first heard about this primal language from the tracker Tom Brown, Jr. Tom had been mentored in his boyhood by his best friend's grandfather, who happened to be an Apache scout. This elder was steeped in the woods, and had an uncanny way of knowing everything that was going on around him, both near and far.

The old man's name was Nuacano, and his people had relied on Nature's language to stay safe from danger back in the days of the wars with the U.S. cavalry and the Mexican army. The need to detect far-off danger honed the scouts' abilities to read the nuanced signs that warned of approaching troops or of hidden threats. They used these skills daily to protect their tribe.

Like a watchful mountain lion, a scout sentinel would perch on a high-up ledge to attune with Nature's patterns and sense for danger or opportunity. It is said that by reading nature's patterns, a good scout could discern the approach of the cavalry at least eight minutes in advance.[1]

Nature's Ripples

Over the course of his apprenticeship with Nuacano, Tom realized that Nature's language works like the ripples on a pond's surface. When the wind is calm, the surface of the water is still and perfectly reflects everything, and it is easy to peer into its depths. Even a slight breeze will disturb this tranquility.

Throw a big rock in the water, and you get a big splash... and a pattern of emanating ripples that work their way across the water. If you trace a ripple back to its center point, you can figure out where it began.

The same thing happens in the woods. Tom speaks of these ripples as "concentric rings,"[2] and he emphasizes that there is a *feeling* to them. If you slow down enough, you can tune into them. When the "water is calm," the animals are feeding, singing, and doing their regular thing. Everything's copacetic, no problemo.

Enter the hunter (or the hiker with the dog, or the noisy campers, or the hungry lion), and suddenly the rock has dropped. *Splash!* The rings ripple out. The squirrel tells the jay, and the jay tells the fox, the fox tells the deer. Within a few moments, all of the animals know someone's coming.

If you've read the ancient Yoga sutras, you might remember the first and most famous of Patanjali's aphorisms: *Yoga chitta, vritti neruda.* Yoga (union) is the cessation of the whirlpools of the mind. Just as the Yogi finds the still place of unity within the waters of the mind, the scout seeks to blend and flow with the currents of Nature. As the chatter of the mind subsides, one's inner harmony emerges. Through this harmony, an attunement with the flow of Nature becomes possible. As always, the realms of Inner and Outer Nature mirror each other in form and expression.

In the spirit of mentoring, a slightly older Tom (at age 21 in 1970) emerged from Nuacano's training and went on to share these skills with his own neighbor, a ten-year-old naturalist named Jon Young. Over many years of observations and fueled by Tom's persistent questions, Jon learned exactly how the animals broadcast these concentric rings, and figured out how to read these patterns, too.

Every bird has a "baseline" behavior (singing, feeding, calling, nest building, etc.) and a set of "alarm" behaviors (fleeing, freezing, mobbing). Any departure from baseline is an *event*, which arises because a ripple is moving through Nature's waters.

My own trail eventually led me to apprentice with Jon, and then to collaborate with him in mentoring others in nature connection through the 8 Shields Institute. During my own apprenticeship with Jon over a number of years, I would learn from his questions and stories (and lots of field time!) how to decode many of these behaviors, as well.

Besides the birds, the mammals (including us humans) each have their own versions of baseline and alarm, too. Not only that, but every predator creates its own "alarm signature" as it moves about the woods. A cat projects a very different concentric ring than does a red-tailed hawk. Further, a hungry cat projects differently than a sleepy, just-ate-lunch kind of cat.

You project these concentric rings, too. Chew on that the next time you get out to your Meditation Spot. What kind of a ring are you sending out? How are the animals responding to you? How does your mood affect your vibe? Or your speed, your posture, your hunger, your intention?

Sit Here...

After I first heard tell about these concentric rings at the ripe old age age of sixteen, I desperately wanted to understand how to read them. When I found my first nature mentor (someone who had learned from Tom and Jon) and explained this to him, he promptly sat me down by a slippery elm tree in the middle of a New York state riparian woodland... and simply left me there, all alone.

No explanation, no nothing. Just, "You want to learn that? Really? Sit here." And then off he went. I didn't know how long I was supposed to stay there. A few minutes? A day? Would I have a long *Castaway* Tom Hanks beard when this guy showed up again?

My desire overcame my uncertainty, and I resolved to stay as long as it took. That first impasse dealt with, now the question was, "What the heck am I supposed be *doing*?"

Gradually, my mind relaxed as my senses expanded to take in the world around me. The late morning air was warm and carried up the scent of the rich loamy soil into my nose. The canopy was still, with only a small ripple of leaves moving in a scant breeze through the treetops. From up above, a scarlet tanager uttered a few whistled buzzy phrases, whiling away the summer day.

Any sense of hurry I might have held faded into the moment, as time seemed to stretch and expand. The quietness of the forest caught my newly awakened attention, and suddenly my ears opened into the distance; the gurgle of an unseen stream seemed to increase in volume, then came the far-away downwards spiraling song of a veery, and finally a cacophonous punctuation offered by what I would later learn to be a Northern flicker. Through this deep listening, the sounds of the forest reached into my being, bringing with them a feeling: all was at peace here in this moment.

This dreamy yet paradoxically wide-awake state continued for some unknown length of time, until finally I heard the soft footsteps of my mentor working his way along the forest trail to retrieve me.

After having been left in the woods, I really wasn't sure what was coming next. Little did I know, my quiet reverie was soon to find its opposite balance. Sitting together by the fire as we prepared some food for lunch, my mentor suddenly peppered me with an endless list of questions. "What did you notice during your sit? What did you hear? What did you see?"

At first I held my own, offering my tidbits about the tanager, the impressive dappled light filtering through to the forest floor, the smell of the loam, and the sounds of the distant veery. But quickly my observations ran out, and the list of unanswered questions grew heavy.

"*What direction was the wind coming from when you first sat, compared to when you got up at the end? How many airplanes flew over? Which way were they going? Were they jet engines or propellor planes? What is the tanager eating right now? Why does he hang out in the treetops? How do you know he wasn't alarmed? What does his alarm sound like?*"

Through these questions, I began to realize how little I had actually paid attention to during my sit. It's not that the information hadn't crossed my senses... certainly, my skin had felt the subtle shift of breeze from south to southwest, and my ears had resonated with the roar of the two jet planes that had flow over. The problem was, none of this had made it to my conscious awareness. My brain wasn't primed until now to track these details. In that moment I determined to sit again, and to notice more.

~ Practice: Tuning the Senses, Near and Far ~

It takes about twenty minutes of sitting calmly before the ripples of your movement fade away. You can reduce this time by blending in even before you reach your destination.

Walk quietly and slowly to your Meditation Spot. Realize that the presence of your Inner Nature is interacting with the rhythm and activities of the Nature around you. Give the birds and animals you encounter enough space so that they remain comfortable in your presence.

Pause often to settle into your *being*, as your *beingness* settles into the rhythms of the land. Scan within yourself for any points of tension in your mind, heart, or body. Allow these points of tension to dissolve with a deep breath when necessary. Feel yourself immersed in the land, filling with the pure energy of Nature through each breath and with each footstep.

After you've arrived at your Spot, tune further into the language of Nature. Allow your senses to spread out across the landscape in all directions.

First, allow your Expanded Vision to open to the earth and sky. Become aware of the movement and flow of Nature — branches swaying in the wind, grasses waving, and birds and animals on the move. Feel yourself as a still point in the center of all this motion.

Then, feel your body resting upon the earth, supported by the living land. Note the condition of the soil, the leaf litter, the moss, the grasses and herbs around you. Feel the life force moving through them.

Feel the breeze touching your skin. Note the direction the breeze is coming from, and its intensity. Feel the breath moving in and out of your lungs, as the power of the sky fills you with its life energy.

Feel the Sun warming you, and note its position in the sky. If it is nighttime, connect with the Moon and Stars for a moment, feeling their subtle light moving through you.

Now, take in the scent of the place with a few slow, deep sniffs. Open your mouth for a moment and breathe in, dragging the air across your the surface of your tongue as you taste it.

With all of these senses tuned, now allow your hearing to spread out, taking in the sounds and rhythms of the life around you.

1. Listen first to sounds close by, within a small circle of 10 or so feet — the scuffling of a squirrel in the leaf litter, the creaks and groans of branches moving in the wind...
2. Then, expand out to listen within the circumference of the larger area that falls within a good stone's throw around you.
3. Finally, let your ears "grow" into the distance, taking in the far-away sounds. The human ear can detect sounds from up to a kilometer away in any direction, tracking 260 million cubic meters of space[3] and around 340,000 unique tones.[4] What sounds are you immersed in?

After you've awakened all of your senses one at a time, now simply *be*, allowing your awareness to remain expanded and attuned. With each breath, feel Nature filling you up with peace and vitality.

As you listen and slip deeper into the stillness of body and mind, note the feelings moving through the landscape. By stilling the waters of your own being, you are making a clear and reflective surface upon which to read the currents rippling through Nature's depths.

The Fox and the Mysterious Ring

Fast forward ten years from my first sit with the tanager and the slippery elm tree, and many questions later. The mysteries I had encountered during my first sit in Nature propelled me on a major life quest. The journey would lead me to focus my college studies on the realm of deep nature connection and mentoring, and then take me across the country to further my understanding of the ancient art of reading Nature's language.

I was now in Bolinas, California on a cool, foggy spring morning, helping Jon Young teach a group about bird language. The cluster of gardens and outdoor classroom space at the Permaculture Institute of Northern California's field site were now uncharacteristically quiet, as most of the eighty-plus participants had travelled across the road and towards the beach for a morning meditation.

Feeling drawn towards the pond, I remained in the camp, settling in just off the trail to enjoy the quiet. A robin fed amongst some wood chips under an apple tree nearby, and the Bewick's wrens sang with their usual frenzied gusto amidst the berry thickets. Time slipped away, and the morning fog began to burn off.

As I gazed towards the horizon, with my vision expanded and my mind at peace, suddenly a *feeling* passed through my body. It was a feeling of being forced into motion, filled with mild irritation and anxiousness. The feeling hit me like a thunderbolt in the clear blue of my stillness.

In that same moment, a strange white transparent "sheet" floated through the air, expanding outward from my right to my left like the leading edge of a giant see-through bubble, coming from the direction of the beach. Although the town of Bolinas is a major hippie hotspot, I hadn't ingested any mind-altering substances. I also didn't have time to question my sanity, because this strange sight was followed by a flurry of activity.

A moment later, some California quail that had been foraging in the distance about 20 yards to the south called tensely and scurried into the brush, and then one of the wrens briefly chattered. In the corner of my eye, I next spied the robin swiftly hooking up off the ground, headed into the branches of the apple tree. The songbird had only flown up to a branch about five feet off the ground, which told me that whatever was coming along the trail did not overly worry it.

Suddenly, one of the resident gray foxes appeared, trotting along the trail. This fox had kits in a den under the foundation of a nearby building, and had been taking advantage of the workshop participants' absence to do some morning foraging. As the fox trotted by, the robin let out a single "Teek! Tut! Tut!" to let the capable predator know he'd been spotted.

I admired the fox's pelage, noting the animal's pepper-gray fur and the distinctive long black streak running down the length of the tail. Twice the fox peered anxiously back over his shoulder as he trotted along, clearly concerned about something in his wake that was pushing him away from his favorite hunting spot. The fox disappeared around the house to my north, and I was left wondering what to make of it all.

Listening into the distance, I sought to pinpoint any further signs of disturbance. About two minutes later, I heard a sound to the south: distant voices. The group was returning, now obviously stirring up all manner of birds in their hurry to get back for the warmth of a cup of tea around the campfire.

Suddenly, I realized two things:

First, the fox had known much sooner than I about the group's return.

Secondly, *the strange expanding light I had "seen" was actually the leading edge of a concentric ring.*

Somehow, I had observed one of these mysterious energetic pulses in action! The undercurrent of anxiousness was coming both from the fox being pushed by the people, and from the people being in a hurry to get back to camp.

Go figure. I then remembered what Tom had said: there's a *feeling* to a concentric ring. I realized then that these rings aren't just broadcast through the obvious calls and behaviors of the birds and animals; the rings are actual energetic movements that ripple through the mysterious ethers of Nature, and the feeling they carry is what triggers the animals' responses, which then further feeds into the energetic broadcast. The ring and the feeling had come first, *followed* by the more tangible quail, wren, and robin alarms.*

*Well, so much for all the scientific references in this book. I know I just lost some of you...maybe some smarty-pants out there can look into Albert Fritz-Pop's biophoton work, and combine it somehow with Sheldrake's morphic fields theory to uncover the mechanisms at work in concentric rings... but we're moving into shaman territory here people, known for the millennia by mystics, but still uncharted by modern science!

Striking the Lion's Tune

The knowledge of Nature's Language extends back to the dawn of time, and has been known intimately by ancient peoples around the world. Surviving hunter-gatherer cultures have kept this understanding alive to this day, spread out now amidst the deserts, mountains, and remote forests of the world that others have found too inhospitable to bother tampering with. That this under-standing has survived the anvil of time, amongst peoples who value that which is truly needful, is a testament to the usefulness of the knowledge.

A few years after my experience with the "Fox and the Ring," I found myself sitting out in the bush of the Kalahari Desert, under the shade of an acacia thorn tree. It was the beginning of the dry season, and already the late morning Sun was baking the land, its heat giving our group strong reason to take pause beneath the cover of the trees.

Boarding a succession of increasingly smaller planes, starting with a transatlantic 747 at San Francisco International and ending up on a tiny 12-seater in the middle of the bush, I had travelled to this remote landscape with Jon Young, Dr. Nicole Apelian, and a small group of friends as part of the Origins Project. Our goal was to visit with a San community whose members are striving to keep the coals of their ancient cultural knowledge alive and burning strong.

On this day, several of us sat in the shade, listening as the San hunters shared observations of life in the bush. Women and children were gathering roots nearby, and the group quietly blended into the place, focused yet relaxed and attentive. In the distance, a flock of pied babblers began making a racket, their calls repetitive and harsh.

The elder hunters noted that one of our number was hearing these agitated calls, and was himself becoming increasingly concerned. The hunters asked why our friend was worried, and he responded, "Didn't you say that babblers make this type of alarm when they see lions? How do you know they are not alarming now at a lion?" (Earlier, we had seen sign of several lions on the move in the greater area, and so our awareness was piqued).

The hunters both laughed with a big smile as they each tapped their solar plexus, saying, "The Babblers are our friends, and they will tell us if they see a lion. When they do, we feel it right here! Right now the birds are just squabbling amongst themselves. The lions are not here."

Because the territorial calls used by certain birds can sound similar to their alarm patterns (think harsh, sharp, and repetitive), it can be tricky at times to tease out what is really an alarm meant for a predator, versus what is simply a heated tussle between flock members or avian neighbors.

A good rule of thumb is to listen for the response from other nearby birds of different species; the presence of a newly discovered predator will often entice other types of birds to join in on the harassment, and you'll hear several species all mobbing an unlucky cat or owl together.[5] Sometimes the predator moves off and the alarms are shorter lived, though. In these moments, one relies on a combination of field experience and gut instinct to decode the meaning.

In this case with the babblers, the San hunters had plenty of both resources at their disposal. Though they tuned into the feeling of annoyance the babblers were broadcasting, they did not sense the degree of tension that comes with the presence of a large predator. The Hunters also noted how the annoyance was contained within the flock; no other bird species got involved — it was only a "babbler concern."

Because decoding bird language has a lot to do with reading the tonality of a bird's call, this skill draws heavily upon the right side of the brain. This hemisphere has the special ability to track the *inflection* of words and other sounds, a neural function called *prosody.*[6]

Once you get how this works, you'll be able to transfer what you already know to decode what the birds in your yard are saying. Here's an everyday example of prosody that you might have experienced for yourself:

Imagine you're sitting in an airport restaurant waiting for your next flight. As you flip idly through the menu, you can't help but notice the fellow to your left conversing on his phone with a heavy Southern drawl. If you've travelled through the southern U.S. states, you might even have a sense of exactly where this man is from. When the waiter walks by, you next hear the woman to your right place her order, instantly recognizing the comparatively clipped and curt statements of a New Englander, probably from New Hampshire.

As you listen, you are dialing into the subtle tonal patterns and rhythms of each speaker's voice. Besides sorting regional dialects, you can probably tell if the speaker is tired or energized, happy or upset. If you listened very closely, you might discern if they are directing their voice upwards to the waiter, or downwards to a child who is scrambling around and vying for their attention, or sideways to another adult at the table.

If either of these people were displeased with their order, you'd also know — perhaps even if you aren't an English speaker. You'd know because their tonal inflection, intensity, and rhythm would shift.

Mild displeasure has its phrases and sounds. A somewhat sharp "Excuse me…" might be first called out, designed to get the waiter's attention.

This opening is followed by a milder but compelling statement of purpose — "They forgot the dressing on this salad…could you please get some for me?" Generally, most people will speak this phrase a bit tentatively, with somewhat placatory and questioning notes (including a slight rise in pitch at the end), but still firm in request.

Meanwhile, extreme displeasure sounds quite different — "Ack! I just saw a ^$!#@*! GIANT RAT in the kitchen! What KIND of a PLACE is this?!"

As the speaker's agitation rises, so does the intensity of their voice. Whether they whisper or shout, the heightened nature of the statement comes through clearly. The speed of their speech picks up, certain words develop a sharp intonation, and the *feeling* behind the words transforms. This is prosody in action, and, in the brain of the listener, the right hemisphere works its magic in decoding the meaning of these subtle tonal inflections.

Prosody is at work when we tune into Nature's language, and

the San hunters put it to good use every day, because it literally saves their lives. The birds' incessant mobbing of a great cat caught stalking in the brush has a potent feeling and a unique sound to it; it's very different than the sporadic alarms that the birds make when a mongoose pops in and out of view in the brush.

Likewise, the birds' close-to-the-earth alarms that warn of ground predators are unique from the mobbing patterns the birds inflict upon a hawk or owl encountered up in the treetops. By reading the patterns of the birds' alarms, the hunters can discern what kinds of animals are in the area, whether they are dangerous, and where they are located. You can learn to do this, too (I did, and I grew up in the suburbs playing video games... come on, no excuses!).

When you understand Nature's language, you come to realize that you are also part of the story. There is no separation. Your movement and actions are broadcasting around you to every earthworm beneath your feet, and rippling out to the owls, foxes, and other creatures listening to your footsteps. Suddenly, mindful awareness takes on a whole new dimension. The first step is learning how the language works.

~ Practice: Listen Once More, With Feeling ~

When the old hunters laughingly tapped on their solar plexuses, they were showing that there is a *feeling* that comes into the body as we decode the prosody of the sounds around us. The feeling of tension registers in the gut, and it's the same inner place I tuned into during the episode with the gray fox.

Start listening to the birds around your Meditation Spot, and as you listen, check in with your gut feeling. Do the birds sound like they are just "doing their thing" (relaxed), or are they upset (tense)? If they are upset, *how* tense are the sounds making you feel?

Quiet can have a feeling, too. Like in the old Westerns, it can be "too quiet around here." Where are the quiet areas? How big are they? Is it *too* quiet there? Everything you hear is fair game for a quick gut check.

If birds seem a bit elusive to start with, begin with an easier guru. Dogs are very accessible teachers that can help you learn to understand and decode tension — their barks are so expressive! An excited dog barks when his owner is coming home, but this bark is very different than the one he uses if an unknown person approaches the house at night. Imagine these two sounds right now — I bet you can, without much effort. That's prosody in action.

Now, imagine each bark again, but also feel your body as you "listen." What feeling does each type of barking produce? That's the ticket to learning Nature's language. Go to a dog park and just listen to the interactions there, *feeling* the energy behind each vocalization.

~ Practice: Tension Check ~

Listen, sense, and feel your surroundings for a minute. Use a scale of 1 to 10 to rate how relaxed or tense the area is. Here's a few key points in the scale to help you begin assessing; with practice, you can figure out your own gradations.

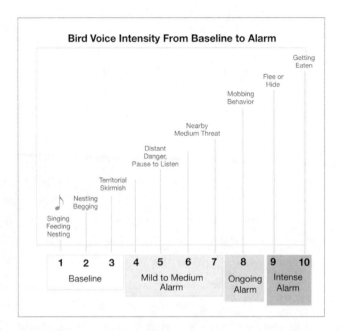

1 is baseline. Animals are singing, maintaining flock or pair contact, feeding, building nests, bathing, preening, and generally doing what they want to be doing.

2 is baseline, but annoying. In the spring, you'll hear young birds petitioning their overworked parents for food. These calls can be persistent and obnoxious (especially the begging calls of woodpecker nestlings, screeching from the safe confines of their nest cavity!).

3 is still baseline, but sporadically noisy and tense as territorial skirmishes are happening amongst neighboring birds. There's no large-scale threat, but the sounds of in-fighting can be sharp and agitated. Fighting tends to happen in the breeding season as rival males challenge each other, or during the off-season in feeding flocks when hungry birds get grabby and angsty. The quick spike of tension soon resolves to the smoother flow of baseline.

4-7 is mild to medium alarm: birds are alarming at low to mid intensity, often because a predator is further away, or because it has just passed through to another area and the birds are still settling back to normal, or because the predator that's there just isn't too big of a deal (think "a well-fed cat"). This is yellow alert zone.

Hearing alarm of any kind should get you on your toes: use this as as opportunity for extra mindfulness. Scan the area far and near for further clues. *Can you remain relaxed yourself, yet aware of the birds' tension?*

8 is persistent, ongoing alarm as birds avidly mob a predator or signal its presence. The harassment exposes the predator's location, taking away its element of surprise. This can also continue for a time after a predator has caught its prey and is more concerned with eating than with attacking anybody else. Stationary alarms indicate that a predator is hunkered down. A "cloud" of birds drifting slowly over the bushes and yelling downwards means a predator is stalking through an area, positioned just below them.

9-10 is gradations of intense alarm, leading to all-out panic. Birds and animals may be fleeing, flying or running fast and away from a predator as they sound a red alert. To get away from danger on the ground, birds fly up. To get away from danger in the skies, birds drop down low or hide. Everything may also be totally silent and still, laced with tension and fear because it's just too dangerous to make a move. This is when everything is "too quiet."

That's my version of the 1-10 scale. It gives you a taste of how much you can learn just through listening to the language of the birds.

You can start simpler, too: One is baseline, five is medium alarm, and ten is all-out alarm. Use those as major reference points and just let your gut tell you how high or low on the scale the area is. Give this a try at least three times every day for the next month, so that you can really engrain this skill into your awareness toolkit.

What's Next

Put all of these tools into practice. Pick one practice to experiment with each day at your Meditation Spot. Use the Arrival and Inner Coherence practices first, and then select one of the Expansion practices to engage your senses with the larger flow of activity around you.

In the next chapter, we'll add to your growing sensory toolkit as we dig deeper into understanding Nature's language. Along the way, we will also explore some of the fascinating neural mechanisms that support these awareness skills.

14

FURTHER EXPANSION INTO NATURE'S CONVERSATION

I n the last chapter, I introduced you to the building blocks of Nature's language. We explored the dynamics of sound, tonality, and the *feeling* moving beneath it all.

Through the practices, you can discover for yourself that each journey into Nature is a *conversation*; your intention and action generates a *response* from the natural world through the voices and behaviors of the animals.

The dialogue with Nature expands our notions of mindfulness. Our awareness grows to encompass a broader field of responsibility as we each engage with the world around us. *How are we showing up in life? How is the world responding? Nature is calling to us to be fully present. Can we hear the call?*

In this chapter, we will further explore the theme of expansion with some new practices and tools. We'll begin with recounting a classic moment in the history of neuroscience.

Mirroring Nature

Besides prosody detection, there's another major thing going on in the brain when all this sensory work is at play; your brain is subtly mirroring the events around you, preparing you to take action. Oddly, this function was discovered by accident in an Italian neuroscience lab, thanks to a monkey and an ice cream cone.[1]

Researchers were observing the monkey, trying to figure out what parts of his brain would activate as he grasped cups and other small objects. The research team figured this is pretty key information to discover, because it could unlock insights into the development of tool use, social behavior, and other perceptual skills that might also apply to humans.

So, the researchers had this poor monkey hooked up to the machine and did their tests. After lunch, one of the grad students came back into the lab with an ice cream cone. Suddenly, the machine unexpectedly let out a "BING!" They had accidentally left the machine running; the monkey's brain somehow activated it when he saw the student holding the cone in his hand.

The strange thing was, the monkey hadn't actually picked up the cone — he had simply observed someone else with it in their hand. This brief view was enough to stimulate the same area of the monkey's brain that gets used for grasping. This accident heralded the discovery of the *mirror neuron*, a special kind of brain cell that helps us model and understand the world around us.

It turns out that when you see others moving and performing actions around you, your brain is secretly mimicking many of these behaviors. If your partner grabs her coffee cup off of the table at breakfast, your mirror neurons light up, as if you've just grabbed the cup yourself.

If you see a football player on the TV zigging and zagging down the field while being pursued by the other team, your mirror neurons put you there holding the ball, too, running madly towards the end zone.

If you watch a dancer moving fluidly across the stage, or a trapeze artist somersaulting through the air, the joy or the thrill that fills you is being narrated and directed by your mirror neurons. These unique brain cells help you sense into the actions around you, modeling and predicting how you might respond in any given moment.

The catch is, your mirror neurons light up the most for actions that you are already familiar with.[2] If you don't know how to play the violin and you go to see an amazing Irish fiddler perform, your mirror neurons won't activate as much as mine will, because I *do* play the fiddle.[3]

I've already laid down the basic wiring in my brain that allows me to make sense of certain key details: the circular motions of the bow, the fluid rolls of the fiddler's fingers during a fast reel, and the emphasized notes on the down beats that give the song its drive and pulse. As I observe each of these actions, my brain is lighting up as if I myself was on the stage. When I get home, my playing will actually be the better for it.

Now, back to the San hunters out in the bush for a moment. They are surrounded by animals every day, from babblers to lions, and beyond. Certain animal behaviors are *similar enough* to human behaviors that I suggest the mirror neuron system might get involved when we encounter them. After all, the monkey saw a person holding the ice cream cone, and it worked for him.

If a bird is craning its head looking down in the bushes, it makes me curious. Of course, humans can crane their heads to look down at things, too. I know it indicates interest in something. What does the bird see? A snake? Food? Something else? I see the bird looking, and I want to know.

If a bird bursts up off the ground and flies up and away, there is a feeling to the movement that I can relate to — similar to the football player running at full speed to the end zone. This prompts questions, which may lead to actions: Why is the bird flying off? Do I need to be concerned? Do I need to run, too?

And if a bird is just putzing around, scratching for seeds, I can connect the dots to my own version of that, too. All is well in bird land.

Are my mirror neurons firing up in these moments, infusing me with data about the flow of life in the woods? I bet they are. This is what was happening for the San hunters as we sat there together under the shade of the acacia tree. Every day, their sensory systems are richly activated by their complex natural surroundings. Their mirror networks are feeding back with a dynamic full-sensory picture of what's happening around them each moment. They are in tune with their place — lions, babblers, and all.

How Nature's Language Expands Your Mind

When we put all this exciting brain activity together, we are in a good spot to begin appreciating how learning Nature's language can expand our senses and awareness to a whole new level.

What's amazing about the mirror neuron research is that not only do these brain cells fire when we see an action taking place, they also activate simply from *listening* to the sounds around us. "Action sounds" engage the parts of the brain related to whatever action causes the sound.[4]

If you've ever scratched around in the leaf litter (even just with a rake in the yard — I'm not implying that you regularly dig around out there, although I have been known to), then when you hear a squirrel stirring up leaves in the distant woods, your brain infers the action that's taking place. You just *know* there's a squirrel over there, even though you can't see it. You might even get a subtle feeling related to the activity of digging, and an image in your mind of what the squirrel is doing.

What's more interesting is how the mirror neurons help you infer the *purpose* of an action.[5]

Why is the squirrel digging? If you've ever watched squirrels in the autumn, you may have seen them foraging for acorns amidst the fallen leaves. They are picking out the choice acorns, chock full of protein and fat, hoarding them away for leaner times. If you looked closely, you might have noticed the rodent's sporadic movements — the quick motion of the forepaws sorting through the leaf litter, and the dolloping bound across the leaves to a proper acorn burial spot, then a frenzy of digging just below the surface to perfectly encapsulate the acorn under the shallow earth, and then the CSI-proof artful hiding of the buried cache.

If you have such a memory, then when you hear the action sounds related to these movements, your mirror neurons will instantly fire up the circuits in your brain connected to this knowledge. You instantly know by the sound that there is a squirrel, and with this next step, you infer by the pattern of sound that the squirrel is foraging acorns. Perhaps you don't even know *how* you know; you just instinctively do.

Let's take this understanding back to the "Babblers and the Lion" story. When the babblers were squabbling amongst themselves, the hunters' brains were keeping track, their mirror neurons and prosody circuits deftly deciphering each action sound and its tonal nuances.

Memories related to similar sounds from their past were called up, along with the visceral feeling connected to the sound. Because of their experience (plus their mindful awareness that helped them register the distant sounds in the first place), the hunters *knew* it was safe. Now *you* know some of the biological mechanics behind this amazing skill.

When you start tuning into Nature's language in this way, the voices of the birds become an extension of your own awareness. Although you can't see the fox sneaking through the bushes, or the hawk buzzing over the distant treetops, the birds can. They become your eyes and your ears. Their calls and movements become a living alphabet, a language of motion and sound that spells out the location and behavior of distant predators and people.

When we add up all of these sophisticated neural gymnastics, we discover a basic pattern to how awareness works: as you experience the outer world, your brain builds an inner model to make sense of it all. The brain then uses this model to predict what's happening around you. The parts of your environment that are most important to you tend to get good representation in this "inner world." These are the things you have learned to pay attention to.

For the San hunters, anything that keeps their families safe from the lions gets tagged with high priority. It makes the cut, and so their neural circuits teem with memories related to the lions and their behavior: the babblers' calls, the lions' footprints (and how to gauge when they were left in the sand, and therefore how nearby the animals may be), the season and what the lions are hunting right now (and thus, where they may be hanging out), and a hundred other ecological nuances.

Through the brain's magic, this complex *knowledge of place* sorts together every moment to paint a story of what's happening on the land, and how to respond. The hunter-gatherer lifestyle truly requires keen observation. This ancient lifeway generates human beings that are deeply attuned to the land, with internal maps of the world that literally mirror the places they live.

This is the ancestral legacy of awareness that is inherent within all of our genes. Many of us may live out of the bush in cities and suburbs, but it's the gift of the lions (and the thousand other concerns faced through generations of close living with the land) that has brought our awareness potential to where it is today as a species. We are still hunter-gatherers in body and brain, finding our way in a new Digital Wilderness.

You can start to develop these kinds of personal connections with the land and animals, too. Your regular visits to your Meditation Spot provide the doorway to this relationship. To step through the door and access your own potential of earth awareness simply requires getting out there, and allowing your senses the chance to engage and connect.

~ Practice: Ear Training ~

Here are several simple practices you can play with to train your listening skills in Nature: *The Sound Count, Follow the Sound*, and *The Space Between the Sounds*. Each exercise will add a new dimension to what you are noticing around you.

The Sound Count

Once you've *arrived* at your Spot (and you know what this truly means, because you've practiced the super-useful skills shared in the previous chapter; and you know through prosody that I'm emphasizing the word *arrived*...), expand your hearing and get a count of the sounds around you. What do you hear to the east? The south? The west? The north? Above? Below? Within your own being?

Use a pocket pad to take notes with if it helps you focus. Heck, use a napkin to write on if you're stuck at Denny's waiting for your "Moon Over My Hammy" to arrive. Any free moment is an opportunity to practice deepening your awareness, and these skills can come with you wherever you go after you've internalized them at your Meditation Spot.

Follow the Sound

Here's a practice that works great at dawn or dusk.

Pick out the song of one particular bird to focus on. You don't even need to know what its name is. Get a bead on where the bird is — what direction, how high up, and where it's facing. Best guess is okay. Try to point to it (really).

Then, for the next however long (five to twenty minutes is good), keep part of your attention on where the bird is. Think of your bird as a movable mantra, drifting through trees and meadow. Sit with Expanded Vision, simply enjoying the time as you listen.

Male songbirds tend to rotate around the edges of their territories in the spring, so you may notice a circular pattern to the bird's location. Common yellowthroats are great ones to try this with.

This little exercise will test your focus. Add challenge like you would in juggling, by next tracking the sounds and positions of two birds at once.

The Space Between the Sounds

Les Fehmi, one of the early titans of biofeedback research, figured out that *space* is the magic key to quickly achieving deep states of relaxation.[6] When you pay attention to the space *between* things, it's like unlocking a cheat-code or back door to the mind.

The brain doesn't quite know how to categorize or get a handle on empty space. It's not a "thing" — space has no color, weight, mass, or direct sensible quality; it must be inferred.

If you stay focused on imagining, say, the space between your two hands, or the space between the top of your head and your feet (or the space between the two robins singing in your yard), the chatty, distractable aspect of the brain just seems to eventually give up and raise its hands in surrender.

Meditating on space is therefore a great way to switch out of mental chatter mode and into the moment. Alpha waves, produced by the brain during periods of relaxation, increase dramatically.

More impressively, Fehmi has found that the alpha waves created in this state synchronize in phase across many regions of the brain, increasing the potency of the meditative experience.[7] It's like getting a 15 minute power reset to refresh all your neural circuits.

There are other benefits, too. This style of meditation can even relieve stress-headaches, soothe gastrointestinal issues, and diminish joint pain.[8]

Another great thing is that with a spatial meditation, you can switch your attention between various things in your environment. You don't have to stay focused the entire time on just one item, which beginning meditators can find daunting. Just stay focused for about 15 seconds at a time on each focal point, and then switch to another.

This satisfies the part of the mind that likes movement and activity (which some traditions call "the monkey mind"), while also helping the brain switch gears into a relaxed mode.

Try this: Pick two sounds you hear around you, and in your mind, simply sense the space between their sources. Spend about 15 seconds on this. Then, pick another two, and do the same. You can continue this pattern with various sounds for 10 to fifteen minutes. Then, notice how you feel after the meditation, compared to before you started.

This type of meditation can be applied to anything, not just sounds. You can also imagine and sense the empty space between trees, plants, rocks, clouds, and even different parts of your body. Try spatial meditation for fifteen minutes, once or twice a day for a period of a month to really experience what this can do for you. Your brain will thank you.

Expansion of the Senses, In Practice

In this chapter, I've offered you a smorgasbord of sensory practices you can enjoy at your Meditation Spot. Experiment with them. Savor them like a variety of fine cheeses laid out on a serving tray. You wouldn't eat them all at once; you'd try them one at a time, with full awareness.

As always, pay attention to how you feel *beforehand* compared to how you feel *after* experiencing each meditation. This will help you understand how each practice can help you to internally shift gears. Are you more alert? More relaxed? Restful but aware? Dreamy and creative? In time, you'll become a connoisseur of awareness, tailoring your meditations to the needs of the moment. Give each practice some time to offer you its fruits.

When you first arrive at your Meditation Spot, use the Arrival and Internal Meditation Sequence from chapters 11 and 12. Then, select one of the Sensory Expansion meditations from this or the previous chapter to use for ten to twenty minutes, as time allows.

You might try each Expansion practice for a week before trying the next, to allow the practice to sink in. Then, rotate through as desired. Of course, you can simply use the practices from this chapter on their own, too, whenever and wherever you feel called.

Meditation Summary

So far, you've developed a meditation routine that helps you tune first into the Nature within yourself, and then to the larger patterns of Nature around you. Here's an outline of your combined meditation sequence up to this point:

1. **Arrival:** Mindfully approach and arrive at your spot (10-15 minutes)

2. **Tuning In:** Activate heart coherence through internal meditation (10-15 minutes)
3. **Expanding Out:** Broaden your awareness with a Sensory Meditation (10 minutes)

In the next chapter, I'll share some simple practices to help you gather and integrate the energy that you've experienced at your Meditation Spot, so that you can transition from your meditation session and carry the peace of Nature with you wherever you go next in your day.

15

GATHERING & RETURNING

Thus far, we've explored meditative techniques for *Arriving* mindfully at your Meditation Spot, *Tuning In* to access the calming power of inner coherence, and *Expanding Out* to connect with Nature's language around you. Through putting these skills to practice, you've been accessing progressively deeper states of consciousness, tuning your attention to Nature's patterns with increasing refinement.

The presence and aliveness that emerges through this attunement is truly the stuff of "First Creation" described by the Bushman shamans. These healing sensations are the gifts of joining in Nature's Great Dance, and they arise when we slough off the stress of daily life and remember the pure awareness that is our core. Whether we turn within or expand to the pulse of life around us, Nature is there as an eager dance partner, waiting for us to catch the rhythm and join the flow.

Now that you've tuned to the frequency of Nature's song at your Meditation Spot, how do you keep the good vibes going with you throughout the day? That's what this chapter is all about. We'll explore how to gather up all the nourishing experiences and energy from your time outdoors, and carry the attunement with you to lift and support whatever is next in your day.

––––––––––

Refining Your Body of Nature

Amongst the ancient Yogic philosophies, there is a teaching called *Mantra Purusha* that works with sound and vibration to refine and uplift the practitioner's consciousness.[1] You may be familiar with the idea of a *mantra* as a phrase that is repeated in meditation to focus the concentration, such as the cosmic OM or AUM sound. *Mantra* literally means "instrument of the mind," and the word's origins date back thousands of years to early Vedic sages who keenly observed the ways of Nature.

In their deep meditations, the sages perceived the Universe as a sea of vibrations, a cosmic medley filled with various sounds and rhythms. Each aspect of Nature was found to contain a primary "seed sound," a basic unit of vibration that shaped and defined its unique growth and development. Mantras were discovered as specific tonal phrases that linked one's consciousness directly with various particular frequencies of the cosmos.

Mantras are basically Nature's apps. Want to link up with a feeling of compassion? There's a mantra for that. Need to deepen your insight? There's a mantra for that, too. Each part of the body is linked to a specific sound that will energize and heal it, too.

The idea is that by working through a meditational cycle of special mantras, a practitioner can build up a Body of Sound that links his or her awareness to deeper and more profound levels of consciousness. Each mantra acts like a tuning fork or a TV antenna, enabling one's awareness to "pick up" different, previously unknown stations.

Awakening and Rewiring

Other mystical traditions such as Kabbalah and Sufism have a similar approach, in which Divine qualities are awakened in the practitioner through meditation upon Sacred Names, or upon various Spheres of Consciousness. Meditate upon *Mercy*, for instance, and you will become merciful. Meditate upon *Severity*, and the power of restriction will become part of your experience. Meditate upon *Balance*, and both of these forces will reach harmony.

With practice, such meditations will literally rewire the brain. Through the Dalai Lama's nudging, a study was done on the effects of the OM mantra in the brain activity of highly experienced Tibetan Buddhist monks. The practitioners meditated on universal compassion as they mentally chanted the OM sound, and their brains showed widespread increases in gamma wave activity, an indicator of enhanced resiliency and plasticity.[2]

Bottom line: by meditating on compassion, the monks increased their ability to consciously *respond* rather than just emotionally *react* during potentially stressful situations (a quality which is part of the foundation of compassion), and their brains adapted to develop this capacity a bit further with each session of meditation.

The journey of connecting with Nature that we are exploring in this book mirrors these ancient insights. Earlier, we saw how each sensory experience that we attend to brings changes to the brain; each song that you consciously experience from the robin in your yard adds to the "robin sound network" in your auditory memory system, and each encounter with the enlivening aroma of the pine tree in the park adds to your olfactory memory of that tree. Every question and curiosity that you cultivate draws linkages between the various neural networks, priming your senses for the next encounter.

The key is to be attentive, and mindfully appreciative of these moments in Nature (and really, what moment is *not* a moment "in Nature"?). The more we embrace the Now with presence and passion, the more we are nourished by the gifts that we are constantly being offered.

Remember the basic formula: *What you put into the brain is what you get out of it.* A life that's lived in close kinship with the land yields a mind full of the rich stories of that place.

As the study with the monks illustrated, these connections actually create physical changes in the brain. The ancient traditions tell us the world is vibrating, and that the patterns we attune to vibrate within us, as well. *What stories and vibrations from Nature are alive for you?*

Building Connections

A Lakota Wisdom Keeper once shared with me a profound understanding about how we come to reflect Nature in our lives. This man had grown up in a small village of Holy men and women, a rural community formed by an extended family of powerful healers who had banded together to maintain their traditional ways after a forced transition to reservation life.

He said, "Amongst my people, we have great respect for elders. We call them *Tonkasila*, which many people translate simply as 'Grandfather.' But really, the word means much more. *Ton* is an energy or emanation, *kan* are ropes or arteries, and *sila* means 'a being that moves independently...'

"When we look at Nature with spiritual vision, we see that everything has energy in it. If you look at the trees at dusk, you can see the energy around their silhouettes. Even a stone has it. You have it, too. The Spirit of Nature has a bundle of arteries that flow with this life force from all things. Everything has an emanation from the Fire Within that holds the world together.

"As a person grows, they form a special relationship with certain parts of the natural world. For one person it could be a connection with a deer, or for another it's with the dragonfly. Too, they get to know the land where they live and spend their time. As that person gets older, they absorb the emanations, the energy, from these parts of Nature. They start to reflect it in the way that they *are* in the world.

"By the time a person becomes an elder, they are steeped in this energy. They have become like the Nature they relate with. This energy now emanates from them as they move about into the community, through their stories, through their presence. So, we honor them and call them *Tonkasila*. Because each person has their own relationship with Nature, the community benefits from many different connections with the natural world."

As you consider the meaning of this story, I invite you to also meditate upon your own special connections with Nature. What aspects of Nature or types of places do you enjoy connecting with? What specific qualities do you observe in these aspects of Nature? How might these qualities be "rubbing off" on you?

Reflect on these patterns, and collect your observations in your journal. Realize that with each visit to your Meditation Spot, you are absorbing the energies and textures of Nature into your own being, and that you are carrying these gifts forward with you wherever you go.

~ Practice: The Centering Form ~

Various wisdom cultures have discovered their own relationships with the life force of Nature. In China, for instance, over 3,500 unique styles of Qi Gong have developed over the past several thousand years. *Qi* ("chee") is the breath or life force of Nature, and *Gong* (like the "kung" in "Kung Fu") indicates skill that is cultivated through practice. Qi Gong is therefore the skill of working with the energy of Nature.

Using breath, posture, sound, and stillness, the practitioner explores his own *being*, realizing his own life as a microcosm of the larger patterns of the universe. As he develops skill, he learns to purify, gather, and circulate the life force for greater health and awareness. This is true Nature Jedi stuff.

Qi Gong practices often end with a closing sequence. After you've awakened your system and tonified your energy, it's good form to center yourself before continuing on to other activities. Centering can also benefit you in the midst of your day if you find yourself getting scattered or overwhelmed.

There are traditionally said to be three special energy centers in the body, called "elixir fields" or *Dan Tien (dahn-tee-en)* by Taoists. The Dan Tien are major hubs that connect to the acupuncture meridians. Each of these areas has a unique function.

The Upper Dan Tien is located in the center of the head, and relates to higher creativity and vision. The Middle Dan Tien dwells in the center of the chest, and relates to the emotions and the flow of the life force. The Lower Dan Tien is in the lower abdomen, located three finger widths below the navel and towards the center of the body, and is considered to be an ideal "battery storage" area for vital chi.

Movement, breath, and meditation practices can all cause qi (life force) to stir and move throughout the body. Heat and energy may be generated, and it's important to sense where the heat is gathering or flowing in the body.

It is said that one should avoid overheating the head and heart, which are sensitive to the energy. For this reason, practices exist to gather qi at the end of a session and direct it towards the Lower Dan Tien, where it can be safely stored and also self-regulate throughout the body as needed.

There is a simple movement and breath pattern that works very well to conclude a meditative cycle based on this theory, and it is called *centering*.[3] This practice can be done either standing or sitting. It is very easy to learn (though a bit detailed to describe), and brings very tangible results.

1   Gather Qi as you scoop in a half circle

2   Bring Qi down the front centerline

3   Direct Qi
    into the
    Dan
    Tien
    beneath
    the
    navel

Hold the left hand with the palm up, just below the navel, with the edge of the hand resting lightly against the lower abdomen. This hand will receive the energy and help direct it inwards to the lower Dan Tien.

As you slowly breath in through the nose, the right hand reaches out to the lower right side and then floats upwards in a half-circle, scooping up the energy until it is above the head (see Figure 1).

At the apex above the head, the hand is now oriented vertically with fingertips pointing upwards, with the palm facing naturally into the centerline of the body (Figure 2).

Next, the hand retains its vertical orientation, but begins slowly dropping downwards as you gradually exhale through the nose, with the hand following the centerline of the front of the torso, fingers still pointing upwards (figure 3).

As the hand drops, it is pulling in the qi that has been gathered, directing it towards the lower Dan Tien. You may feel a tingly sensation, or sensations of warmth or coolness as the energy moves down through your torso and to the Dan Tien.

Once the hands come close to meeting, they trade roles and now you use the "new" hand to gather energy similarly on the other side of the body. Sense the pure, healing energy coming to you from all around in Nature. Smile as you gather up the energy.

Continue with the same breathing pattern, alternating hands on each side, until you've done three, six, or nine repetitions on each side.

As you do the movement, simply intend that you are gathering all the good energy from your meditation experience and bringing it now into your core, where it will integrate and harmonize into your system. If you feel called, you may remember specific moments from your day's journey that you wish to carry forward, inviting the lessons and energy of those interactions to harmonize into your being.

Once you've gathered the energy, you can place both palms over the lower Dan Tien (just below the navel), resting one on top of the other. Different Qi Gong schools have varying preferences as to which hand should go over the other; I suggest simply letting your hands choose whatever position feels most natural.

Now, simply feel the warmth and movement of the lower abdomen as you breathe in and out, allowing the energy to settle in the Dan Tien.

You may choose to envision the Dan Tien glowing like a giant red coal as the energy gathers, but it is enough simply to feel the sensations there (in fact, cultivating awareness of the sensation is the most important aspect, as this attunement directs the chi to the area).

Breathe fully and relaxedly in this manner for 2-3 minutes as you smile down to your Dan Tien, feeling it fill with warmth and vitality; five minutes is even better.

Just as you took your time in getting to your Meditation Spot, once you have completed your practices, take your time returning, if possible. Allow the peace and presence cultivated through your session to remain with you as you return to whatever is next in your day.

If you need a re-presencing moment during the day, you can imagine yourself at your Meditation Spot, enjoying the relaxing sights, sounds and other sensations. Even one minute of this imagined visitation can be deeply nourishing. If you are on lunch break and stuck inside, put on a sleep mask or close your eyes and enjoy five to ten minutes of this meditation. Or, do the Centering movements for a minute or two to gather your energy. Remember, your connections with Nature are with you wherever you go.

Meditation Summary

Having now experienced the various stages of meditating in Nature, here's an outline of your complete Meditation Spot sequence:

1. **Arrival:** Mindfully approach and arrive at your spot (10-15 minutes)
2. **Tuning In:** Activate heart coherence through internal meditation (10-15 minutes)
3. **Expanding Out:** Broaden your awareness with a Sensory Meditation (10 minutes)
4. **Gathering & Returning:** Centering and integrating your experiences (5-10 minutes)

When you have the time, go through the entire sequence for a good 35 minutes to an hour. Of course, each component can be used on its own as an effective meditation, too. But I'd recommend doing the whole shebang three times a week if you can, or at least once each week.

Do mini-sessions if you have to. A minute of pure awareness here and there adds up. Just like with weight lifting, focus on quality repetitions versus shoddy attempts at quantity. Remember, you're building actual neural pathways through your practice. How do you want to develop your brain?

After all, you're going to carry these connections forward with you in your gray matter, and what you put into the process is what you will get out of it. Every intentional step you take will lead you towards where you want to go... but enjoy the journey each step of the way. There's no rush, and no "end point" to the journey of awareness; rather, there's simply new discoveries to be made around every corner.

SECTION III

ADVANCED PRACTICE

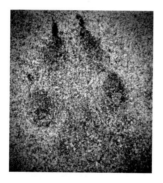

Now, it's time to take the meditation skills you've acquired to the next level, with the practice of *Being Nature*:

- **Learn how the attuned imagination** transforms your awareness and empowers your intent

- **Explore a special eight-day series of active meditations,** designed to help you strengthen positive mind-states and cultivate new qualities in your life

- **Realize how you can consciously carry Nature's gifts and teachings with you everywhere you go,** from the workplace to home and beyond...

16

BEING NATURE

The Great Dance of Nature is a realm of ceaseless transformation. In this mysterious place where a rhino can become a zebra, a zebra can become a lion, and a lion can become a man, we find ourselves swept up in the flow state, effortlessly meeting each change with full gusto.

When we get onto the cosmic dance floor of transformation, we are faced with a core truth discovered by sages throughout time: we are awareness, pure consciousness, experiencing form but not truly defined by it. We are like the water, experiencing the ripples of sensation that come and go. Does the ocean define itself as the wave breaking on the shore, or as the whitecaps whipped up by the wind far out to sea? No, the great ocean encompasses all of the waves and currents alike.

Through awareness of our thoughts and feelings, we become more intentional creators of the perceptual ripples that filter our human experience of Infinity. When we tap into the Dance, we expand our frozen notions of who and what we truly are. The animals can help us remember this knowledge.

Lessons From the Weasel

One of my clients, Steve, loved being outside in Nature, but he often felt a bit trapped and confined while at work. The office environment just seemed a bit dulling to his senses, and he experienced fatigue and loss of focus at various points throughout the day.

During our coaching sessions, which were focused on the ancient art of wildlife tracking, we had been exploring the skill of "becoming" the animal one is tracking.

Steve had been following deer tracks, and was growing familiar with their habitat and how they traversed the land. I had suggested that as he track, he imagine his arms becoming covered with fur, his head sprouting antlers, and his hands and feet turning into the sharp hooves of the deer. With the lengthened ears of the deer, he would pause often to scan into the distance for subtle sounds that might indicate danger.

Through these and other practices, Steve's relationship with the deer and with the landscape deepened quickly. Each tracking outing became an adventure. Since he had been doing well with the deer, I sensed that "becoming an animal" might serve Steve nicely for transforming his experience at work. The question was, which animal?

The deer are great for teaching us about relaxation and deep listening, but it seemed like Steve needed something to wake him up and energize him in the dull work environment. Then I remembered that Steve had also shared a story with me of some mystery tracks he'd found in the snow. The footprints seemed to bound all over the place, zigging and zagging and disappearing in tunnels under the snow. Hmm, something small with high energy and an insatiable awareness... a weasel. Perfect!

On our next call, I guided Steve into "becoming" a weasel. First, I had him imagine that a weasel had gotten into the room. As he gazed forward in Expanded Vision, I prompted Steve to imagine seeing the weasel in the corner of his eye, darting beneath the furniture, a blur of fur. When I asked him how this made him feel, Steve promptly replied, "Alive!" I knew we had found the right animal for the situation.

Next, I invited Steve to imagine himself shrinking down to weasel size, peering around the room from this vantage point close to the floor. Where could he go for cover to move without being seen? What would draw his attention and interest? Where would he feel safe, where would he feel exposed to danger? How could he get outside if he wanted to leave the building?

After a few minutes of imaginally exploring the house as a weasel, I asked Steve to return to his original perceptual position, growing back to regular size and stepping out of the weasel mind-set, with appreciation for the gifts given, knowing he could return to that awareness in the future when needed.

After a minute of "shaking it off" with some light movement, I asked Steve about his experience and what he discovered. He told me that he felt incredibly energized, and that he was surprised at how his perception of the room had expanded in many new ways.

Over the next few weeks, Steve experimented with "putting on the mind of the weasel" for a few minutes before stepping into the office, or during lunch breaks. He found that his awareness was energized for longer periods throughout the day, and his interactions with co-workers also improved from the mood shift.

Steve had discovered that he could "be Nature" and expand beyond his own usual perceptual range and experience of the world, simply by transforming into one of the animals he had encountered at his Meditation Spot. *Being Nature* is an effective way you can apply the art of *becoming* to real life, everyday situations in order to to enhance your awareness.

Part of what made this experience so powerful for Steve was that he already had some personal connection with the weasel through his tracking adventures (even though he wasn't sure yet exactly whose footprints he was following in the snow, he had experienced the energy and quality of the animal through its tracks).

The more that you build your relationship with the animals and other aspects of Nature around your spot, the more deeply you can draw upon this connection to inspire your creativity.

Likewise, the more that you explore the arts of *Being Nature* and *Becoming*, the more you will discover about the hidden gifts of Nature all around you. For this reason, I have placed this practice at the end of the book. *Being Nature* draws upon all of your previous experiences at your Meditation Spot, and deepens these relationships.

Long ago, the animals could turn into people, and the people could turn into animals...

~ Practice: The Art of Being Nature ~

Now it's time to put *Being Nature* into practice. We will use a special eight day meditation cycle for this journey. The first four days is about identifying and honing a quality you wish to develop, and beginning to awaken it within you. The second four days is about exploring this trait through your connection with the animals and other aspects of Nature.

Phase 1: Inviting Transformation

To start the first phase, make a short list of qualities that you would like to develop in your life. What are some traits that would benefit you the most at this moment in your life — Determination? Relaxed presence? Stealth? Speed and endurance? Gracefulness?

List three to five qualities. Then, pick one that jumps out to you the most in this moment. Set your intention to connect with this trait and activate it more strongly inside yourself at this time.

To add depth to this process, carry this intention with you to your Meditation Spot each day for four days.

Build your focus and energy around the question each day as you hold it lightly in your heart. Spend a few minutes at your spot accessing the state of heart coherence, and then use the appropriate tool for each day as shared below.

~ Day 1 Practice: Identify the Transformation ~

Ponder your current manifested qualities and traits. Bring a notebook and briefly jot down any key thoughts or insights that arise. Where do you feel open, where do you feel stuck? In what ways do you wish to grow?

Examine how this new quality that you've selected might help you to expand your experience of life. Ask yourself:

- Why is this trait calling to me now?
- What is this desire teaching me about myself and my journey in life?
- How will this help me to develop myself as a human being?
- How will this quality help me to serve others more effectively?

These questions are designed to clarify your motivation for change. By asking them, you are walking a trail that leads to greater self-knowledge.

This inquiry also helps you to examine if this transformation is something you really wish to call forth into your life. By the end of the four days, you will have clearly identified the trait that you wish to develop, and already begun the process of activating it in your consciousness.

~ Day 2 Practice: Activate the Shift ~

With your purpose clearly defined, imagine and feel that you have this quality now, and sense what your life feels like as a result.

- If there is a challenge or obstacle you are currently experiencing, imagine yourself empowered by this trait... how does this situation dissolve or transform accordingly?
- Sense how you are now empowered to enjoy new experiences, and how your capacity to help others increases, too. What do you see, hear, feel, smell, and taste in your newly transformed perceptions? Who are the people you encounter, and how are you interacting? What are the places you experience? What activities you are engaged in, and how do you feel while doing them?

By imagining yourself experiencing this trait, you are engaging the neural circuitry that supports the desired experience. By adding in all of your inner senses to this envisioning, you are expanding the map of this trait to reach into diverse areas of your brain. As you imagine the larger effects of this transformation, such as the responses of your family, friends, and co-workers to this positive change, you are anchoring this new trait with even more existing neural nets.

~ Day 3 Practice: Strengthening Your Intention ~

Today you will further strengthen the vision and energy of the trait you are awakening inside yourself. Again, restate your intention. You might even say it out loud, with conviction!

Envision yourself immersed in this new quality, enjoying the sense of accomplishment and satisfaction that comes with its presence in your life. Smile and feel your life healing and transforming as you step further into this new experience of yourself.

By re-experiencing this new condition, you are strengthening the neural web that you have already established. Quality repetition builds stronger neural pathways, making it more likely for you to activate this quality in the midst of your regular daily life.

~ Day 4 Practice: Vision & Release ~

On this fourth day, spend a little more time envisioning yourself enjoying this new quality in your life. Most importantly, *feel* the impact it makes for you and for those you care for. Revisit the reason *why* behind your desire:

- What's really at stake here? What's driving this change? If you have a lot of work-related stress in your life that you tend to carry home, how would it feel to let go of it and enjoy a deep state of peace each evening?
- How would this personal transformation affect your relationship with your spouse, or with your kids, or with your friends? *Why* does this change matter?

Smile into your heart as you feel this energy build. Then, release your intention to Nature, trusting that your process is already unfolding. Realize and feel the positive ripples of your intention moving out in the world. Again, keep a watch on any flashes of insight, dreams, conversations, or encounters in the days to come.

Phase 2: Learning From the Animals

With this foundation in place, you are ready to move into Phase 2. During these next four days, you'll further empower your new trait by exploring its connection to an animal that lives in your area. Now, we're entering the realm of the shaman. Like Samuel L. Jackson said in his classic line in *Jurassic Park*, "Hold onto your butts, people!"

While the animals can help you access your own capacities to nourish and heal yourself, they can also take you out of your comfort zones and stretch you in new directions. Every animal carries both its positives and negatives (not in a "good" or "bad" sense, but in terms of tendency and habit); what they teach has a lot to say about your current state of being, shining a light on both your gifts and shadows.

Bears look cute and cuddly, and carry a profound healing presence, but when their curiosity gets aroused with a tantalizing smell of food, they can tear a place up until they are satisfied. They'll knock down bird feeders and strew garbage bins about, leaving a trail of chaos in the wake of their feeding.

How could adopting the bear's insatiable drive to experience life support any healing or change you may need? Or, is there any over-indulgence or extremity in your life that Bear may be nudging you to consider? When Bear comes around, what is she saying? The animals and their actions can mirror what's already moving inside yourself, serving as potent reminders to look within.

With any connection that arises, ask yourself, "What is this experience teaching me? What is this perception mirroring for me? What do I need to pay attention to right now about myself or my surroundings?"

Consider these lessons of polarity during your interactions with Nature. The positive polarity of trait development is a building force, harmonizing and enhancing your life. Like attracts like, so if you are surrounded by loving people, you will likely mirror these emotional patterns. You can also cultivate positive traits by studying and emulating positive role models, and by surrounding yourself with examples of the patterns you seek to develop.

Every animal displays aspects of this positive polarity that you can study and learn from, even if this is not obvious to you at first glance. Most people will probably not think of "love" when imagining an alligator, an animal with a reputation for toughness and reptilian coldness. Yet, a mother gator will fiercely protect her young from danger.

Philosophers will debate whether that response is love or simply instinct, but I personally sense a demonstration of love in such caring. This connection process is really what *you* make of it. As you connect with a trait through an animal role model, you really are discovering and activating a quality whose potential already dwells inside yourself. In this way, the Outer Nature around you leads towards realization of your Inner Nature.

Because the forces of opposites are constantly at play in the realm of Nature, development of a quality can also come about through experience of its opposite. This is the teaching capacity of the *negative polarity* at work. Skunk, for example, has a lot to teach about developing confidence. Very few animals will mess with this squat, slow moving mammal. The skunk can take its time and walk with impunity because it knows it is respected. The skunk only sprays when it really has to, but when it does, watch out!

This animal's teaching expresses as you learn to become secure in your own self. This confidence may come about through situations that require you to stand in your own unique skills and power, which may not always be pleasant. These are true rites of passage that you must learn to navigate on your way to discovering the place of personal truth. Through experience, with skunk as your teacher, you learn to hold your center and your vision, even if those around you would try to knock you off balance.

Setting Intentions

This example illustrates the importance of honing your intent with clear understanding. As one Wisdom Keeper shared with me, "If you set the intention to have strength in your life, how will you get it? By being knocked down and having to get back up? Therefore, consider what you are really intending, and how you would truly like to reach your goals."

As you set your intentions, consider what the most positive, joyful route might be towards developing the qualities you seek. When tough times come up, it's also an opportunity to look within and ask what hidden gifts the situation might be calling forth from you in order to move forward.

Ultimately, though, your deepest Self decides what you will experience, so you get what you need (even if your ego doesn't always like or understand why it's happening at the time), and your inmost intention guides your way.

The time you've taken in Phase One to clarify what you truly need will now reap further dividends as you connect with an animal teacher. With this greater context in mind, let's get into the practices for this second cycle of meditation.

~ Day 5 Practice: Meeting an Animal Ally ~

Go to your Meditation Spot today with the intent to connect with an animal that will support you in growing your chosen quality in a healthful, joyous way (later, you might feel called to work with stones, plants, trees, creeks, clouds, and more. For now, stick with an animal for this first experience, unless you are called otherwise).

- As you settle into your spot, slip first into Expanded Vision to open your field of perception.
- Next, move into the place of inner coherence to anchor yourself in a peaceful, relaxed state.
- Once relaxed, presence your intention in your heart space for a moment. Smile and breathe life into your intention until it feels vibrant and empowered.
- Then, with a sense of wonder and curiosity, release your intention to connect with an animal helper. Let your intention ripple out in all directions around you, knowing it is being heard by the realms of Nature.

As you hold your intention, or at any point after you release it, you may get a sudden flash of creativity indicating that your awareness is being drawn towards a certain animal. This flash can come as an image of the animal in your mind's eye, a memory of a past experience with the animal, or at times as a physical encounter with the animal at some point in your day. Simply rest in your awareness, observing whatever information comes through.

Once you've honed in on an animal to connect with, now it's time to open a conversation. Though at times a physical interaction with the animal may occur, more often, this exchange takes place within the imaginal field of Inner Nature. You may choose to remain in Expanded Vision with eyes open, or if it's more comfortable, to close your eyes.

At this point, you may envision the animal interacting with you. Send out an imaginal greeting. Envision yourself talking to the animal; introduce yourself, and explain what your intention is. Note what the animal does in response, and sense the quality of *being* it is displaying to you at this time; there is a lesson in this for you to discover.

Ask the animal to show you things about its life and what it can teach you. Allow your imaginal power to deepen and connect you with the animal's gifts as the conversation unfolds. As you get further into the day-dreamy state, the imagery may intensify and take on a life of its own; observe relaxedly and see where the journey leads you.

As the visit comes to a natural close, share your thanks for the gifts of understanding and well-being the animal offers you. Invite the animal to visit again in your meditations and in the dreamtime.

When you get home, write an account in your journal of anything that happened or that stood out to you. Reaffirm your intention tonight as you go to sleep, and be on the lookout for any dream encounters with your animal friend. You have a new ally who can teach you in many ways.

~ Day 6 Practice: A Walk of Discovery ~

We've existed side-by-side with the animals long before our species developed language; animals quickly evoke our deeper emotional and instinctive selves. Family crests, team mascots, and even caffeine beverage logos draw upon the primal power of animal imagery to summon enthusiasm and elicit our attention. In this meditation cycle, you are learning to use this instinctual "mind-hack" to enhance your own self-awareness and capacities.

Imagine a buffalo plowing through chest-deep snow, and you can instantly tap into a powerful full-sensory mental code for "determination." Or, envision a red-tailed hawk soaring circles on a windy day, and realize a natural code for the essence of "easeful grace." Notice how the activity of the animal activates a feeling and an energy within you when you envision it in motion. This feeling is evidence of this awesome mind-hack at work.

The animal that you're connecting with in this meditation cycle will become a powerful focal point for your awareness. The animal helps you access the change in perception that you are intending, which provides leverage for your new trait to develop more fully. Just like Steve did with the weasel, you can envision yourself becoming this animal, experiencing the world through its senses. When you do this, you'll gain new insights and an expanded mindset that can help you creatively meet life in new ways. In fact, we are gradually building towards that experience in this eight-day process.

Today, you're going to go on a walk with your animal! This practice will grow your capacity to envision, while teaching you new ways of understanding the landscape. Before you step foot towards your Meditation Area, pause and get into your senses. Expand your vision and hearing, sense your body, and tune into the landscape. Become aware of the four directions, the earth and sky, and yourself in the center of them all.

Once you are present and relaxed, extend your intent and invite your animal friend to come to you. Envision the animal next to you. Remember your intention to awaken the new trait you wish to develop. Request that the animal help you develop understanding of this trait in a healthy, joyous way. Feel the trait coming alive within you, subtly (or not so subtly) shifting your perception.

Ask the animal to teach you something about this trait today, by showing you how it interacts with the landscape — how does the animal move through the area? What does the area offer to the animal — food, shelter, water, concealment? Envision the animal moving through the landscape, and follow along as you walk. Realize that the animal's way of being is telling you something deeper about the trait you are developing. On this walk, you may or may not end up at your usual Meditation Spot.

Do keep track of where you are, so that you don't get lost or do anything too silly (true story — I once followed a live striped skunk around my college campus, taking notes on everything it was getting into. My neighbors had their door open during dinner and it walked right in, with me trailing ten feet behind! They were surprised by the skunk, but perhaps even more so by the crazy long-haired naturalist following behind it with notebook in hand. The two of us proceeded through the room, past the stock-still neighbors, and out the front door, which was also wide open. I still wonder what they thought about the whole thing...but I did learn a lot about the skunk that day!).

Particularly, tune into the *feeling* the animal's behavior evokes in you. Is the animal tentative, or aggressive and powerful in its motion? If tentative, how does the animal blend into its place, and where does it feel most comfortable? What does the animal cue into with its senses? Simply go with the flow, and notice how the animal draws you into a new awareness of your place and your self.

When the session feels complete, thank the animal and allow it to go back to wherever it came from, with the invitation to return again to help you in your life when needed. Take notes in your journal about what happened, and what you learned today. Again, set the intention to connect with the animal in your dreams, and be ready to catch any new stories when you awaken in the morning.

~ Day 7 Practice: Putting on the Mind of the Animal ~

So far, you've met your animal friend, and you've walked with it and discovered new insights about your place. Today is a chance to *become* the animal and step further into its unique gifts and teachings.

Like wearing a mask, San Bushman trackers talk about "putting on the mind of the animal" when they track. When a tracker puts on the antelope's mind, she is resonating with the animal's essence.

Because of this intentional filtering, the tracker pays special attention to the things that attract or repel her as an antelope — the succulent greens that call her with their protein, and the dangerous places where predators could lie in wait.

The tracker becomes attuned to the animal's unique way of being, and then the landscape sings out with the trails and sign of the antelope. This is a practice you can explore, too, even if you don't have a long set of tracks to follow.

- Arrive at your Meditation Spot. Attune to the four directions, earth above, sky below, and yourself in the center of the flow of life around you. Expand your senses.
- Invite your animal ally to appear once again, and re-presence your intention to cultivate the desired trait you are working with at this time. Again, take a moment to feel this trait coming alive in you and informing your awareness.
- Request now that the animal may merge with you, so that you can experience the world through its senses and further develop your understanding.
- Envision and sense yourself merging with the animal, like two vibrational spheres of being overlapping with each other in space and time. Hold your hands at chest level, as you look ahead in Expanded Vision. In your peripheral vision, see your hands and envision them becoming covered with fur, growing hooves or claws.

Feel the softness or coarseness of the fur with one hand
running along the other.

- Envision your face transforming into the face of the
  animal. Feel your snout lengthening, your ears
  growing, and your teeth changing shape. Feel the
  pattern of the animal's face on your own face.
- Feel the rest of your body changing into the shape of
  the animal as you become imbued with its qualities.
  Sense your tail, and envision it flicking and moving.
  Feel your feet as the feet of the animal.

Now that your transformation is complete, test your senses.
What is your attention drawn towards on the landscape? Go
where you are drawn to. Move at a pace that feels right for this
animal.

As you move, how do the birds and other animals relate to you
— do they alarm? Do they remain calm? What are you doing as
you move — do you relaxedly forage for greens here and there?
Do you trot through an area looking to flush prey? Do you hide in
the shadows in concealment? The lessons you learned on yester-
day's walk will now help you step further into the world of the
animal, yielding further insights.

As you move and interact with your environment in this way,
notice how you feel. Do you feel strong, or vulnerable in certain
places? Where? What is the overall feeling you experience as this
animal? How does this feeling inform and empower the trait you
are cultivating? Allow the energy you feel in this state to infuse
your being with aliveness.

When you feel complete, sense the two spheres of animal and
human parting from each other, each mutually enriched through
the experience. Sense your perceived body returning to its usual
state, with the fur gone and your features back to "normal." Thank

the animal for the day's teachings, and invite your friend to visit again when needed.

Take a few deep breaths and release anything that needs releasing. Sense your heartbeat for a moment, and then stamp your feet on the ground a bit to ground yourself. Be aware again of the four directions around you, the vast sky above, the earth beneath your feet, and yourself held and supported in the center. Return home and journal about the day's events.

The Importance of Closure

By the way, don't skip out on the closure piece of this experience. I learned the importance of "taking off the mind of the animal" many years ago in a funny but instructive way.

It was a cold overcast day, at the end of a long winter that wouldn't quite give way to the spring. We'd had fresh snow a few days before, followed by several meltings and freezings cycling one after the other. Realizing it was probably the last chance of the year to track in the snow, I went in search of whatever prints I could find that were left to trail.

At the edge of a red pine forest bordering a farm field, I picked up a coyote trail. The tracks showed the animal was trotting along, covering ground. I started jogging lightly alongside the trail, looking to the horizon in Expanded Vision.

Allowing my peripheral vision to keep the tracks in view, I would glance down for more information whenever a change occurred in the track pattern. With each step, my consciousness morphed further into the mind of the coyote. I could feel my bushy dark-tipped tail and long muzzle, my strong toe-pads and claws gripping the crunchy snow for traction.

The snow was patchy, with prints evident for 25 yard stretches at the most, disappearing often into forest leaf litter. The best-preserved prints occurred under the protective shade of the hemlock trees, whose dark boughs kept the sunlight at bay.

During these stretches, I noted which kinds of gaps and openings the animal preferred. I used my vector and momentum to guide me forward on the long patches of trail when the snow disappeared under the open canopy of the red oaks and maples. After a couple hours of trailing, my senses and awareness became very attuned to the movement of the coyote; the tracks had opened a doorway into a powerful moving meditation.

As evening set in, the sky grew dark and I realized home was still quite a ways to go from this place. Reluctantly, I knew it was time to leave the coyote's trail and head back while there was still some light to work with. As I walked quickly through the hemlock forest, a strange thing happened.

Alarm calls sounded, coming from various songbirds around me. Chickadees and titmice and even kinglets were uttering a frantic flurry of tones. Was there a predator nearby? Suddenly, I realized the birds were alarming at *me*; in fact, the foraging flock had swarmed around me, directing their angst right at my location. This had never happened before. What was going on?

In that moment, sensing my focused posture and fast movement, I noticed that I was still moving as a hungry coyote on the hunt, and that I hadn't actually "let go" of that connection from the day's trailing. To remedy this, I took a deep breath, thanking the coyote and releasing myself from the coyote mind as I exhaled fully.

Instantly, my posture shifted and the feeling in my body changed to a more relaxed state. With this inner shift, the birds stopped alarming and went back to their last few minutes of feeding before the darkness set it. The response from the birds to my inner transformation was palpable. Since that day, I have always made it a point to consciously shift out of the "vibe" of whatever I've been tracking, and re-center myself in my own base-line state.

~ Day 8 Practice: Application ~

Today's your chance to test your mettle. You're going to take what you've learned and apply it in "real life." What's one moment during your day when you'd like your new trait to really shine — that particular time and place when you know you'll need some extra resolve, more inner peace and spaciousness, or whatever it is you've been cultivating?

Set the intention now that when that moment arises, you will be ready to meet it. Put out the request to your animal ally to help you in that moment by invigorating the quality you need to succeed. Send your awareness forward for a moment and envision yourself in that situation. Sense and feel yourself merging with your animal ally in that moment, filled with the qualities you need to meet your goals. Feel the satisfaction and joy and of success. Take a deep breath to charge this intent with life, and as you exhale, know that it will be so.

During the day, take small pauses to maintain your presence and awareness. Slip into Expanded Vision each time you walk through a doorway. Pause outside your house or place of work as you enter or leave and listen into the distance for a moment. Take a deep Complete Breath or two every hour.

Know that these little "resets" are giving you extra fuel to maintain your internal well-being. Then, when the moment arrives, you are ready to rise to the occasion. When you most need your new trait, the momentum provided by your animal ally (and all of your training) will be there to support you.

Sense your connection with your ally in this moment, and feel the trait emanating forth from you. Let this energy support whatever you've intended, and simply *be* and allow the success to manifest.

Some might call this event *the moment of challenge*, but I like to think of it as a *moment of opportunity*. These are the times when we get a chance to define how we are being in life, and to step forward with mindful intention. Sometimes we wildly succeed, and other times we don't engage the way we would have liked to. Either way, it's a chance to learn more about ourselves as we journey towards who we are becoming next.

At the end of the day, review what happened:

- How did priming yourself in the morning affect the your capacity to meet the challenge later in the day?
- What feelings, sensations, and energy did you experience when you faced your challenge?
- How did it go? What happened?
- What is this moment teaching you? What worked well? What would you do differently the next time you apply this process?
- Is there anything you want to ask your animal ally about what happened?
- What other places in your life could benefit from this application?

Tending To Your Animal Ally

Traditional shamans in many cultures recommend periodically *feeding* your animal ally. This can be done by occasionally putting out a small bit of food in honor of your animal, and also enjoying the food yourself. Select something that your animal would like to eat.

You can *exercise* your animal by doing activities or going places that your animal enjoys.[1] Invite your ally to walk beside you or merge with you during portions of these outings. Because your animal helper reflects an aspect of your own essence, doing these things will nourish these parts of yourself, too.

Bringing it All Together

You can see now how all of the skills in this book come together in this section on *Being Nature*. Once you've experienced this process for yourself, you'll have put into practice the fusion of the realms of Inner Nature and Outer Nature. You'll have experienced how these seemingly dual aspects of Nature dynamically interweave and affect one another.

Some readers might wonder about the nature of the animal ally. Does this being dwell purely in your mind, or does it exist in its own right on some ethereal level, with its own volition and existence? Ask three different people, and you will be sure to get three very different answers.

The psychologist might argue, "We are simply dealing with our own mind stuff here in the guise of a symbol that we can relate to effectively." The shaman would smile and say, "Everything is alive, whether a stone or a person or whatever else. Besides, don't ask me... find out for yourself!" The practitioner of non-dual awareness might offer, "Ultimately all manifestations are expressions of the One reality beyond all form."

From each vantage point, the answer becomes obvious in its own way. The teachings of the Great Dance remind us that there is room for fluidity of thought in life. No matter what we are engaging with, can we keep our awareness open and flexible enough to admit light beyond the limited filters of our beliefs and prejudices?

Long ago, the Ch'an Buddhist master Qingyuan Weixin wrote: "Before I had studied Ch'an for thirty years, I saw mountains as mountains, and rivers as rivers. When I arrived at a more intimate knowledge, I came to the point where I saw that mountains are not mountains, and rivers are not rivers. But now that I have got its very substance, I am at rest. For it's just that I see mountains once again as mountains, and rivers once again as rivers."

Truly, you are one with the pond, with the stone that splashes through it, and with the ripples that move across the water's surface and in the depths. You are one with the forest, as you are with the animals that roam within it, whether on the visible landscape or in its mysterious Inner pathways. Through participating in the ecology of Nature's imagination, you can discover your own deepest purpose and story, and infuse every day with adventure and wonder.

The practices shared in this book demonstrate that by harmonizing consciously with the forces within and around you, you can more effectively create a joyful path for yourself and those you care for in your life. These tools have served me well over the years, as they have done for those before me, and my wish is that they may do the same for you.

By meditating in Nature, may you directly realize your interdependence and connection with all of life. Have fun along the way! Be well, and enjoy your journeys as you explore and expand into your fullest potential of Conscious Nature.
—*Josh Lane*

SECTION IV

APPENDICES

Contents:

APPENDIX A. LIST OF ALL PRACTICES

Hone your Conscious Nature skills by choosing a routine each day from the 36+ core practices shared in this book:

Chapter 2. Going Into Nature: Researching Local Hazards

Scanning for Natural Hazards

Chapter 3. How Meditating in Nature Helps Us Feel & Be Our Best

Taking a Restorative Nature Walk

Chapter 4. Finding a Meditation Spot in Nature: Mapping Your Meditation Spot

Tension Check

APPENDIX B. PRACTICE JOURNAL TEMPLATE

Keep a record of your experiences & set goals for your practice with this Daily Practice Journal.

Download a printable version:

https://www.consciousnature.net/readers-extras

Day # ___ of ___. Date ___/___/___/ .

Time: _____ Session Length: _____

Today's Intention:

_____
_____
_____
_____
_____
_____

Practices/Meditations:

_____

_____

_____

_____

_____

_____

Outer Nature Observations:

_____

_____

_____

_____

_____

_____

_____

_____

Inner Nature Observations:

_____

_____

_____

_____

_____

_____

_____

_____

Lessons Learned/Key Takeaways:

_____

_____

_____

_____

_____

_____

_____

_____

_____

_____

_____

Next Steps:

_____

_____

_____

_____

_____

_____

_____

_____

_____

_____

_____

APPENDIX C. PRACTICES & RELATED BRAIN STATES

Peruse this list for awareness practices and meditations that support each of the five primary brain states.

Activities in this Book that Support Delta States:

- **Going to your Meditation Spot (Chapter 4).** If you have a nice comfy spot where you can nap, catch some z's in the great outdoors; take a dip into delta for essential rest and rejuvenation. The afternoon is a natural time to recoup.
- **Tuning the Senses & Listen Once More, with Feeling (Chapter 13).** Interacting with unexpected sounds, or selecting a particular sound to focus on amidst others, can engage delta activity.

Activities in this Book that Support Theta States:

- **Expanded Vision & Passive Awareness (Chapter 6).** As your practice deepens you may begin to tap into theta brainwaves.
- **The Mind Walk (Chapter 8) & The Art of Becoming (Chapter 9).** Internal imagery comes to life as you relax and engage the theta state.
- **Remembering How to Play (Chapter 9).** Play is a natural state of flow that promotes theta activity.
- **Radiance of the Inner Sun (Chapter 12) & The Space Between Sounds (Chapter 14).** The spatial awareness that enfolds your connection with the earth beneath you and the Sun above can open your awareness into theta states of meditation. Likewise, tracking the spatial relationships in the soundscape can also awaken deep states of being.

Activities in this Book that Support Alpha States:

- **Restorative Nature Walk (chapter 3) & Going to Your Meditation Spot (chapter 4).** Simply being in green spaces boosts your alpha waves.
- **Expanded Vision & Passive Awareness (chapter 6).** Access whole brain alpha synchrony.
- **Fox Walking (Chapter 8).** Walking meditation is an engaging pathway to deeper states of presence.
- **The Art of Becoming (Chapter 9).** Relaxed states of imagination awaken alpha waves.

- **Getting Your Earth On (Chapter 10).** Grounding promotes alpha states.
- **The Complete Breath (Chapter 11).** Deep breathing is a potent way to access relaxed states.
- **Radiance of the Inner Sun (Chapter 12).** Heart coherence supports the mind to relax.
- **Listen Once More, with Feeling (Chapter 13) & the Space Between Sounds (Chapter 14).** The spatial awareness afforded through deep listening may support alpha synchrony.

Activities in this Book that Support Beta States:

- **Active Awareness (Chapter 6).** Engages top-down attention circuits.
- **Asking Questions & Reflecting (all of the practices in Chapter 7).** Engages frontal lobe and executive network activity, and promotes integration with sensory and memory circuits across the brain.
- **Fox Walking (Chapter 8).** Slow, intentional movement may support SMR response.
- **Current Needs Inventory & Setting Your Intention (Chapter 11).** Engages frontal lobe/executive network and connections with deeper emotional circuits.

Activities in this Book that Support Gamma States:

- **The Power of Curiosity & Wandering, Soaking It In (Chapter 6); Empower Your Motivation & Curiosity (Chapter 7).** Gamma is stimulated by new observations, which are fueled by curiosity and presence.
- **Meditation in Motion (Chapter 8).** Moving meditations are a great way to engage your senses, supporting gamma connectivity.
- **Current Needs Inventory (Chapter 11).** Emotions are linked to increased gamma waves, which help you tune into what's moving within your inner world.
- **Expanding Through the Senses (Chapter 13) & Further Expansion (Chapter 14).** All of the practices in these two chapters are designed to nourish your sensory connections, which rely on gamma coordination to make a unified experience of the world.

APPENDIX D. HOLISTIC MEDITATION SEQUENCE

Practice the key exercises as listed from the following chapters to create your own daily holistic Inner and Outer Nature meditation sequence.

Suggested timings for each piece of the sequence are also included.

Arrival:
Mindfully approach and arrive at your Meditation Spot (10-15 minutes)
See Chapter 8, "Moving Mindfully in Nature"
& Chapter 11, "I'm Here - Arriving to Meditate"

Tuning In:

Activate heart coherence through internal meditation (10-15 minutes)
See Chapter 12, "Tuning In"

Expanding Out:
Broaden your awareness with a Sensory Meditation (10 minutes)
See Chapter 13, "Expanding Through the Senses"
& Chapter 14, "Further Expansion Into Nature's Conversation"

Gathering & Returning:
Center and integrate your experience (5-10 minutes)
See Chapter 15, "Gathering & Returning"

At Home Practices:
Journal & research to support your field awareness (5-15 minutes)
See Chapter 7, "Flex Your Question Muscle"

ACKNOWLEDGMENTS

Thank you to my family for always encouraging me to follow my vision, and for all the continuing support along the way.

Thank you to my mentors and teachers who have shared the ancient (and emerging) wisdom teachings that have helped me to more deeply realize my primal connection with the Nature within and around me:

Special gratitude to Jon Young and Tom Brown, Jr. for your dedication to helping the next generations connect with the language of Nature (and thank you Jon for the timeless mentoring wisdom you've shared with me over the past two decades). Big thanks to Mark Morey and Scott Eldridge for initiating the journey and helping me establish strong taproots of nature connection and mentoring skills, right from the start.

Much appreciation to Gilbert Walking Bull for role modeling so many times that "Nothing is impossible with the Great Spirit!" Thank you to Xanama for sharing your oneness with the Kalahari and the *beingness* expressed in your presence as we tracked together. Gratitude to Salvatore Gencarelle for sharing hard-learned healing wisdom, and to Fredd Lenn for teaching me to vision forward from the deepest power of the heart.

Thank you to my friends, teachers, and ancestors of the Tao who pass forward good practices that remind us of the unity of body, heart, and spirit, and of our mysterious place bridging the earth and heavens; thank you especially to Lee Holden, Mantak Chia, and One Cloud; to H.B. and to B.P. Chan; and to Wendy Ballen, Sid Fontana, and Chong I Chung.

Thank you to my relatives in the world of Nature who are my teachers and inspiration each day, from the Earth to the sky and beyond, to the spark of Creativity that we each bring forward with our dreams and gifts.

Thank you to those who have helped me bring this book into existence. Gratitude to first draft readers Siddika Angle, Ken Clarkson, Matthew Fogarty, and Matt Jarman for your essential constructive feedback on the initial manuscript. Big thanks to my sweetheart Rebekah for your patience with me throughout the many late nights and early mornings of writing this book, for your love, and for sharing the inspiration and beauty you find in Nature with all who cross your path.

Thank you to stellar content editor Melissa Kirk for helping me refine and shape the storyline, and to artists and designers Fabiana Treré for the meditation posture line drawings, Tyler Lieberthal for the brain wave EEG graphics, Melissa Glorieux (TheRitualMandala@Instagram) for the perfect cover photo, and Rebecca LeGates for fantastic cover design.

Thank you to those who have honored me with the chance to share what I have learned along the way, and to the readers of the present and future who feel called to put these skills to use.

NOTES

1. We Are Nature

1. Prechtel, Martin. *Secrets of the Talking Jaguar: A Mayan Shaman's Journey to the Heart of the Indigenous Soul.* Tarcher, 1998.
2. Nabhan, Gary Paul. *Cultures of Habitat.* Counterpoint, 1997.

2. Going Into Nature

1. Lovgren, Stefan. "Chimps, Humans 96 Percent the Same, Study Says." *National Geographic* website. Internet article, published August 31, 2005. Retrieved online October 15, 2018: https://news.nationalgeographic.com/news/2005/08/chimps-humans-96-percent-the-same-gene-study-finds/
2. Cheng, Ze, et al. "A genome-wide comparison of recent chimpanzee and human segmental duplications." *Nature* 437.7055 (2005): 88.
3. Simakov, Oleg, et al. "Hemichordate genomes and deuterostome origins." *Nature* 527.7579 (2015): 459.
4. Becker, Gavin de. *The Gift of Fear: Survival Signals That Protect Us From Violence.* London: Bloomsbury (1997).
5. Brown, Tom. *The Science and Art of Tracking.* Berkley Trade, 1999.

3. How Meditating in Nature Helps Us Feel & Be Our Best

1. Feit, Noah. "Study Reveals Most-Googled Medical Symptoms By State." *The Chicago Tribune.* Newspaper article, Oct. 2, 2018. http://www.chicagotribune.com/lifestyles/health/ct-hlth-most-googled-medical-issue-1002-story.html. Accessed 10.01.2018.
2. Benson, Herbert, and William Proctor. *Relaxation Revolution: The Science and Genetics of Mind Body Healing.* Simon and Schuster, 2010. Page 28.
3. Park, Bum Jin, et al. "The physiological effects of Shinrin-yoku (taking in the forest atmosphere or forest bathing): evidence from field experiments in 24 forests across Japan." *Environmental Health and Preventive Medicine* 15.1 (2010): 18.
4. Li, Q., et al. "Forest bathing enhances human natural killer activity and expression of anti-cancer proteins." *International Journal of Immunopathology and Pharmacology* 20.2_suppl (2007): 3-8.

5. Sop Shin, Won. "The influence of forest view through a window on job satisfaction and job stress." *Scandinavian Journal of Forest Research* 22.3 (2007): 248-253.

6. Berman, Marc G., John Jonides, and Stephen Kaplan. "The cognitive benefits of interacting with nature." *Psychological Science* 19.12 (2008): 1207-1212.

7. Faber Taylor, Andrea, and Frances E. Kuo. "Children with attention deficits concentrate better after walk in the park." *Journal of Attention Disorders* 12.5 (2009): 402-409.

8. Hartig, Terry, Marlis Mang, and Gary W. Evans. "Restorative effects of natural environment experiences." *Environment and Behavior* 23.1 (1991): 3-26.

9. Atchley, Ruth Ann, David L. Strayer, and Paul Atchley. "Creativity in the wild: Improving creative reasoning through immersion in natural settings." *PloS One* 7.12 (2012): e51474.

10. Kaplan, Stephen. "The restorative benefits of nature: Toward an integrative framework." *Journal of Environmental Psychology* 15.3 (1995): 169-182.

11. Kaplan, Stephen. "Meditation, restoration, and the management of mental fatigue." *Environment and Behavior* 33.4 (2001): 480-506.

12. Lazar, Sara W., et al. "Meditation experience is associated with increased cortical thickness." *Neuroreport* 16.17 (2005): 1893.

4. Finding a Meditation Spot in Nature

1. Kaplan, Stephen. "Meditation, restoration, and the management of mental fatigue." *Environment and Behavior* 33.4 (2001): 480-506.

2. Kaplan, Stephen. "The restorative benefits of nature: Toward an integrative framework." *Journal of Environmental Psychology* 15.3 (1995): 169-182.

3. Berman, Marc G., John Jonides, and Stephen Kaplan. "The cognitive benefits of interacting with nature." *Psychological Science* 19.12 (2008): 1207-1212.

4. Young, Jon, Ellen Haas, and Evan McGown. *Coyote's Guide to Connecting with Nature: For Kids of All Ages and Their Mentors.* OWLink Media/Wilderness Awareness School, 2008.

5. Li, Qing. "Effect of forest bathing trips on human immune function." *Environmental Health and Preventive Medicine* 15.1 (2010): 9.

6. Young, Jon. *What the Robin Knows: How Birds Reveal the Secrets of the Natural World.* Houghton-Mifflin Harcourt, 2012.

7. Tomatis, Alfred. *The Ear and the Voice.* Scarecrow Press, 2005. Page 6.

8. Wilson, T., and A. Tomatis. "Chant: The Healing Power of Voice and Ear." *Music Physician For Times to Come: An Anthology.* Wheaton, Illinois: Quest Books (1991): 11-28.

9. Alfred Tomatis in *Super-Learning 2000* by Sheila Ostrander & Lynn Schroeder with Nancy Ostrander. Dell, New York. 1994. Pages 92-95.

5. The Nature of Action & Stillness

1. Schutter, Dennis JLG, and Gennady G. Knyazev. "Cross-frequency coupling of brain oscillations in studying motivation and emotion." *Motivation and Emotion* 36.1 (2012): 46-54.
2. Collura, Thomas F., and Jon A. Frederick, eds. *Handbook of Clinical QEEG and Neurotherapy.* Taylor & Francis, 2016.
3. Steriade, Mircea, David A. McCormick, and Terrence J. Sejnowski. "Thalamo-cortical oscillations in the sleeping and aroused brain." *Science* 262.5134 (1993): 679-685.
4. Hiltunen, Tuija, et al. "Infra-slow EEG fluctuations are correlated with resting-state network dynamics in fMRI." *Journal of Neuroscience* 34.2 (2014): 356-362.
5. Hofle, Nina, et al. "Regional cerebral blood flow changes as a function of delta and spindle activity during slow wave sleep in humans." *Journal of Neuroscience* 17.12 (1997): 4800-4808.
6. Başar-Eroglu, Canan, et al. "P300-response: possible psychophysiological correlates in delta and theta frequency channels. A review." *International Journal of Psychophysiology* 13.2 (1992): 161-179.
7. Sivananda, Swami. "The Three Avasthas." The Divine Life Society website. Internet article, retrieved November 1, 2018: http://sivanandaonline.org/public_html/?cmd=displaysection&section_id=851
8. Klimesch, Wolfgang. "EEG alpha and theta oscillations reflect cognitive and memory performance: a review and analysis." *Brain Research Reviews* 29.2-3 (1999): 169-195.
9. Knyazev, Gennady G. "Motivation, emotion, and their inhibitory control mirrored in brain oscillations." *Neuroscience & Biobehavioral Reviews* 31.3 (2007): 377-395.
10. Cantero, Jose L., et al. "Sleep-dependent θ oscillations in the human hippocampus and neocortex." *Journal of Neuroscience* 23.34 (2003): 10897-10903.
11. Neher, Andrew. "Auditory driving observed with scalp electrodes in normal subjects." *Electroencephalography and Clinical Neurophysiology* 13.3 (1961): 449-451.
12. Maxwell, Melinda. "Abstract: Effects of Rhythmic Drumming On EEG and Subjective Experience." Retrieved on November 18, 2018 from https://web.stanford.edu/group/brainwaves/2006/MaxfieldABSTRACT.pdf
13. Collura, Thomas F., and Jon A. Frederick, eds. *Ibid.,* page 101.
14. Kirk, Ian J., and James C. Mackay. "The role of theta-range oscillations in synchronising and integrating activity in distributed mnemonic networks." *Cortex* 39.4-5 (2003): 993-1008.
15. Buzsáki, György. "Theta rhythm of navigation: link between path integration and landmark navigation, episodic and semantic memory." *Hippocampus* 15.7 (2005): 827-840.
16. Bjørk, Marte Helene, et al. "Interictal quantitative EEG in migraine: a blinded controlled study." *The Journal of Headache and Pain* 10.5 (2009): 331-339.
17. Collura, Thomas F., and Jon A. Frederick, eds. *Ibid.,* page 101.

18. Walker, Jonathan E. "QEEG-guided neurofeedback for recurrent migraine headaches." *Clinical EEG and Neuroscience* 42.1 (2011): 59-61.

19. Aftanas, L. I., and S. A. Golocheikine. "Human anterior and frontal midline theta and lower alpha reflect emotionally positive state and internalized attention: high-resolution EEG investigation of meditation." *Neuroscience Letters* 310.1 (2001): 57-60.

20. Csikszentmihalyi, Mihaly, and Isabella Csikszentmihalyi. *Beyond Boredom and Anxiety*. Vol. 721. San Francisco: Jossey-Bass, 1975.

21. Katahira, Kenji, et al. "EEG Correlates of the Flow State: A Combination of Increased Frontal Theta and Moderate Frontocentral Alpha Rhythm in the Mental Arithmetic Task." *Frontiers in Psychology* 9 (2018): 300.

22. Sadaghiani, Sepideh, et al. "Intrinsic connectivity networks, alpha oscillations, and tonic alertness: a simultaneous electroencephalography/functional magnetic resonance imaging study." *Journal of Neuroscience* 30.30 (2010): 10243-10250.

23. Goldman, Robin I., et al. "Simultaneous EEG and fMRI of the alpha rhythm." *Neuroreport* 13.18 (2002): 2487.

24. Ulrich, Roger S. "Natural versus urban scenes: Some psychophysiological effects." *Environment and Behavior* 13.5 (1981): 523-556.

25. Nobre, Anna C., Anling Rao, and Gail N. Owen. "L-theanine, a natural constituent in tea, and its effect on mental state." *Asia Pacific Journal of Clinical Nutrition* 17.S1 (2008): 167-168.

26. Klimesch, Wolfgang. "Alpha-band oscillations, attention, and controlled access to stored information." *Trends in Cognitive Sciences* 16.12 (2012): 606-617.

27. Klimesch, Wolfgang. "Memory processes, brain oscillations and EEG synchronization." *International Journal of Psychophysiology* 24.1-2 (1996): 61-100.

28. Klimesch, Wolfgang. "EEG alpha and theta oscillations reflect cognitive and memory performance: a review and analysis." *Brain Research Reviews* 29.2-3 (1999): 169-195.

29. Vakalopoulos, Costa. "The EEG as an index of neuromodulator balance in memory and mental illness." *Frontiers in Neuroscience* 8 (2014): 63.

30. Lind-Kyle, Patt. *Heal Your Mind, Rewire Your Brain*. Energy Psychology Press, 2010.

31. Buschman, Timothy J., and Earl K. Miller. "Top-down versus bottom-up control of attention in the prefrontal and posterior parietal cortices." *Science* 315.5820 (2007): 1860-1862.

32. Güntekin, Bahar, and Erol Başar. "Event-related beta oscillations are affected by emotional eliciting stimuli." *Neuroscience Letters* 483.3 (2010): 173-178.

33. Pizzagalli, Diego A., et al. "Brain electrical tomography in depression: the importance of symptom severity, anxiety, and melancholic features." *Biological Psychiatry* 52.2 (2002): 73-85.

34. Lind-Kyle, Patt. *Ibid.*, page 143.

35. Davidson, Richard J. "What does the prefrontal cortex "do" in affect: perspectives on frontal EEG asymmetry research." *Biological Psychology* 67.1-2 (2004): 219-234.

36. Li, Yuezhi, et al. "Beta oscillations in major depression–signalling a new cortical circuit for central executive function." *Scientific Reports* 7.1 (2017): 18021.

37. Jenkinson, Ned, and Peter Brown. "New insights into the relationship between dopamine, beta oscillations and motor function." *Trends in Neurosciences* 34.12 (2011): 611-618.
38. Lind-Kyle, Patt. *Ibid.*, pages 143-144.
39. Engel, Andreas K., Daniel Senkowski, and Till R. Schneider. "Multisensory integration through neural coherence." (2012).
40. Gray, Charles M., et al. "Oscillatory responses in cat visual cortex exhibit intercolumnar synchronization which reflects global stimulus properties." *Nature* 338.6213 (1989): 334.
41. Lee, Hosuk Sean, et al. "Astrocytes contribute to gamma oscillations and recognition memory." *Proceedings of the National Academy of Sciences* 111.32 (2014): E3343-E3352.
42. Rodriguez, Eugenio, et al. "Perception's shadow: long-distance synchronization of human brain activity." *Nature* 397.6718 (1999): 430.
43. Tiitinen, H. T., et al. "Selective attention enhances the auditory 40-Hz transient response in humans." Nature 364.6432 (1993): 59.
44. Pantev, C., et al. "Human auditory evoked gamma-band magnetic fields." *Proceedings of the National Academy of Sciences* 88.20 (1991): 8996-9000.
45. Sederberg, Per B., et al. "Hippocampal and neocortical gamma oscillations predict memory formation in humans." *Cerebral Cortex* 17.5 (2006): 1190-1196.
46. Headley, Drew Battenfield, and Denis Paré. "In sync: Gamma oscillations and emotional memory." *Frontiers in Behavioral Neuroscience* 7 (2013): 170.
47. Womelsdorf, Thilo, and Pascal Fries. "The role of neuronal synchronization in selective attention." *Current Opinion in Neurobiology* 17.2 (2007): 154-160.
48. Pizzagalli, Diego A., et al. "Resting anterior cingulate activity and abnormal responses to errors in subjects with elevated depressive symptoms: A 128–channel EEG study." *Human Brain Mapping* 27.3 (2006): 185-201.
49. Lee, Pin-Shiuan, et al. "Distinct neuronal oscillatory responses between patients with bipolar and unipolar disorders: a magnetoencephalographic study." *Journal of Affective Disorders* 123.1-3 (2010): 270-275.
50. Fitzgerald, Paul J., and Brendon O. Watson. "Gamma oscillations as a biomarker for major depression: an emerging topic." *Translational Psychiatry* 8.1 (2018): 177.
51. Traub, Roger D., et al. "Gamma-frequency oscillations: a neuronal population phenomenon, regulated by synaptic and intrinsic cellular processes, and inducing synaptic plasticity." *Progress in Neurobiology* 55.6 (1998): 563-575.
52. Gilsinan, Kathy. "The Buddhist and the Neuroscientist: What Compassion Does to the Brain." *The Atlantic.* Published July 4, 2015. Accessed online November 1, 2018: https://www.theatlantic.com/health/archive/2015/07/dalai-lama-neuroscience-compassion/397706/
53. Lutz, Antoine, et al. "Long-term meditators self-induce high-amplitude gamma synchrony during mental practice." *Proceedings of the National Academy of Sciences* 101.46 (2004): 16369-16373.
54. Engel, Andreas K., and Pascal Fries. "Beta-band oscillations—signalling the status quo?." Current opinion in neurobiology 20.2 (2010): 156-165.
55. Brunet, Nicolas, et al. "Visual cortical gamma-band activity during free viewing of natural images." Cerebral cortex 25.4 (2013): 918-926.

56. Grothe, Iris, et al. "Switching neuronal inputs by differential modulations of gamma-band phase-coherence." Journal of Neuroscience 32.46 (2012): 16172-16180.

57. Ulrich, Roger S., et al. "Stress recovery during exposure to natural and urban environments." Journal of Environmental Psychology 11.3 (1991): 201-230.

58. Young, Jon. *What the Robin Knows: How Birds Reveal the Secrets of the Natural World*. Houghton Mifflin Harcourt, 2012.

59. Herbert Benson, M. D., and Miriam Z. Klipper. *The Relaxation Response*. Harper Collins, New York, 1992.

60. Ulrich, Roger S. "Natural versus urban scenes: Some psychophysiological effects." Environment and behavior 13.5 (1981): 523-556.

61. McCraty, Rollin, et al. "The Coherent Heart Heart-Brain Interactions, Psychophysiological Coherence, and the Emergence of System-Wide Order." Integral Review: A Transdisciplinary & Transcultural Journal for New Thought, Research, & Praxis 5.2 (2009).

62. Servan-Schreiber, David. *The Instinct to Heal*. Rodale, 2003.

63. Bair, Puran. *Living From the Heart: Heart Rhythm Meditation for Energy, Clarity, Peace, Joy, and Inner Power*. Three Rivers Press, 1998.

64. Benson, Herbert. *Ibid.*

65. Park, Bum-Jin, et al. "Physiological effects of shinrin-yoku (taking in the atmosphere of the forest)—using salivary cortisol and cerebral activity as indicators—." Journal of Physiological Anthropology 26.2 (2007): 123-128.

6. Empowering Your Sensory Awareness

1. Mason, C., & Kandel, E. R. (1991). Central visual pathways. In E. R. Kandel, J. H. Schwarz, & T. M. Jessell (Eds.), *Principles of Neural Science* (3rd ed., pp. 420–439). Norwalk, Connecticut: Appleton & Lange.

2. Tatler, Benjamin W., et al. "Yarbus, eye movements, and vision." *i- Perception 1.1* (2010): 7-27.

3. Zull, James Ellwood. *The Art of Changing the Brain: Enriching Teaching By Exploring the Biology of Learning*. Stylus Publishing, LLC., 2002.

4. Barrett, Lisa Feldman. *How Emotions Are Made: The Secret Life of the Brain*. Houghton Mifflin Harcourt, 2017.

7. Flex Your Question Muscle

1. Ochsner KN, Bunge SA, Gross JJ, Gabrieli JD. "Rethinking feelings: an FMRI study of the cognitive regulation of emotion." *Journal of Cognitive Neuroscience.* 2002;14(8):1215–1229.

2. Zull, James Ellwood. *The Art of Changing the Brain: Enriching Teaching by Exploring the Biology of Learning*. Stylus Publishing, LLC., 2002. Page 97.

3. Rozin, Paul, and Edward B. Royzman. "Negativity bias, negativity dominance, and contagion." *Personality and Social Psychology Review* 5.4 (2001): 296-320.

4. David, James P., et al. "Differential roles of neuroticism, extraversion, and event desirability for mood in daily life: An integrative model of top-down and bottom-up influences." *Journal of Personality and Social Psychology* 73.1 (1997): 149.

5. Emmons, Robert A., and Michael E. McCullough. "Counting blessings versus burdens: an experimental investigation of gratitude and subjective well-being in daily life." *Journal of Personality and Social Psychology* 84.2 (2003): 377.

6. Kraft, Tara L., and Sarah D. Pressman. "Grin and bear it: The influence of manipulated facial expression on the stress response." *Psychological Science* 23.11 (2012): 1372-1378.

7. Lin, Wenyi, Jing Hu, and Yanfei Gong. "Is it helpful for individuals with minor depression to keep smiling? An event-related potentials analysis." *Social Behavior and Personality: An International Journal* 43.3 (2015): 383-396.

8. Ekman, Paul, and Richard J. Davidson. "Voluntary smiling changes regional brain activity." *Psychological Science* 4.5 (1993): 342-345.

9. Wenk, Gary. "Addicted to Smiling." *Psychology Today.* https://www.psychologytoday.com/us/blog/your-brain-food/201112/addicted-smiling. Online article. Retrieved October 20, 2018.

10. Iwase, Masao, et al. "Neural substrates of human facial expression of pleasant emotion induced by comic films: a PET study." *Neuroimage* 17.2 (2002): 758-768.

11. Chia, Mantak. *Taoist Ways to Transform Stress Into Vitality: The Inner Smile, Six Healing Sounds.* Universal Tao Publications, 1985.

12. Koepp, Matthias J., et al. "Evidence for striatal dopamine release during a video game." *Nature* 393.6682 (1998): 266.

13. Schultz, Wolfram. "Predictive reward signal of dopamine neurons." *Journal of Neurophysiology* 80.1 (1998): 1-27.

14. Fiorillo, Christopher D., Philippe N. Tobler, and Wolfram Schultz. "Discrete coding of reward probability and uncertainty by dopamine neurons." *Science* 299.5614 (2003): 1898-1902.

15. Treadway, Michael T., et al. "Dopaminergic mechanisms of individual differences in human effort-based decision-making." *Journal of Neuroscience* 32.18 (2012): 6170-6176.

16. Gruber, Matthias J., Bernard D. Gelman, and Charan Ranganath. "States of curiosity modulate hippocampus-dependent learning via the dopaminergic circuit." *Neuron* 84.2 (2014): 486-496.

17. The school is based on the 8 Shields Institute's model of nature connection mentoring, developed by Jon Young and a number of other collaborators. See the book, *Coyote's Guide to Connecting with Nature* to learn more.

8. Moving Mindfully in Nature

1. Young, Jon. *Kamana Two: The Path of the Naturalist.* OWLink Media, 1998.

2. Brown, Tom, and Brandt Morgan. *Tom Brown's Field Guide to Nature Observation and Tracking.* New York: Berkley Books, 1983.

3. Cisek, Paul, and John F. Kalaska. "Neural correlates of mental rehearsal in dorsal premotor cortex." *Nature* 431.7011 (2004): 993.

4. Taylor, Shelley E., et al. "Harnessing the imagination: Mental simulation, self-regulation, and coping." *American Psychologist* 53.4 (1998): 429.

5. Ryan, E. Dean, and Jeff Simons. "Efficacy of mental imagery in enhancing mental rehearsal of motor skills." *Journal of Sport Psychology* 4.1 (1982): 41-51.

6. Lotze, Martin. "Kinesthetic imagery of musical performance." *Frontiers in Human Neuroscience* 7 (2013): 280.

9. The Great Dance & Trickster's Cave

1. Keeney, Bradford. *The Bushman Way of Tracking God: The Original Spirituality of the Kalahari People.* Simon and Schuster, 2010.

2. Ibid., page 81.

3. Ibid., page 13.

4. Crow, Fools, and Thomas E. Mails. *Fools Crow: Wisdom and Power.* Council Oak Books, 2001.

5. Hill, Bill. *The Magic of Reading.* April 1999. Microsoft Corporation.

6. Liebenberg, Louis. *The Art of Tracking.* David Philip Publishers, 1990.

7. Foster, Craig and Damon. *The Great Dance: A Hunter's Story.* 2000. Sense-Africa.com

8. Crow, Fools, and Thomas E. Mails. Ibid., page 64.

9. Crow, Fools, and Thomas E. Mails. Ibid., page 64.

10. Somé, Malidoma Patrice. *The Healing Wisdom of Africa: Finding Life Purpose Through Nature, Ritual, and Community.* New York: Jeremy P. Tarcher/Putnam, 1998.

11. Lenn, Fredd. *Inner Marketing: The Non-Competitive Approach to Success.* Three Hearts Society, 2015.

10. Getting Grounded

1. Feynman, Richard. "Electricity in the Atmosphere." *The Feynman Lectures on Physics.* 1963. Web. http://www.feynmanlectures.caltech.edu/II_09.html

2. Geophysics Study Committee, and National Research Council. *The Earth's Electrical Environment.* National Academies Press, 1986.

3. Volland, Hans. *Atmospheric Electrodynamics.* Vol. II. Springer Science & Business Media, 2013.

4. Harrison, R. Giles. "The carnegie curve." *Surveys in Geophysics* 34.2 (2013): 209-232.

5. Underwood, E. (2017), Ocean showers power the global electric circuit, *Eos, 98,* https://doi.org/10.1029/2017EO085441. Published on 26 October 2017.

6. Feynman, Richard. Ibid., Internet site: http://www.feynmanlectures.caltech.edu/II_09.html

7. Blakeslee, Richard J., et al. "Seasonal variations in the lightning diurnal cycle and implications for the global electric circuit." *Atmospheric Research* 135 (2014): 228-243.

8. Peterson, Michael, et al. "A TRMM/GPM retrieval of the total mean generator current for the global electric circuit." Journal of Geophysical Research: Atmospheres (2017).

9. These storm-driven energies are named *Wilson currents*, after C.T.R. Wilson, who first theorized their existence in a 1903 *Nature* article.

10. Helman, Daniel S. "Earth electricity: a review of mechanisms which cause telluric currents in the lithosphere." *Annals of Geophysics* 56.5 (2014): 0564.

11. Ober, Clinton, Stephen T. Sinatra, and Martin Zucker. *Earthing: The Most Important Health Discovery Ever?* Basic Health Publications, Inc., 2010.

12. Ghaly, Maurice, and Dale Teplitz. "The biologic effects of grounding the human body during sleep as measured by cortisol levels and subjective reporting of sleep, pain, and stress." *Journal of Alternative & Complementary Medicine* 10.5 (2004): 767-776.

13. Chevalier, Gaétan, Kazuhito Mori, and James L. Oschman. "The effect of earthing (grounding) on human physiology." *European Biology and Bioelectromagnetics* 2.1 (2006): 600-621.

14. Linkowski, Paul, et al. "The 24-hour profile of adrenocorticotropin and cortisol in major depressive illness." The Journal of Clinical Endocrinology & Metabolism 61.3 (1985): 429-438.

15. Ober, Clinton. *Ibid.*

16. Oschman, James L.. *The Journal of Alternative and Complementary Medicine.* November 2007, 13(9): 955-967. https://doi.org/10.1089/acm.2007.7048

17. Chevalier, Gaétan. "The effect of grounding the human body on mood." *Psychological Reports* 116.2 (2015): 534-542.

18. Sokal, Karol, and Pawel Sokal. "Earthing the human organism influences bioelectrical processes." *The Journal of Alternative and Complementary Medicine* 18.3 (2012): 229-234.

19. Sinatra, Stephen T. "Emotional stress, heart rate variability, grounding, and improved autonomic tone: clinical applications." *Integrative Medicine* 10.3 (2011): 16.

20. Huikuri, Heikki V., et al. "Heart rate variability and progression of coronary atherosclerosis." *Arteriosclerosis, Thrombosis, and Vascular Biology* 19.8 (1999): 1979-1985.

21. Chevalier, Gaétan, et al. "Earthing (grounding) the human body reduces blood viscosity—a major factor in cardiovascular disease." *The Journal of Alternative and Complementary Medicine* 19.2 (2013): 102-110.

22. Chevalier, Gaétan, Kazuhito Mori, and James L. Oschman. "The effect of earthing (grounding) on human physiology." *European Biology and Bioelectromagnetics* 2.1 (2006): 600-621.

23. Fukushima, Masanori, et al. "Evidence of Qi-gong energy and its biological effect on the enhancement of the phagocytic activity of human polymorphonuclear leukocytes." *The American Journal of Chinese Medicine* 29.01 (2001): 1-16.

24. He, Yijie, et al. "A primary study on meridian-stretching of injected FDG using PET MPItool." *Chinese Journal of Nuclear Medicine* 22.3 (2002): 145-146.

25. Zhang, Wei-Bo, et al. "A discovery of low hydraulic resistance channel along meridians." *Journal of Acupuncture and Meridian Studies* 1.1 (2008): 20-28.

11. "I'm Here..." Arriving to Meditate

1. Frantzis, Bruce. *Opening the Energy Gates of Your Body: Qigong for Lifelong Health.* North Atlantic Books, 2006.

12. Tuning In

1. Tiller, William A., Rollin McCraty, and Mike Atkinson. "Cardiac coherence: A new, noninvasive measure of autonomic nervous system order." *Alternative Therapies in Health and Medicine* 2.1 (1996): 52-65.

2. McCraty, Rollin, and Maria A. Zayas. "Cardiac coherence, self-regulation, autonomic stability, and psychosocial well-being." *Frontiers in Psychology* 5 (2014): 1090.

3. Langhorst, P., G. Schulz, and M. Lambertz. "Integrative control mechanisms for cardiorespiratory and somatomotor functions in the reticular formation of the lower brain stem." *Cardiorespiratory and Cardiosomatic Psychophysiology.* Springer, Boston, MA, 1986. 9-39.

4. McCraty, Rollin, et al. "The effects of emotions on short-term power spectrum analysis of heart rate variability." *The American Journal of Cardiology* 76.14 (1995): 1089-1093.

5. Rein, G., R. M. McCraty, and M. Atkinson. "Effects of positive and negative emotions on salivary IgA." *J. Adv. Med* 8.2 (1995): 87-105.

6. McCraty, Rollin, Mike Atkinson, and Dana Tomasino. "Impact of a workplace stress reduction program on blood pressure and emotional health in hypertensive employees." *The Journal of Alternative & Complementary Medicine* 9.3 (2003): 355-369.

7. Lloyd, Anthony, David Brett, and Keith Wesnes. "Coherence training in children with attention-deficit hyperactivity disorder: cognitive functions and behavioral changes." *Alternative Therapies in Health & Medicine* 16.4 (2010).

8. Rein, G., R. M. McCraty, and M. Atkinson. *Ibid.*

9. McCraty, Rollin, et al. "The impact of a new emotional self-management program on stress, emotions, heart rate variability, DHEA and cortisol." *Integrative Physiological and Behavioral Science* 33.2 (1998): 151-170.

10. Poponin, V. "Nonlinear stochastic resonance in weak EMF interactions with diamagnetic ions bound within proteins." Allen MJ, Cleary SF, and Sower AE. *Charge and Field Effects in Biosystems.* New Jersey: World Scientific (1994): 306-319.

11. Litovitz, T. A., D. Krause, and J. M. Mullins. "Effect of coherence time of the

applied magnetic field on ornithine decarboxylase activity." *Biochemical and Biophysical Research Communications* 178.3 (1991): 862-865.

12. McCraty, Rollin, et al. "The electricity of touch: Detection and measurement of cardiac energy exchange between people." *Brain and Values: Is a Biological Science of Values Possible* (1998): 359-379.

13. In the prayer posture, the fingertips lightly touch one another. The base of the thumbs lightly touch the center of the chest. This mudra (hand position) connects the body's meridians with the supportive flow of the heart center.

13. Expanding Through the Senses

1. Young, Jon. *Advanced Bird Language: Reading the Concentric Rings of Nature*. Audio series. OWLink Media, 1999.

2. Brown, Tom. *Tom Brown's Field Guide to the Forgotten Wilderness*. Vol. 6. Berkley Publishing Group, 1987.

3. Horowitz, Seth S. *The Universal Sense: How Hearing Shapes the Mind*. Bloomsbury Publishing USA, 2012.

4. Stevens SS, Davis H. *Hearing, its Psychology and Physiology*. John Wiley; New York: 1938. pp. 152–154.

5. Young, Jon. *What the Robin Knows: How Birds Reveal the Secrets of the Natural World*. Houghton Mifflin Harcourt, 2012.

6. Johnsrude, Ingrid S., Virginia B. Penhune, and Robert J. Zatorre. "Functional specificity in the right human auditory cortex for perceiving pitch direction." *Brain* 123.1 (2000): 155-163.

14. Further Expansion into Nature's Conversation

1. Lametti, Daniel. "Mind - Mirroring Behavior: How Mirror Neurons Let Us Interact With Others." *Scientific American* online. June 9, 2009.

2. Heyes, Cecilia. "Where do mirror neurons come from?." *Neuroscience & Biobehavioral Reviews* 34.4 (2010): 575-583.

3. Haslinger, Bernhard, et al. "Transmodal sensorimotor networks during action observation in professional pianists." *Journal of Cognitive Neuroscience* 17.2 (2005): 282-293.

4. Kohler, Evelyne, et al. "Hearing sounds, understanding actions: action representation in mirror neurons." *Science* 297.5582 (2002): 846-848.

5. Iacoboni, Marco, et al. "Grasping the intentions of others with one's own mirror neuron system." *PLoS Biology* 3.3 (2005): e79.

6. Fehmi, Les, and Jim Robbins. *The Open-Focus Brain: Harnessing the Power of Attention to Heal Mind and Body*. Shambhala Publications, 2008.

7. Ibid., page 75.

8. McKnight, J. T., and L. G. Fehmi. "Attention and neurofeedback synchrony train-

ing: Clinical results and their significance." *Journal of Neurotherapy* 5.1-2 (2001): 45-61.

15. Gathering & Returning

1. Frawley, David. *Mantra Yoga and Primal Sound: Secrets of Seed (Bija) Mantras.* Lotus Press, 2010.
2. Davidson, Richard J., and Antoine Lutz. "Buddha's brain: Neuroplasticity and meditation [in the spotlight]." *IEEE Signal Processing Magazine* 25.1 (2008): 176-174.
3. Holden, Lee. *Qi Gong: The Flow Continues.* DVD. Exercise to Heal, 2007.

16. Being Nature

1. Harner, Michael. *The Way of the Shaman.* Harper, 1990 edition.

CONTINUE YOUR JOURNEY

Ready to go further in your explorations of the Nature within and around you?

Join me for one of my online trainings, in-person retreats or one-on-one coaching experiences, available at:
https://ConsciousNature.net

**A Wayfinder's Journey
Audio Toolkit**

The Vision Tree - A Wayfinder's Journey:
Audio Toolkit with Josh Lane

Shamans and mystics have long maintained that the entire world is alive — every stone, creek, cloud, and tree has stories to tell, if we have the ears to hear them speak.

Further, the patterns of the world of Nature can offer us guidance and awaken our intuition, if we are present to what wisdom is being offered at each turn of the trail.

Once a connection with Nature's language is established, it becomes possible to enter into a creative dialogue with the metaphors and insights awakened through the attuned senses.

The ancient and enduring Wisdom Cultures around the globe all have their own methods and philosophies of entering this dialogue; the archetypal Hero's Journey itself points towards clues that support this enlivening conversation.

The Vision Tree Journey is a modern Wayfinder's guide back to this world of mystery and creative guidance that is our human birthright.

Learn through engaging stories and gain a unique toolset in how to awaken and deepen your own dialogue with Nature.

The Primal Awareness Training Course:
Connecting with the Five Elements in Nature

A Six-Week Home Study Course, with Josh Lane

The ancient Mystery Schools recognized that Outer Nature is a reflection of the Inner Nature that dwells within each of us.

At the same time, we are a microcosm of the larger world of Nature. For most of our history as human beings, we've lived close to the Earth's rhythms and cycles. This closeness creates harmony and well-being.

When we remember and attune to this primal connection with Nature, our own regenerative wellness and highest creativity emerges.

This unique six-week online course offers training in many "lost arts" of awareness that have been long-known to those who live close to the patterns of the land.

By attuning to the mysteries of Outer Nature, we get into touch with the deeper patterns moving within us. And, as we become aware of the deeper instincts and intuitions moving within us, we gain insights into the places and connections we make in the world around us.

This is an in-depth training with daily outdoor meditations. The practices are designed to open the modern consciousness to new (and ancient) dimensions of awareness and relationship with Nature.

Transformative Coaching

For those who want a deep immersion and one-on-one support in awakening connection with the Nature within and around you, I offer a limited number of private coaching spots throughout the year.

Experience custom guidance in primal awareness training, as you cultivate your relationship with the Nature of your place through meditations, sensory practices, and other integral skills.

Group trainings are also available on a limited basis, both virtually and in person.

Learn More at https://www.consciousnature.net/

**Stay Connected &
Get Your Reader's Only Bonus Content**

**Get Your FREE learning tools, including guided meditations
and awareness practices, at:**

https://www.consciousnature.net/readers-extras

ABOUT THE AUTHOR

Josh Lane is an avid explorer of Nature's mysteries. He brings forward a depth of experience from his journeys in the realms of ancient Earth connection skills, Qi Gong, and visionary meditation.

Josh has mentored and trained people of all ages around the world for the past twenty years in the inner and outer arts of mindful, whole-being connection with Nature.

(photo by Virginia Dunn)

Josh's vision is to bridge the healing power of Nature into the modern experience, sharing the gifts of grounding, presence, and passion for life that a primary connection with the Earth offers us all.

Visit Josh's website at https://www.ConsciousNature.net

facebook.com/ConsciousNature

instagram.com/consciousnaturecoach

THANK YOU

Thank you for reading this book, and for journeying with me through these pages into a greater conscious exploration of the Nature within and around us.

Your feedback is important to me. Please take a moment to leave me a helpful review on your favorite bookseller's website - what did you learn from the book? How did the stories and practices shared here help you on your journey?

Thanks so much, and I wish you many magical moments of connection with Nature's endless mysteries.

-Josh Lane

Made in United States
North Haven, CT
07 December 2024

61771266R00198